North of Slavery

NORTH

LEON F. LITWACK

OF SLAVERY

THE NEGRO IN THE FREE STATES, 1790–1860

 THE UNIVERSITY OF CHICAGO PRESS
CHICAGO AND LONDON

The University of Chicago Press, Chicago 60637
The University of Chicago Press, Ltd., London

© 1961 by The University of Chicago. All rights reserved
Published 1961. Printed in the United States of America

ISBN: 0–226–48585–4 (clothbound); 0–226–48586–2 (paperbound)
Library of Congress Catalog Card Number: 61–10869

80 79 78 77 76   12 11 10 9 8

To My Father and Mother
JULIUS AND MINNIE LITWACK

Preface

The Mason-Dixon Line is a convenient but an often mislead-
ing geographical division. It has been used not only to distinguish the Old South from the North and the Confederacy
from the Union but to dramatize essential differences in the
treatment of, and attitudes toward, the Negro — to contrast
southern racial inhumanity with northern benevolence and
liberality. But the historian must be wary of such an over-
simplified comparison, for it does not accord with the realities
of either the nineteenth or the twentieth century. The inherent
cruelty and violence of southern slavery requires no further
demonstration, but this does not prove northern humanity.
Although slavery eventually confined itself to the region below
the Mason-Dixon Line, discrimination against the Negro and
a firmly held belief in the superiority of the white race were
not restricted to one section but were shared by an overwhelming majority of white Americans in both the North and the
South. Abraham Lincoln, in his vigorous support of both white
supremacy and denial of equal rights for Negroes, simply
gave expression to almost universal American convictions.

In the ante bellum North racial discrimination was not as
subtle or as concealed as it has been in more recent decades.

Politicians, whether Democrats, Whigs, or Republicans, openly and blatantly professed their allegiance to the principles of white supremacy; indeed, they tried to outdo each other in declarations of loyalty to the ante bellum American Way of Life and its common assumption that this was a white man's country in which the Negro had no political voice and only a prescribed social and economic role. Inasmuch as most northern states had disfranchised the Negro, politicians were responsible only to the whims, prejudices, and pressures of a white electorate; few of them cared to risk political suicide.

The same popular pressures that forced political parties to embrace the doctrine of white supremacy demanded and sanctioned the social and economic repression of the Negro population. Racial segregation or exclusion thus haunted the northern Negro in his attempts to use public conveyances, to attend schools, or to sit in theaters, churches, and lecture halls. But even the more subtle forms of twentieth-century racial discrimination had their antecedents in the ante bellum North: residential restrictions, exclusion from resorts and certain restaurants, confinement to menial employments, and restricted cemeteries. The justification for such discrimination in the North differed little from that used to defend slavery in the South: Negroes, it was held, constituted a depraved and inferior race which must be kept in its proper place in a white man's society.

The position of the Negro in the ante bellum North invites obvious comparison with that of the slave in the South. Indeed, many publicists and politicians in both sections repeatedly made and exploited that comparison, claiming that slaves and free Negroes shared an identical existence. Such a position, however, is as gross an oversimplification as is the traditional contrast between northern racial benevolence and southern intolerance. For, as this study suggests, important distinctions did exist between northern free Negroes and southern slaves, just as there were fundamental differences between the condition of northern white industrial workers and southern bondsmen. Above all, the northern Negro was a free man; he was not subject to the whims and dictates of the master or overseer; he could not be bought and sold; he could not be arbitrarily separated from his family. Although a victim of racial proscription, he could — and on several occasions did — advance his political and economic position in the ante bellum period; he could and did organize and petition, publish newspapers and tracts, even join with white sympathizers to advance his cause; in sum, he was able to carry on a variety of activities directed toward an improvement of his position. Although subjected to angry white mobs, ridicule, and censure, he made substantial progress in some sections of the North and, at the very least, began to plague the northern conscience with the inconsistency of its antislavery pronouncements and prevailing racial practices. And although confined largely to menial employments, some Negroes did manage to accumulate property and establish thriving businesses; by 1860, northern Negroes shared with white workers the vision of rising into the middle class. Finally, on the eve of the Civil War, an increasing number of Negroes were availing themselves of educational opportunities, either in the small number of integrated schools or in the exclusive and usually inferior Negro schools.

The northern Negro, then, proved to be neither as passive nor as meek and subservient as the conventional stereotype portrayed him; nor, for that matter, did the southern slave. But the free society of the North and the slave society of the South dictated different forms of Negro protest. While the pre-eminent Negro of the ante bellum North was undoubtedly Frederick Douglass, an active abolitionist organizer, speaker,

and editor, the most symbolic product of the ante bellum
South was Nat Turner, the unsuccessful slave insurrectionist.
Therein lies the difference.

During its various stages of development, this book has
benefited from the suggestions and criticisms of many friends.
My indebtedness to Kenneth M. Stampp is considerable. Since
the inception of this study, he has given it direction, encouragement, and searching criticism. I am also grateful to Vernon
Carstensen and Leslie H. Fishel, Jr., for their careful reading
of the entire manuscript and their helpful comments and cor-
rections. Early in the study I profited from the suggestions of
Richard Drinnon, John Hope Franklin, Seymour M. Lipset,
and William R. Stanton. In the final stages Gaspare Saladino
and Rupert Loucks rendered some valuable assistance. Finally, to my good friends James Kindregan and Arthur Zilver-
smit I would like to express my special gratitude for the
interest, time, energy, and insights which they so generously
bestowed upon this work. Bowing to one of the traditions of
acknowledgments, and to protect the innocent, I assume full
responsibility for any stylistic errors or misinterpretations of
facts.

The Sigmund Martin Heller Traveling Fellowship, awarded
by the University of California, enabled me to conduct my
research in various parts of the United States. A summer grant
from the University of Wisconsin Graduate School permitted
me to prepare the manuscript for publication. I am also appreciative of the co-operation and courtesies extended to me by
the staffs of the University of California Library, Berkeley;
the University of California, Santa Barbara Library, Goleta;
the Henry E. Huntington Library, San Marino; the Library of
Congress and Howard University Library (Moorland Foundation), Washington, D.C.; the 135th Street Branch of the New
York Public Library (Schomburg Collection) and the Columbia University Library, New York City; the Boston Public

Library; the Harvard University Library, Cambridge; the Cornell University Library, Ithaca; the University of Michigan Library and the William L. Clements Library, Ann Arbor; the Historical Society of Pennsylvania Library, Philadelphia; the Friends Historical Library of Swarthmore College, Swarthmore; and the State Historical Society of Wisconsin Library, Madison. For permission to reprint materials that have appeared in their publications, I am grateful to the editors of the *Journal of Negro History* and the *New England Quarterly*.

Finally, the debt that this study owes to my wife, Rhoda, can never be measured adequately. It must suffice to say that her encouragement, patience, and understanding — not to mention her valuable assistance on the long research trek — helped to make this book possible.

Contents

preface quote!

"We shall not make the black man a slave; we shall not buy him or sell him; but we shall not associate with him. He shall be free to live, and to thrive, if he can, and to pay taxes and perform duties; but he shall not be free to dine and drink at our board — to share with us the deliberations of the jury box — to sit upon the seat of judgment, however capable he may be — to plead in our courts — to represent us in the Legislature — to attend us at the bed of sickness and pain — to mingle with us in the concert-room, the lecture-room, the theatre, or the church, or to marry with our daughters. We are of another race, and he is inferior. Let him know his place — and keep it." This is the prevalent feeling, if not the language of the free North.

— Charles Mackay, *Life and Liberty in America: or, Sketches of a Tour in the United States and Canada in 1857–1858.*

Slavery to Freedom

On the eve of the War of Independence, American Negro slavery knew no sectional boundaries. Every colony recognized it and sharply defined the legal position of free and enslaved blacks. The Declaration of Independence boldly asserted the natural rights of man but made no mention of slavery; the Constitution subsequently sanctioned and protected the institution without naming it. By that time, however, the Revolution had worked some important changes. Human bondage, it seemed certain, would henceforth assume a sectional character, for the North had sentenced it to a slow death. By 1800, some 36,505 northern Negroes still remained in bondage, most of them in New York and New Jersey, but almost every northern state had either abolished slavery outright or had provided for its gradual extinction.[1]

State statutes, constitutions, and court decisions recorded

[1] Slavery was abolished by the constitutions of Vermont (1777), Ohio (1802), Illinois (1818), and Indiana (1816); by a judicial decision in Massachusetts (1783); by constitutional interpretation in New Hampshire; and by gradual-abolition acts in Pennsylvania (1780), Rhode Island (1784), Connecticut (1784 and 1797), New York (1799 and 1817), and New Jersey (1804).

the methods of northern abolition but said little about the
motives. Why did northern slaveholders surrender, with little
apparent opposition or compensation, a valuable investment
in human property? Perhaps, some have argued, it was not
that valuable. In the complex economy and uncongenial climate of the North, slave labor presumably proved to be unprofitable; savage Africans lacked the mental capacity to learn
anything more than how to tend a single crop. Climate and
geography thus prompted the employing class to turn to the
more profitable use of free white laborers, thereby dooming
slavery. "The winter here was always unfavourable to the
African constitution," one New Englander explained. "For
this reason, white labourers were preferable to blacks." [2]

Although commonly accepted, the economic explanation for
northern abolition has not been adequately demonstrated.
Plantation capitalism did not root itself in the North; the economy of that region came to be based largely on commerce,
manufacturing, and small-scale agriculture. But this did not
necessarily preclude the profitable use of slave labor. On the
contrary, evidence suggests that the scarcity and expense of
free white labor prompted ambitious northerners to make a
profitable use of slaves and that these Negro bondsmen could
and did perform successfully a variety of tasks — agricultural
and mechanical, skilled and unskilled — in a diversified economy. On farms, slaves assisted in the production of foodstuffs
and dairy products and in sheep and stock raising; in the cities,
they worked in various skilled trades — as bakers, carpenters, cabinetmakers, sawyers, blacksmiths, printers, tailors,
and coopers — and perhaps most prominently in the maritime
industry.[3]

[2] Jeremy Belknap, "Queries Respecting the Slavery and Emancipation of Ne-
groes in Massachusetts, Proposed by the Hon. Judge Tucker of Virginia, and
Answered by the Rev. Dr. Belknap," *Massachusetts Historical Society Collections*
(Ser. 1, 10 vols.; Boston, 1795), III, 199. See also Thomas J. Wertenbaker, *The
First Americans, 1607–1690* (New York, 1927), pp. 61–63.
    [3] Lorenzo J. Greene, *The Negro in Colonial New England, 1620–1776* (New

Wherever utilized, slave labor was still cheap labor. Free labor, on the other hand, involved additional expense. In comparing the economic value of the two groups, John Adams admitted that his personal abhorrence of slavery had cost him "thousands of dollars for the labor and subsistence of free men, which I might have saved by the purchase of Negroes at times when they were very cheap." Moreover, some northern slaveholders appeared unconvinced that abolition would rid them of an economic encumbrance. Vigorously opposing a proposed duty on the importation of Negroes, a group of Pennsylvania merchants cited the scarcity of laborers and artisans and argued that additional slaves would reduce "the exorbitant price of Labour, and, in all probability, bring our Staple Commoditys to their usual prices." Despite public abolition sentiment, a Massachusetts physician recalled in 1795, it took legal action to force many slaveholders to part with their human chattel. Such reluctance would seem to suggest that slaves at least performed some useful and profitable services.[4]

If slave labor was indeed unprofitable, not only did some masters reluctantly give up their property, but white workers protested often and bitterly against the Negro's competitive position. By the end of the seventeenth century, for example, workers in New York City had already complained that Negro labor had "soe much impoverisht them, that they Cannot by their Labours gett a Competency for the Maintenance of themselves and Family's." In 1737, the lieutenant governor of New York asked the Assembly to consider the justifiable complaints of "honest and industrious tradesmen" that skilled slave labor

York, 1942), pp. 100–123; Samuel McKee, Jr., *Labor in Colonial New York, 1664–1776* (New York, 1935), pp. 125–27.

[4] Charles F. Adams (ed.), *The Works of John Adams* (10 vols.; Boston, 1850–56), X, 380; *Colonial Records of Pennsylvania, 1683–1790* (16 vols.; Harrisburg, 1852–53), VIII, 576; "Letters and Documents Relating to Slavery in Massachusetts," *Massachusetts Historical Society Collections* (Ser. 5, 10 vols.; Boston, 1877), III, 400.

had reduced them to unemployment and poverty. Twenty years later, when Lieutenant Governor James Delancey proposed a poll tax on slaves, he argued that this would attract more white laborers and occasion little local resistance. "[T]he price of labor is now become so high," he explained, "and hence the owners of slaves reap such advantage, that they cannot reasonably complain of a tax on them." In Massachusetts, John Adams recalled, the opposition of white labor assured the extinction of slavery, for it "would no longer suffer the rich to employ these sable rivals so much to their injury." Had slavery not been abolished, Adams observed, the white laborers would simply have removed the Negro by force. In any case, their hostility had already rendered the institution unprofitable. "Their scoffs and insults, their continual insinuations, filled the negroes with discontent, made them lazy, idle, proud, vicious, and at length wholly useless to their masters, to such a degree that the abolition of slavery became a measure of economy." [5]

If contemporary explanations have any validity, the liquidation of slavery in the North should not be considered simply on the grounds of profits and losses, climate, or geography.[6] Abolition sentiment generally ignored these factors and chose instead to emphasize one particular theme: that the same principles used to justify the American Revolution, particularly John Locke's natural-rights philosophy, also condemned and doomed Negro slavery. Such an institution could not be reconciled with colonial efforts to resist English tyranny; indeed,

[5] Richard B. Morris, *Government and Labor in Early America* (New York, 1946), p. 183; Charles Z. Lincoln (ed.), *Messages from the Governors* (11 vols.; Albany, 1909), I, 260, 618; *Mass. Hist. Soc. Colls.*, Ser. 5, III, 402.

[6] Although a full investigation of northern slavery is outside the proposed scope of this study, sufficient evidence exists to warrant a reassessment of the traditional reasons assigned for the abolition of bondage in the North. My examination, though it does not pretend to be exhaustive, suggests the need to balance the economic argument with a more careful consideration of cultural and ideological influences.

its existence embarrassed the American cause. "To contend for liberty," John Jay wrote, "and to deny that blessing to others involves an inconsistency not to be excused." Until America ridded herself of human bondage, "her prayers to Heaven for liberty will be impious." [7]

During the Revolution, official pronouncements reiterated the incompatibility of slavery and the struggle for independence. In Pennsylvania, for example, the Executive Council suggested to the Assembly in 1778 that the further importation of slaves be prohibited as a first step toward eventual abolition. Such a move, the Council pointed out, would not only be humane and just but would raise American prestige among the Europeans, "who are astonished to see a people eager for Liberty holding Negroes in Bondage." One year later, the Council contended that slavery disgraced a people supposedly fighting for liberty and urged a plan for gradual abolition. In 1780, the state legislature incorporated these sentiments in the preamble to a gradual-abolition act. Inasmuch as Americans had gone to war to obtain their freedom, the legislature asserted, such a blessing should be shared with those who had been and were being subjected to a similar state of bondage. In neighboring New Jersey, the governor urged the legislature in 1778 to provide for gradual abolition on the grounds that slavery conflicted with the principles of Christianity and was especially "odious and disgraceful" for a people professing to idolize liberty.[8]

Perhaps the most radical extension of the Revolutionary ideology to Negro rights was made in New York. In 1785,

[7] William Jay, *The Life of John Jay* (2 vols.; New York, 1833), I, 231; Henry P. Johnston (ed.), *The Correspondence and Public Papers of John Jay* (4 vols.; New York, 1890), I, 407.

[8] Samuel Hazard (ed.), *Pennsylvania Archives* (Ser. 1, 12 vols.; Philadelphia, 1852–56), VII, 79; *Colonial Records of Pennsylvania*, XI, 688; James T. Mitchell and Henry Flanders (eds.), *The Statutes at Large of Pennsylvania from 1682 to 1801* (16 vols.; Harrisburg, 1896–1911), X, 67–73; Henry S. Cooley, *A Study of Slavery in New Jersey* (Baltimore, 1896), p. 23.

the New York legislature passed a gradual-abolition act. The Council of Revision, however, rejected the bill because of a clause which prohibited Negroes from exercising the franchise. Contending that the freedmen should be granted full citizenship, the Council found this clause contrary to basic liberties and "repugnant to the principle on which the United States justify their separation from Great Britain," for it "supposes that those may rightfully be charged with the burdens of government, who have no representative share in imposing them." If free Negroes failed to secure the vote, the Council warned, a time might come when they would be numerous, wealthy, and powerful, and they might then turn against a constitution which deprived them of their just rights. The legislature failed to override the Council's veto and delayed gradual abolition for another fourteen years.[9]

Massachusetts, where resistance to British authority had been the most dramatic and far-reaching, perhaps reflected most clearly the troublesome conflict between the Revolutionary ideals and slavery. Few public pronouncements had been made on the subject of Negro bondage, Dr. Jeremy Belknap of Boston recalled, "till we began to feel the weight of oppression from 'our mother country' as Britain was then called. The inconsistency of pleading for our own rights and liberties, whilst we encouraged the subjugation of others, was very apparent; and from that time, both slavery and the slave-trade began to be discountenanced." Early in the Revolutionary struggle, James Otis struck at both colonial and Negro bondage. Although *The Rights of the British Colonies Asserted and Proved* has had more enduring fame as a forceful statement of the colonial constitutional position, that same tract applied John Locke's natural-rights philosophy not only to the current troubles with England but also to Negro slavery. "It is a clear truth," Otis wrote, "that those who every day

[1] Lincoln (ed.), *Messages from the Governors*, II, 237–39.

barter away other mens liberty, will soon care little for their own."[10]

As the colonial crisis became more intense and headed for a showdown, many New Englanders felt even more conscious of the inconsistency of opposing English tyranny and practicing slavery. "It always appeared a most iniquitous scheme to me," Abigail Adams wrote her husband in 1774, "to fight ourselves for what we are daily robbing and plundering from those who have as good a right to freedom as we have." Massachusetts town meetings began to couple their protests against royal and Parliamentary usurpation with pleas that slavery be abolished.[11] Two months after the Declaration of Independence, the state house of representatives climaxed this growing sentiment by resolving that human bondage violated the natural rights of man and was "utterly inconsistent with the avowed principles in which this and other States have carried on their struggle for liberty." Meanwhile, several Massachusetts towns did not wait for legislative or judicial action but simply voted to have no slaves in their midst and to bear any expense that might arise from the emancipated Negroes' old age, infirmities, or inability to support themselves. By the end of 1776, one observer wrote, public opinion had virtually extirpated slavery.[12]

In Massachusetts, unlike Pennsylvania, New Jersey, and New York, court action legally ended slavery. Prior to 1783, several slaves collected money among themselves and success-

[10] *Mass. Hist. Soc. Colls.*, Ser. 1, III, 198; James Otis, *The Rights of the British Colonies Asserted and Proved* (3d ed.; Boston, 1766), pp. 43–44.

[11] Charles F. Adams (ed.), *Letters of Mrs. Adams* (2 vols.; Boston, 1841), I, 24; Franklin P. Rice (ed.), "Worcester Town Records," *Collections of the Worcester Society of Antiquity* (25 vols.; Worcester, 1881–1912), IV, 149; Emory Washburn, *Historical Sketches of the Town of Leicester, Massachusetts* (Boston, 1860), pp. 442–43.

[12] Joseph B. Felt, *Annals of Salem* (2d ed.; 2 vols.; Salem, 1849), II, 417; George H. Moore, *Notes on the History of Slavery in Massachusetts* (New York, 1866), pp. 149–53; *Mass. Hist. Soc. Colls.*, Ser. 5, III, 392–93.

fully sued for their freedom. Some even secured compensation for their services. John Adams, who represented several bondsmen in such cases, recalled that he "never knew a jury, by a verdict, to determine a negro to be a slave. They always found them free." Those arguments most commonly used to obtain a Negro's freedom, Adams stated, were based on "the rights of mankind, which was the fashionable word at that time." Successful court action encouraged the voluntary liberation of other slaves. To avoid court litigation, some slaves simply took the new constitution at its word when it affirmed the freedom and equality of all men, and either asked for and received their release or took it without consent.[13]

Against this favorable background, the Massachusetts Supreme Court dealt Negro slavery a final blow. Quork Walker, a Negro slave, claimed his freedom on the basis of his master's verbal promise. Although this would ordinarily have been insufficient evidence to release him from bondage, Walker's attorneys found other grounds, the most important of which stressed the natural rights of man, the newly adopted Massachusetts Declaration of Rights, and the need for a more consistent stand against tyranny. "Can we expect to triumph over G. Britain," counsel Levi Lincoln asked, "to get free ourselves until we let those go free under us?" Chief Justice William Cushing's subsequent charge to the jury reiterated much of this argument. Regardless of previous practices, he declared, the American people had demonstrated a greater devotion to the natural rights of man "and to that natural, innate desire of Liberty, with which Heaven (without regard to color, complexion, or shape of noses, features) has inspired all the human race." The new constitution, Cushing concluded, made this quite clear; consequently, "the idea of slavery is inconsistent with our own conduct and Constitution." This decision,

---

[13] *Mass. Hist. Soc. Colls.*, Ser. 1, III, 202; Ser. 5, III, 386, 393, 401.

handed down in 1783, ended slavery in the Puritan Commonwealth.[14]

Exploiting the abolition sentiment aroused by the Revolution, Negro slaves and their white allies sought to dramatize the conflict between colonial principles and practices.
Obviously aware of the symbolic value of the War of Independence for the cause of emancipation, Negro petitioners
claimed a natural, a God-given, right to freedom and asserted
"that Every Principle from which America has Acted in the
Cours of their unhappy Dificultes with Great Briton Pleads
Stronger than A thousand arguments in favours of your
petioners." In the New London *Gazette*, "a Negro" made this
point even more forcefully,

> Is not all oppression vile?
> When you attempt your freedom to defend,
> Is reason yours, and partially your friend?
> Be not deceiv'd — for reason pleads for all
> Who by invasion and oppression fall.
> I live a slave, and am inslav'd by those
> Who yet pretend with reason to oppose
> All schemes oppressive; and the gods invoke
> To curse with thunders the invaders yoke.
> O mighty God! let conscience seize the mind
> Of Inconsistent men, who wish to find
> A partial god to vindicate their cause,
> And plead their freedom, while they break its laws.[15]

If such theoretical or poetic appeals did not suffice, an estimated five thousand Negroes — most of them northerners —

[14] *Ibid.*, Ser. 5, III, 439–42; *Massachusetts Historical Society Proceedings*
(Ser. 1, 20 vols.; Boston, 1859–84), XIII, 298; Helen T. Catterall, *Judicial Cases
concerning American Slavery and the Negro* (5 vols.; Washington, D.C., 1926–
37), IV, 481.

[15] *Mass. Hist. Soc. Colls.*, Ser. 5, III, 432–37; Isaac W. Hammond, "Slavery in
New Hampshire in the Olden Time," *The Granite Monthly*, IV (1880), 108–10;
Herbert Aptheker (ed.), *A Documentary History of the Negro People in the
United States* (New York, 1951), pp. 5–12; New London *Gazette*, May 1, 1772.

fought with white men for American independence. Despite colonial laws excluding Negroes from the militia and an early hesitancy to enlist them in the war, military expediency finally broke down these barriers and prompted the Continental Congress and most of the states to enlist slaves and free Negroes. Between 1775 and 1781, Negro soldiers participated in virtually every major military action. In return for their military services, most states either freed them upon enlistment or at the end of hostilities.[16]

In several states, religious organizations played an active and sometimes decisive role in the work of emancipation. After all, the pulpit was still a most influential and authoritative position from which to mold public opinion. Colonial parishioners had long been indoctrinated with the ideas of John Locke and their implications for the struggle with the mother country. Consistency and moral rectitude demanded, many churchmen insisted, that the laws of God and Nature also be directed at the glaring sin of human slavery. Otherwise the Revolutionary struggle had little significance. "Would we enjoy liberty?" a Massachusetts minister asked in 1774. "Then we must grant it to others. For shame, let us either cease to enslave our fellow men, or else let us cease to complain of those, that would enslave us." Quoting directly from the Scriptures, one churchman deplored the inconsistency of colonial practices and professions: "Happy is he saith the apostle Paul that condemneth not himself in that thing which he alloweth." [17]

Most conspicuous among the antislavery religious groups were the Quakers. Abolition sentiment in Pennsylvania, for example, resulted largely from early and persistent Quaker opposition to slavery as inconsistent with the true spirit of Christianity. In 1758, the Philadelphia Yearly Meeting voted

[16] John Hope Franklin, *From Slavery to Freedom* (2d ed.; New York, 1956), pp. 130–38.

[17] Joshua Coffin, *A Sketch of the History of Newbury, Newburyport, and West Newbury, from 1635 to 1845* (Boston, 1845), pp. 338–41.

13

to exclude anyone who bought or sold slaves from participation in the meetings and affairs of the church; in 1774, it increased the penalty to disownment, and two years later it directed its members to "testify their disunion" with any member who resisted a last entreaty to free his slaves. The Quaker antislavery stand was not limited to any one state, however. Following the lead of Pennsylvania, yearly meetings in New England, New York, Baltimore, Virginia, and North Carolina soon adopted similar condemnations of slaveholding. After completing their work of emancipation, Quakers shifted their attention to improving the educational and economic level of the free Negro population.[18]

Quakers also participated actively in the organization, leadership, and activities of the Pennsylvania Society for the Abolition of Slavery. Organized in 1775, the Society first directed its efforts toward securing an abolition law in Pennsylvania and protecting the free Negro from being kidnaped and sold into slavery. The victims of kidnaping were usually ignorant of legal remedies or unable to secure competent legal assistance. After a successful campaign for adequate protective legislation, the Society helped to enforce the new laws through the organization of committees of correspondence and by hiring competent counsel to secure the conviction of offenders. Although the Society suspended its work during the war, individual members continued to be active. Reorganized in 1787 as the Pennsylvania Society for Promoting the Abolition of Slavery, the Relief of Free Negroes Unlawfully Held in Bondage, and for Improving the Condition of the African Race, the Society joined the Quakers in granting assistance to freedmen.[19]

[18] Thomas E. Drake, *Quakers and Slavery in America* (New Haven, 1950).
[19] Edward Needles, *An Historical Memoir of the Pennsylvania Society, for Promoting the Abolition of Slavery, the Relief of Free Negroes Unlawfully held in Bondage, and for Improving the Condition of the African Race* (Philadelphia, 1848), pp. 13–15, 29.

In celebrating the abolition of slavery in New York, a Negro leader singled out for particular praise the Quakers and the New York Manumission Society, which he termed "the most powerful lever, or propelling cause." That society had organized in 1785 with John Jay as president and Alexander Hamilton as vice-president, thus reflecting the strong Federalist interest in abolition. As early as 1777, Jay had felt that Revolutionary consistency required the abolition of Negro bondage; twenty-two years later, as governor, Jay signed a bill providing for the gradual emancipation of New York's twenty-one thousand slaves. Having fulfilled its major goal, the Manumission Society concerned itself with enforcing and liberalizing the provisions of the abolition act and also joined with the Pennsylvania Society to secure improved anti-kidnaping laws and educational facilities for free Negroes.[20]

By 1830, whether by legislative, judicial, or constitutional action, Negro slavery had been virtually abolished in the North. Only 3,568 Negroes remained in bondage, and more than two-thirds of these resided in New Jersey. Although the Revolutionary ideology had also penetrated the South, particularly Virginia, emancipation had made little headway there. Powerful social and economic factors, the most obvious being Eli Whitney's cotton gin, made slavery the cheapest and most productive form of labor in the South. During the Revolution, some southerners had indeed joined with their northern compatriots to deplore the inconsistency of slavery and the struggle for liberty, but the postwar years brought only disappointment and finally complete disillusionment. After congratulating New England on its successful elimination of bondage, one Virginia judge sadly confessed in 1795 that

[20] William Hamilton, *Oration Delivered in the African Zion Church, on the Fourth of July, 1827, in Commemoration of the Abolition of Domestic Slavery in this State* (New York, 1827), pp. 6–10; Johnston (ed.), *Correspondence and Public Papers of John Jay*, I, 136; Alice D. Adams, *The Neglected Period of Anti-Slavery in America, 1808–1831* (Boston, 1908), p. 14?.

deep rooted white prejudices, the fear of large numbers of
free Negroes, the impossibility of assimilating them into
white society, and the need for a large and cheap servile labor
force had combined to frustrate and defeat any plan for
gradual abolition. "If, in Massachusetts," he wrote, "where
the numbers are comparatively very small, this prejudice be
discernable, how much stronger may it be imagined in this
country, where every white man felt himself born to tyran-
nize, where the blacks were regarded as of no more importance than the brute cattle, where the laws rendered even venial
offences criminal in them, where every species of degradation
towards them was exercised on all occasions, and where even
their lives were exposed to the ferocity of the masters." [21] By
the turn of the century, human bondage had become a "peculiar institution."

Freedom did not suddenly confer citizenship on the Negro.
Emancipation, although enthusiastically welcomed by the
northern slave, had its limitations. Until the post–Civil War
era, in fact, most northern whites would maintain a careful
distinction between granting Negroes legal protection — a
theoretical right to life, liberty, and property — and political
and social equality. No statute or court decision could immediately erase from the public mind, North or South, that long
and firmly held conviction that the African race was inferior
and therefore incapable of being assimilated politically, socially, and most certainly physically with the dominant and
superior white society. Despite the absence of slavery in the
North, one observer remarked, "chains of a stronger kind
still manacled their limbs, from which no legislative act could
free them; a mental and moral subordination and inferiority,

[21] St. George Tucker to Jeremy Belknap, June 29, 1795, in *Mass. Hist. Soc.
Colls.*, Ser. 5, III, 405–7.

to which tyrant custom has here subjected all the sons and
daughters of Africa." [22]

In Massachusetts, for example, where the Revolutionary
ideals had played such an important part in emancipation,
public sentiment appeared much less unanimous on the question of political rights for the freedmen. Despite the protest
of one legislator that Negro disfranchisement violated those
principles upon which the Revolution was being fought, the
proposed state constitution of 1778 excluded "negroes, Indians and mulattoes" from the suffrage. Massachusetts voters
rejected the constitution, but for other reasons. Two years
later, a popularly ratified constitution based voting qualifications only on sex, age, and property. That the Negro's
political position remained unclear, however, was amply demonstrated by the demands of two colored residents that they be
granted either tax relief or the right to vote and hold office.
For several years, contemporaries differed over whether or
not the new constitution accorded political rights and privileges to Negroes.[23] After the elimination of bondage, the
Massachusetts legislature voted to bar interracial marriages
and to expel all Negroes who were not citizens of one of the
states. In 1800, Boston authorities sought to implement this
measure by ordering the immediate deportation of 240 Negroes, most of them natives of Rhode Island, New York, Philadelphia, and the West Indies.[24] By this time, a Negro leader
could only advise his brethren to be patient and "bear up
under the daily insults we meet on the streets of Boston,"

[22] John M. Duncan, *Travels through Part of the United States and Canada in
1818 and 1819* (2 vols.; New York, 1823), I, 60.

[23] Moore, *Notes on the History of Slavery in Massachusetts*, pp. 185–99;
Aptheker (ed.), *Documentary History*, pp. 14–16; Henry N. Sherwood, "Paul
Cuffe," *Journal of Negro History*, VIII (1923), 163–66; *Mass. Hist. Soc. Colls.*,
Ser. 1, III, 208–9; Ser. 5, III, 393, 400.

[24] Some newspapers contended that fears aroused by the Gabriel slave conspiracy in Virginia had prompted the expulsion move. Moore, *Notes on the
History of Slavery in Massachusetts*, pp. 231–37.

though "we may truly be said to carry our lives in our hands, and the arrows of death are flying about our heads." But be not downcast, he concluded, for "the darkest hour is just before the break of day." [25] As subsequent events in Massachusetts would reveal, this optimism was not misplaced. Elsewhere in the North, the Negro's position at the turn of the century generally resembled that of his Massachusetts brethren, but the future did not seem as bright. In New York and Pennsylvania, for example, instead of a gradual liberalization of his rights, the Negro faced a long period of political disfranchisement, economic discrimination, and social ostracism.

Although encouraged by the progress of emancipation, northern antislavery societies realized that much work remained to be done, that freedom had to be given a more solid base, and that the cause of abolition, especially in the South, required an improvement in the moral and economic level of the freedmen. By 1790, the Pennsylvania Society adopted an ambitious plan to deal with these problems; it appointed committees to supervise the morals and general conduct of the freedmen, to place Negro children with persons who could teach them a trade, to promote Negro education in either the regular or separate schools, and to help free Negroes find employment. Despite local opposition, the Society made some notable progress, particularly in the realm of education, where it not only supported colored schools but successfully pressed for state assistance. By 1821, the Society could report that, notwithstanding the Negro's degraded condition — "excluded from most of the respectable and profitable employments of life, confined to the humblest and least gainful occupations, with strong prejudices to surmount, and labouring under every species of difficulty" — he still formed a smaller proportion

[25] Prince Hall, "Extract from a Charge delivered to the African Lodge, June 24th, 1797, at Menotomy, Massachusetts," in Benjamin Brawley (ed.), *Early Negro American Writers* (Chapel Hill, 1935), p. 99.

of the paupers of the state than the whites. In view of the strong prejudices existing among white workers, this was no mean accomplishment.[26]

Since 1794, southern and northern antislavery societies had met periodically as the "American Convention of Delegates from Abolition Societies." The number of states represented and their geographical distribution varied from year to year; the consistent presence of the Pennsylvania and New York societies, however, gave them a dominant voice in the organization. The American Convention appeared to be a highly informal group and largely confined its activities to resolutions, legislative memorials, and moralistic messages to the free Negro population. Perhaps its most important function was to afford opportunities for various state abolition societies to exchange information about the economic and educational status of free Negroes and about steps that had been taken to improve their condition. Although the member societies maintained an independent existence, the American Convention as a unit pressed for a more speedy emancipation of slaves, for strong antikidnaping legislation, and for the right of alleged fugitive slaves to testify and be tried by a jury.[27]

Hoping to create a more favorable atmosphere for abolition, the American Convention also stressed the need for some noticeable improvement in the free Negro's condition. This would be the best proof of the wisdom of emancipation. In its advice to the colored population, published periodically as tracts, the American Convention made it quite clear that the future ad-

[26] MSS Minutes of the Committee for Improving the Condition of the Free Blacks, 1790–1803, Pennsylvania Abolition Society Papers, Historical Society of Pennsylvania, Philadelphia; *Address of the Committee for Improving the Condition of the Free Blacks, to the Members of the Pennsylvania Abolition Society, and to the Public in General* (Philadelphia, 1800) ; *Minutes of the Seventeenth Session of the American Convention for Promoting the Abolition of Slavery, and Improving the Condition of the African Race . . . 1821* (Philadelphia, 1821), p. 13.

[27] American Convention for Promoting the Abolition of Slavery and Improving the Condition of the African Race, *Minutes* . . . (Philadelphia, 1794–1829).

vancement of abolition depended in great measure on how Negroes utilized their newly won freedom. In an effort to guide the Negro along the correct social and moral path, the American Convention included in its appeals homilies which subsequent abolitionist literature would simply standardize: attend public worship regularly; encourage the reading of the Holy Scriptures; acquire instruction in reading, writing, and the fundamentals of arithmetic; teach your children useful and virtuous trades; be diligent in your respective callings and faithful in your relations with society; acquire habits of industry, sobriety, and frugality and avoid dissipation and vice; abstain from spirituous liquors; perform your marriages legally and maintain them; avoid lawsuits, expensive and idle amusements, and noisy and disorderly conduct on the Sabbath; and always conduct yourself with other people in a civil and respectable manner. By following this spotless life of virtue, honesty, sobriety, and industry, the Negro was told, he could effectively refute the objections which had been raised against him as an inferior being and at the same time justify the cause of abolition everywhere.[28]

By 1830, the American Convention remained largely in the hands of the New York and Pennsylvania societies. After a seven-year suspension of meetings, delegates from New York, Pennsylvania, and Delaware agreed in 1838 that the continuation of the organization was not likely to promote its original objectives and therefore voted to dissolve.[29] In the North, Garrisonian abolitionism had, in the meantime, established itself by reputation, if not by numbers; in the South, perhaps even more significantly, antislavery societies had virtually disappeared — victims not so much of Garrison's fiery editorials in

[28] *Minutes of the Proceedings of the Third Convention of Delegates from the Abolition Societies . . . 1796* (Philadelphia, 1796), pp. 12–15. Subsequent conventions repeated this advice with only slight variations.

[29] For a comprehensive account of the work of the American Convention, see Adams, *Neglected Period of Anti-Slavery*, pp. 154–94.

The Liberator as of the growing conviction that internal security required the suppression of all abolitionist activity and pronouncements. In a further effort to protect their "peculiar institution," several southern states stiffened their restrictions against that increasingly obnoxious anomaly, the free Negro. Such legislation, along with the continued proscription of northern free Negroes, also encouraged a newly formed organization, the American Colonization Society, to press its contention that prevailing prejudices made the elevation of the free Negro in the United States — now and ever — impossible.

Since the colonial period various proposals to colonize the Negro had been discussed and advocated, but the steady growth of the free Negro population indicated to many the need for more vigorous action. Accordingly, delegates from several states convened in Washington, D.C., in December, 1816, and organized the American Colonization Society. They voted to take immediate steps to promote and execute a plan for colonizing Negroes, on a voluntary basis, in Africa or any place that Congress might deem expedient. The Society promised not to interfere with slavery; in fact, it termed emancipation and amelioration subjects outside its jurisdiction. A committee — whose membership included such illustrious men as John Randolph, Francis Scott Key, and Richard Rush — was appointed to prepare a memorial to Congress requesting that body to take steps to procure a territory in Africa or elsewhere for the colonization of free Negroes.[30] Meanwhile, the Society set out to win public support through pamphlets, legislative petitions, public meetings, and its own journal, *The African Repository*.

Basing their arguments largely on the condition of the free Negro population, colonizationist speakers and tracts painted a dreary picture of general degradation and wretchedness.

[30] *The African Repository, and Colonial Journal*, I (1825), 1–3; *A View of Exertions Lately Made for the Purpose of Colonizing the Free People of Colour, in the United States, in Africa, or Elsewhere* (Washington, D.C., 1817).

"[I]ntroduced among us by violence, notoriously ignorant, degraded and miserable, mentally diseased, brokenspirited, acted upon by no motive to honourable exertions, scarcely reached in their debasement by the heavenly light," the freedmen "wander unsettled and unbefriended through our land, or sit indolent, abject and sorrowful, by the streams which witness their captivity." Such conditions, colonizationists contended, prevailed everywhere, North and South. Even in Philadelphia — "the pride and ornament of our country" — a Virginia congressman and Colonization Society officer found "scenes of squalid and hopeless misery — such as he had never witnessed in any part of the globe — neither among the wretched paupers of England, nor the woodenshod peasantry of France." [31]

Against this depressing background, colonizationists argued that theirs was the only humane and just solution. As long as Negroes remained in the United States, public opinion would bar them from the polls, the jury box, and the white man's schools, church pews, workshops, and dining tables. Besides this legal and social proscription, the Negro had to contend with an obviously "superior knowledge, wealth and influence . . . a competition to which he is unequal." Such distinctions, be they justifiable or not, made it impossible at any foreseeable time to assimilate the two races, or to ameliorate the Negro's political and social position, or to alter substantially the white man's racial attitudes. "This is not the fault of the coloured man, nor of the white man, nor of Christianity," the Colonization Society explained, "but an ordination of Provi-

[31] *African Repository*, I (1825), 68; *The Twelfth Annual Report of the American Society for Colonizing the Free People of Colour of the United States* (Washington, D.C., 1829), p. vi. See also *An Address to the Public by the Managers of the Colonization Society of Connecticut* (New Haven, 1828), p. 4; Cyrus Edwards, *An Address Delivered at the State House, in Vandalia, on the Subject of Forming a State Colonization Society* (Jacksonville, Ill., 1831), p. 6; J. K. Converse, *A Discourse on the Moral, Legal, and Domestic Condition of our Colored Population, preached before the Vermont Colonization Society* (Burlington, 1832), pp. 6–7.

22

SLAVERY TO FREEDOM

dence, and no more to be changed than the laws of nature."
Throughout the United States, a "broad and impassible" line
divided blacks and whites and "neither refinement, nor argument, nor education, nor religion itself" could successfully
soften or obliterate the customs and prejudices of white
society.[32]

This dismal evaluation of the Negro's position in American
society largely explains the persistent refusal of colonizationists to speak or act against legislation designed to keep the
black man in his place. In fact, many colonizationists favored
such measures and argued that "inevitable necessity" and the
excesses of freedom justified them. In northern legislatures
and constitutional conventions, speakers often coupled demands for Negro disfranchisement, anti-immigration laws,
and other racial restrictions with proposals to promote African
colonization. Equal political rights, they argued, would hardly
encourage Negroes to leave the United States; instead, they
would present "an everlasting obstacle . . . in the way of
colonization" and "chain them to us." Moreover, any attempt
to improve the Negro's position would defy public sentiment,
threaten, if not destroy, the very fabric of American society,
and inevitably produce "commotion, effervescence, collision
and bloodshed."[33]

If no conceivable amount or type of legislation could suc-

[32] *Address of the Managers of the American Colonization Society, to the
People of the United States* (Washington, D.C., 1832), pp. 3–4; *The Fifteenth
Annual Report of the American Society for Colonizing the Free People of Colour
of the United States* (Washington, D.C., 1832), pp. 17–18; *Address of the Colonization Society of Connecticut*, p. 5; *Address to the American Society for Colonizing the Free People of Colour of the United States* (Washington, D.C., 1818),
pp. 27–28.

[33] Edwards, *Address Delivered at the State House*, p. 6; *Proceedings and Debates of the Convention of the Commonwealth of Pennsylvania, To Propose
Amendments to the Constitution* (14 vols.; Harrisburg, 1837–39), X, 24; *Report
of the Debates and Proceedings of the Convention for the Revision of the Constitution of the State of Indiana* (2 vols.; Indianapolis, 1850, 1935), I, 247–48,
457–58, 461, 604; II, 1793, 1794–96; *Proceedings of the Colonization Society of the
City of New York* (New York, 1835), p. 34.

cessfully temper white prejudices, colonizationists maintained, neither could Negro education and economic independence. These might be commendable virtues, but they could not alter a man's color or innate character; consequently, the Negro's general status would remain unchanged. To educate the Negro, then, was merely to tease, frustrate, and finally disillusion him. "Educate him," the Connecticut Colonization Society declared, "and you have added little or nothing to his happiness — you have unfitted him for the society and sympathies of his degraded kindred, and yet you have not procured for him, and cannot procure for him, any admission into the society and sympathy of white men." Voicing an almost identical sentiment, Elias B. Caldwell, secretary of the American Colonization Society, concluded that it would be best to keep Negroes "in the lowest state of degradation and ignorance," for it was futile to raise their hopes and give them "a higher relish for those privileges which they can never attain." [34]

Humanity and justice — not to mention the desirable elimination of a social and political anomaly and nuisance — thus demanded colonization. In Africa, where "the fierce sun . . . scorches the complexion and withers the strength of the white men," the American Negro would have no superior; he would cultivate the fertile soil, proclaim the message of Christianity to the heathen savages, and restore the ancient glories of his race. In the meantime, the United States could rejoice in the gradual extinction of slavery and prejudice and assume a more consistent and influential position in the world community as "the great moral and political light-house." [35]

This was the colonizationist appeal, and the national and state societies directed it to all classes. Each might profit by

[34] *Address of the Colonization Society of Connecticut*, p. 5; *A View of Exertions Lately Made for the Purpose of Colonizing the Free People of Colour*, p. 7.

[35] American Colonization Society, *Annual Reports, 3rd* (Washington, D.C., 1820), p. 24; *14th* (Washington, D.C., 1831), p. xviii; *19th* (Washington, D.C., 1836), p. 8.

the removal of the free Negro population — from the southern
landowner, who would "enhance the value of his property,"
to the patriot, who would "contribute to the immortal honour
of his country . . . by flinging off from the community an
intolerable burden." [36] That this appeal was highly attractive
might be demonstrated by the number of leading public figures
who gave it their support, including many who were acutely
conscious of prevailing public sentiment. Adorning the Society's list of officers during the ante bellum period were such
men as James Madison, Andrew Jackson, Henry Clay, Daniel
Webster, Stephen Douglas, William H. Seward, Richard Rush,
John Marshall, Roger Taney, Francis Scott Key, General Win-
field Scott, Matthew Carey, Edward Everett, Benjamin Silli-
man, Abbot Lawrence, William Appleton, and many religious
leaders and college presidents. "Men of all parties and of all
religions and of no religion have zealously espoused its cause,"
one critic sadly admitted. "The legislatures of fourteen states
have passed resolutions in its favor. . . . Politicians have
declaimed, ministers have preached and Christians have
prayed in its behalf." Although critical of colonization, the
American Convention of Abolition Societies stated in 1829
that most Americans appeared to favor it, particularly as a
means of emancipation. Even New England was sound on this
subject, a southern visitor reported in 1834. "Colonization is
popular here — with those, I mean, who know or reflect at all
about it." [37]

One important, indeed necessary, source of support was con-
spicuously missing: the ostensible objects of colonizationist
benevolence, the free Negroes. One month after the organization of the Colonization Society, approximately three thousand
Negroes crowded into Philadelphia's Bethel Church to give

    [36] *African Repository*, I (1825), 68.
    [37] William Jay, *Miscellaneous Writings on Slavery* (Boston, 1853), p. 79;
Journal of Negro History, VI (1921), 354; [Lucian Minor], "Letters from New
England," *Southern Literary Messenger*, I (1834), 88.

their reply: the colonization scheme violated professed American principles, it sought to stigmatize the free Negro population, and it countenanced the perpetuation of human bondage and encouraged it by seeking to remove the free blacks. Under these circumstances, it deserved to be repudiated by all Negroes, who should, instead, reaffirm their determination never to part voluntarily from their enslaved brethren. As for those Negroes who indorsed the idea, a subsequent protest meeting denounced them as "a few obscure and dissatisfied strangers among us . . . in favor of being made presidents, governors and principals, in Africa." [38]

In state and national conventions, published tracts, and newspapers, northern Negroes periodically reiterated their vigorous opposition to African colonization and maintained that their lot could be improved in this country. Nothing "in the burning sun, the arid plains, and barbarous customs of Africa" peculiarly fitted them for improvement. "This is our home," they repeatedly asserted, "and this is our country. Beneath its sod lie the bones of our fathers; for it some of them fought, bled, and died. Here we were born, and here we will die." No grandiose schemes for alleged Christianization of Africa, they insisted, would deter them from maintaining a steady campaign to gain political recognition and the abolition of slavery in the United States. [39]

What particularly disturbed Negro leaders, however, was that the colonizationist appeal might make such a campaign

[38] William Lloyd Garrison, *Thoughts on African Colonization* (Boston, 1832), pp. 9–10; *The Liberator*, August 1, 1835; *Niles' Weekly Register*, XVII (November 27, 1819), 201–2.

[39] *Resolutions of the People of Color . . . 1831* (New York, 1831) ; Samuel E. Cornish and Theodore S. Wright, *The Colonization Scheme Considered, in Its Rejection by the Colored People* (Newark, 1840) ; Garrison, *Thoughts on African Colonization*, pp. 8–67; *Freedom's Journal*, May 18, June 8, 1827; *The Liberator*, July 2, 23, August 13, 20, September 17, 24, October 8, 29, December 17, November 5, 1831, February 4, March 10, November 3, 1832. For some favorable response from Negroes, most of them southerners, see Carter G. Woodson (ed.), *The Mind of the Negro as Reflected in Letters Written during the Crisis, 1800–1860* (Washington, D.C., 1926), pp. 1–158.

increasingly difficult. Although colonizationists repeatedly denied any intention to remove them by force, many Negroes
realized that colonization propaganda, particularly its almost
lurid descriptions of Negro degradation and licentiousness,
might increase racial prejudice to a point where their continued presence in this country would be intolerable. The Negro would then have no choice but to depart. "They cannot
indeed use force," a New York Negro meeting declared. "That
is out of the question. But they harp so much on 'inferiority,'
'prejudice,' 'distinction,' and what not, that there will no
alternative be left us but to fall in with their plans." If the Colonization Society sincerely desired to help the Negro, then let it
protest those prejudices which blocked their political, economic, and social progress and which furnished the Society
with its dismal pictures of Negro life. This required no large
expenditures or hazardous overseas projects, they explained,
but only that those who professed to believe in Negro improvement should treat them as equals.[40]

After the Negro had made his position quite clear, white
abolitionists began to deprecate the objectives and prejudiced
propaganda of the Colonization Society. In 1817, the usually
mild-mannered American Convention of Abolition Societies
indicated that it was suspicious but not yet hostile; it praised
"the dignified and benevolent intentions" of the Society but
insisted that any colonization scheme had to be preceded by
the gradual and total emancipation of all slaves and by the
literary and moral education of the free Negro. Four years
later, the American Convention circulated an address among
the various antislavery societies expressing its disapproval of
colonization and called it "incompatible with the principles of

[40] *Minutes and Proceedings of the Third Annual Convention, for the Improvement of the Free People of Colour in these United States* (New York, 1833), pp.
27–28; *Resolutions of the People of Color, 1831*, pp. 6–8; Sarah Forten to Angelina Grimke, April 15, 1837, in Gilbert H. Barnes and Dwight L. Dumond (eds.),
Letters of Theodore Dwight Weld, Angelina Grimke Weld, and Sarah Grimke (2
vols.; New York, 1934), I, 380. Cited hereafter as *Weld-Grimke Correspondence.*

our government, and with the temporal and spiritual interests of the blacks." [41]

After 1831, the abolitionist movement and press vigorously denounced colonization. Although once sympathetic to that solution, such antislavery leaders as William Lloyd Garrison, Arthur and Lewis Tappan, Gerrit Smith, and James Birney soon declared their unalterable opposition. To dramatize the allegedly true and sinister designs of the Society, abolitionist journals and tracts reprinted colonization material that spoke of the Negro as a nuisance and menace to white society. [42] So severe was much of this abolitionist criticism that some Garrisonians, still sympathetic with the professed benevolence of colonization, deplored the attack as unfair and too brutal. "You have gone too far," Samuel J. May wrote to Garrison. "Your language has been too severe — your censures too indiscriminate. I fear you have already injured greatly a cause for which, I doubt not, you are ready to sacrifice every thing but your hope of Heaven." But to Garrison, opposition to colonization, as to slavery, permitted no retreat; indeed, he concluded, no loyal abolitionist could indorse the colonization scheme and at the same time profess a sympathy for the Negro's plight. "They can love and benefit them four thousand miles off," he wrote, "but not at home. They profess to be, and really believe that they are, actuated by the most philanthropic motives; and yet are cherishing the most unmanly and unchristian prejudices." [43]

[41] Minutes of the Proceedings of the Fifteenth American Convention for Promoting the Abolition of Slavery, and Improving the Condition of the African Race (Philadelphia, 1817), pp. 30–31; Minutes of the Seventeenth Session of the American Convention, p. 57.

[42] Francis and Wendell P. Garrison, William Lloyd Garrison (4 vols.; Boston and New York, 1894), I, 290–302; Garrison, Thoughts on Colonization; William Jay, Inquiry into the Character and Tendency of the American Colonization, and American Anti-Slavery Societies (New York, 1835); Anti-Slavery Reporter, I (June, 1833), 5–15.

[43] Samuel J. May to William Lloyd Garrison, March 26, July 18, 1831, Garrison Papers, Boston Public Library; Garrison to Ebenezer Dole, July 11, 1831, Garrison to Henry E. Benson, July 30, 1831, Garrison Papers.

Persistent Negro and abolitionist criticism had its desired effect. Unless "agents of zeal and talent" could be found to defend the colonization cause, Secretary R. R. Gurley sadly noted in 1834, the abolitionists would carry the North.[44] But external criticism proved to be only one factor, though a major one, in the decline of the Colonization Society. Internal dissension, financial difficulties, Liberian troubles, and the failure to secure governmental assistance further weakened its influence and effectiveness. Moreover, only a small percentage of the Negro population had been converted to the scheme, most of them recently manumitted southern slaves who gladly agreed to colonization in return for freedom. Noting this failure to win Negro support, some colonizationists concluded that the Society had swerved from its original course and had alienated the colored people by repeatedly describing them as an evil and dangerous class. After all, one Society director declared, "the people of color are not ignorant of this aspect of the subject; they read — they hear — and when they are spoken of as a nuisance to be got rid of, they prove themselves men, men of like passions with us, by resenting it. Their prejudices are roused. They stand aloof from the design." Unfortunately, he added, colonizationists would have to face the fact that partly through their own errors, "the free people of color, taken as a community, look on our undertaking with disaffection."[45]

Although colonization probably appealed to most ante bellum northerners as the ideal solution to the problem of race

[44] Early L. Fox, *The American Colonization Society, 1817–1840* (Baltimore, 1919), p. 94.

[45] *Fifteenth Annual Report of the American Colonization Society*, pp. viii–ix. For a more complete account of the organizational development and problems of the Society and the Liberian colony, see Charles I. Foster, "The Colonization of Free Negroes in Liberia, 1816–1835," *Journal of Negro History*, XXXVIII (1953), 41–66; Frederic Bancroft, "The Colonization of American Negroes, 1801–1865," in Jacob E. Cooke, *Frederic Bancroft* (Norman, Okla., 1957), pp. 147–91; Fox, *American Colonization Society*; and Charles H. Huberich, *Political and Legislative History of Liberia* (2 vols.; New York, 1947).

relations, strong Negro resistance, governmental apathy, and southern suspicion, if not hostility, made any significant achievements almost impossible. The successful establishment of a colony in Liberia, for example, had little impact or influence on the free Negro community. In the 1850's, colonization enjoyed a brief renascence, including practical indorsement by the Republican party and its first presidential victor, Abraham Lincoln. By that time, several Negro leaders had concluded that emigration, preferably to Central America rather than Africa, constituted the sole alternative to continued repression, that this, unfortunately but realistically, was the only way in which the Negro people might give their freedom political significance and economic content. That a substantial body of Negroes should have agreed with this dismal conclusion is not surprising, for it was based on long years of frustration and defeat, broken only in some New England states where few Negroes resided anyway. It had its basis in the proscriptive legislation of most states and territories; in the tacit recognition given such statutes by the federal government; in the decision of the Supreme Court which stripped the Negro of any claim to the rights and privileges of American citizens; in the failure to secure adequate or equal educational and economic opportunities; in the drabness of those urban sections and white-owned shacks reserved for Negroes; in the violence of white mobs and the public sentiment that incited and refused to punish such mobs; in those forms of popular entertainment which caricatured the black man as clownish, carefree, and irresponsible; and, finally, in the futile efforts to gain recognition from any of the major political parties. Such had been the limitations of emancipation and the plight of the American Negro in the age of Jeffersonian and Jacksonian democracy.

II

The Federal
Government and
The Free Negro

Since the Constitution made no mention of race or color, the states and the federal government separately defined the legal status of free Negroes. Both generally agreed, however, that the Negro constituted an inferior race and that he should occupy a legal position commensurate with his degraded social and economic condition. If God had not ordained such an inferior status, public opinion at least demanded it. "The federal constitution is silent about race or colour," an English visitor observed, "but in interpreting it, American lawgivers arrive at the conclusion, that the United States are the property of whites, and that persons with a tinge of dark colour in their countenance, though born free, are not citizens. . . . There seems, in short, to be a fixed notion throughout the whole of the states, whether slave or free, that the coloured is by nature a subordinate race; and that in no circumstances, can it be considered equal to the white." [1]

While most states were circumscribing the Negro's legal position, federal authorities frequently questioned his claim to exercise the rights and privileges of American citizens. Not until 1857, however, when the Supreme Court ruled on the case of *Dred Scott* v. *Sanford,* did the federal government finally dispel all doubts concerning Negro citizenship. By then, Chief Justice Roger B. Taney could find appropriate precedents in the actions of Congress and "the conduct of the Executive Department."

Reflecting the popular conception of the United States as a white man's country, early Congressional legislation excluded Negroes from certain federal rights and privileges and sanctioned a number of territorial and state restrictions. In 1790, Congress limited naturalization to white aliens; in 1792, it organized the militia and restricted enrollment to able-bodied white male citizens; in 1810, it excluded Negroes from carrying the United States mails; in 1820, it authorized the citizens of Washington, D.C., to elect "white" city officials and to adopt a code governing free Negroes and slaves.[2] Moreover, it repeatedly approved the admission of states whose constitutions severely restricted the legal rights of free Negroes.[3] On the basis of such legislation, it would appear that Congress had resolved to treat Negroes neither as citizens nor as aliens. But consistency did not distinguish the actions of

[1] William Chambers, *American Slavery and Colour* (London, 1857), p. 37, and *Things as They Are in America* (London and Edinburgh, 1854), p. 354.

[2] *Appendix to the Annals of Congress,* 1 Cong., 2 sess., pp. 2205–6; 2 Cong., 1 sess., p. 1392; 11 Cong., 1 and 2 sess., p. 2569; 16 Cong., 1 sess., pp. 2600–10; *Appendix to the Congressional Debates,* 18 Cong., 2 sess., p. 91.

[3] After the admission of Maine in 1819, for example, every state that came into the Union before the end of the Civil War confined the suffrage to whites. Charles H. Wesley, "Negro Suffrage in the Period of Constitution Making, 1787–1865," *Journal of Negro History,* XXXII (1947), 154.

the national legislature. On at least one occasion, it recognized — perhaps inadvertently — that Negroes might qualify
as citizens. Against a background of increasing foreign difficulties, including the impressment of American seamen into
the British navy, the House of Representatives resolved in
1803 "to enquire into the expediency of granting protection
to such American seamen citizens of the United States, as are
free persons of color." [4] Protecting the rights of Negro seamen
in foreign waters apparently posed no threat to white supremacy at home.

The failure of Congress to legislate in certain areas also
raised doubts about the Negro's legal position. Although an
early act excluded Negroes from the militia, no such legislation barred them from the Army, Navy, or Marines. In 1798,
the Secretaries of War and Navy issued separate directives
forbidding Negro enlistments in the Marine Corps and on
naval warships. Military necessity, however, apparently negated this policy, for Negro soldiers and sailors served prominently, and often courageously, during the naval war with
France (1798–1800) and the War of 1812. "I have yet to
learn," Captain Oliver H. Perry wrote, "that the color of a
man's skin or the cut and trimmings of the coat can affect a
man's qualifications or usefulness." (Of Perry's four hundred
men, an estimated one hundred were Negroes.) [5] The absence
of any congressional prohibition and the subsequent enlistment of Negro troops raised at least one troublesome question
in the postwar years: Could Negroes qualify for land bounties
promised the veterans of the War of 1812? Attorney General
William Wirt replied in 1823 that they could, although he felt

[4] *Journal of the House of Representatives*, 8 Cong., 1 sess., p. 224. Ten years
later, however, Congress barred from employment on public or private vessels
"any person or persons except citizens of the United States, *or* persons of color,
natives of the United States." 2 *U.S. Stat. at Large* 809.

[5] Rayford W. Logan, "The Negro in the Quasi War, 1798–1800," *Negro History Bulletin*, XIV (1951), 128–31; Lorenzo J. Greene, "The Negro in the War
of 1812 and the Civil War," *ibid.*, p. 133.

"that it was not the intention of Congress to incorporate negroes and people of color with the army any more than with the militia of the United States." [6]

In an effort to clarify congressional policy regarding Negro troops, Senator John C. Calhoun moved in 1842 to exclude Negroes from the Navy, except as cooks, stewards, and servants. "It was wrong," the South Carolinian declared, "to bring those who have to sustain the honor and glory of the country down to a footing of the negro race — to be degraded by being mingled and mixed up with that inferior race." Although several northern congressmen cited the valuable military service of Negroes in the War of 1812, the Senate agreed to Calhoun's proposal, rejected an amendment which would have permitted the employment of Negro sailors "in unhealthy climates," and, for good measure, voted to exclude Negroes from the Army. The House, however, took no action on these measures. [7]

Occasional congressional lapses did not nullify the intent and impact of earlier legislation. By 1820, free Negroes could not legally exercise certain rights and privileges guaranteed to American citizens and aliens. Moreover, the adoption of these restrictions had prompted little or no debate, and no real effort was made in the ante bellum period to change or repeal them. Although free Negroes failed to secure any alteration of legislative policy, they did succeed on several occasions in arousing the wrath of Congress by exercising one of their few remaining rights, that of petitioning the national legislature for a redress of grievances. In 1800, for example, a group of Philadelphia free Negroes, headed by the Reverend Absalom Jones, petitioned Congress to take appropriate steps to correct the evils of the African slave trade and the fugitive-slave act and to provide for the gradual abolition of slavery.

[6] *Official Opinions of the Attorneys General of the United States* (40 vols.; Washington, D.C., 1791–1948), I, 602–3. The acts under which these Negro troops were raised called only for free, able-bodied men.
[7] *Congressional Globe*, 27 Cong., 2 sess., pp. 805–7; 27 Cong., 3 sess., p. 175.

Although the petition admitted the impropriety of immediate emancipation and couched its appeal in very mild terms, it threw the House of Representatives into momentary turmoil. Representative Harrison Gray Otis of Massachusetts immediately opposed referring the petition to committee, as was the normal practice, because to encourage such a measure "would have an irritating tendency, and must be mischievous to America very soon. It would teach them the art of assembling together, debating, and the like, and would soon . . . extend from one end of the Union to the other." Henry Lee of Virginia agreed; indeed, it should not even be tabled but simply returned to its authors. So improper was the petition, John Rutledge, Jr., of South Carolina added, that several states would never have ratified the Constitution had they imagined that such sentiments might be entertained as a proper subject of debate. Only one member of the House, George Thacher of Massachusetts, pressed for congressional consideration on grounds that slavery was "a cancer of immense magnitude, that would some time destroy the body politic, except as proper legislation should prevent the evil." After a two-day debate, the House voted 85 to 1 (Thacher) that those portions of the petition asking Congress "to legislate upon subjects from which the General Government is precluded by the Constitution, have a tendency to create disquiet and jealousy, and ought therefore to receive no encouragement or countenance." [8]

Free Negroes had much greater reason to be concerned with the legislative debates of 1820–21 on the admission of Missouri, for Congress now had an opportunity to clarify once and for all the matter of Negro citizenship. In November, 1820, the prospective state submitted its constitution for the necessary approval of Congress. The right of Missourians to own slave property had been conceded in the previous session, but a new issue had now been raised. The proposed constitution,

[8] *Annals of Congress*, 6 Cong., 1 sess., pp. 229–45.

written and adopted by an aggressively proslavery convention, not only sanctioned slavery but enjoined the state legislature to pass such laws as might be necessary "to prevent free negroes and mulattoes from coming to and settling in this state, under any pretext whatsoever." This had not been conceded or expected, and many found it impossible to reconcile such a clause with the guarantee of the federal constitution that "the citizens of each state shall be entitled to all privileges and immunities of citizens of the several states." If Congress agreed to such a measure, Secretary of State John Quincy Adams told a Pennsylvania representative, it would, in effect, alter the terms of the Constitution and deprive thousands of citizens of their just rights. "Already cursed by the mere color of their skin," Adams remarked, "already doomed by their complexion to drudge in the lowest offices of society, excluded by their color from all the refined enjoyments of life accessible to others, excluded from the benefits of a liberal education, from the bed, from the table, and from all the social comforts of domestic life, this barbarous article deprives them of the little remnant of right yet left them — their rights as citizens and as men." [9]

Since Congress had adopted no consistent position on Negro citizenship, Missouri's congressional defenders searched elsewhere for appropriate precedents. Why not consult the state constitutions and statutes, Senator William Smith of South Carolina urged, for these had given "a decisive character" to the legal status of free Negroes, and they demonstrated beyond a doubt that neither the North nor the South had ever regarded them as suitable members of the political community. Nearly every state barred the Negro from voting, giving evidence in court, and marrying with white persons; no state admitted him into the militia or made him a citizen by legislative act; and

[9] Charles F. Adams (ed.), *Memoirs of John Quincy Adams, Comprising Portions of His Diary from 1795–1848* (12 vols.; Philadelphia, 1875), V, 209–10.

at least one northern state, Pennsylvania, had only recently considered prohibiting further Negro immigration. Moreover, in admitting new states, Congress had already approved racial restrictions. Indeed, the very act that had authorized Missouri to elect delegates to a constitutional convention had limited the suffrage to free white male citizens. "This is unanswerable proof," Senator Smith concluded, "of the degraded condition in which Congress consider free negroes and mulattoes ought to be placed. With this strong and peculiar example before their eyes, well might the people of Missouri conceive they had a right to provide against this evil." [10]

Advocates of Missouri's unqualified admission saw no inconsistency between the anti-free Negro clause and the guarantees of the federal constitution. Using the evidence accumulated by Senator Smith, they simply noted that every state had found it necessary to legislate against the free Negro. Someone, of course, might charge that all such state measures were, in fact, unconstitutional. In this regard, however, Missouri's defenders could find comfort in the remarks of the venerable Representative Charles Pinckney of South Carolina. A delegate to the Constitutional Convention in 1787, Pinckney claimed that he had been responsible for the disputed section on the privileges and immunities of citizens. Now — thirty-four years later — he explained to Congress what he had meant by this clause: "I perfectly knew that there did not then exist such a thing in the Union as a black or colored citizen, nor could I then have conceived it possible such a thing could ever have existed in it; nor notwithstanding all that is said on the subject, do I now believe one does exist in it." Turning his attention to the degraded position of the northern Negro, Pinckney charged that the free states were seeking to rid themselves of the black population "by treating them, on every occasion with the most marked contempt" and excluding them from any

[10] *Annals of Congress*, 16 Cong., 2 sess., pp. 57–71.

political privileges. Not until northerners altered their constitutions and laws and granted Negroes a full enjoyment of the
rights of white citizens could they expect the southern states
to recognize Negro citizenship.[11]

Were Congress to ignore state precedents, reject Missouri's
racial bar, and thus elevate the Negro to citizenship, several
congressmen predicted disastrous consequences. Emancipated
and fugitive slaves would inundate the free states, where they
would vote and send black representatives to sit in the state
and federal legislatures. Was this not "a supposition too
absurd to be for a moment entertained?" Senator John Holmes
of Maine asked. "Gentlemen, with all their humanity, to be
obliged to sit in this Senate by a black man, would consider
their rights invaded." In the face of increasing pressure on
southern free Negroes, Holmes warned his northern colleagues
that every state might be well advised to retain its power to
check the movements of such "a troublesome or dangerous
population." Self-protection also demanded that the South be
able to adopt appropriate controls, for free Negroes posed
serious dangers there. "They are just enough elevated to have
some sense of liberty," a Virginia representative declared,
"and yet not the capacity to estimate or enjoy all its rights,
if they had them — and being between two societies, above
one and below the other, they are in the most dissatisfied state.
They are themselves perpetual monuments of discontent, and
firebrands to the other class of their own color. And if the time
ever came when the flames of servile war enwrap this Union
in a general blaze, perhaps we may have to look to them as
the primary cause of such horrors." Under such circumstances,
had not any state "a right to get rid of them"? [12]

Those who assailed Missouri's free-Negro proviso generally
argued that the Constitution, unlike various state laws, made

[11] *Ibid.*, pp. 1134–39.
[12] *Ibid.*, pp. 83–86, 549.

no distinctions based on color. Moreover, some states accorded their black citizens equal rights with whites. How, then, could the Negroes of New York, Massachusetts, Vermont, and New Hampshire constitutionally be prohibited from settling in Missouri? Southern critics had charged that various northern states prohibited interracial marriages, but how could this be considered discriminatory when it applied to both races? Although they defended the Negro's legal position, few northern congressmen denied the existence of strong racial prejudices in their constituencies. "Custom has made a distinction between them and other men," a New Hampshire senator remarked, "but the constitution and laws make none." Noting the fear that Negroes might be elected to public office, a Pennsylvania representative reminded the House that this had never occurred in states that acknowledged Negro citizenship and undoubtedly never would occur. "The manners and practical distinctions in private life," he asserted, "will form a barrier, in this respect, as insurmountable as if engrafted in the constitution itself; and no danger need be feared that there will be any other commixture of community than we see at present." Nevertheless, Negroes should be accorded "such rights of citizenship as our customs and habits may approve of as suitable to their condition." [13]

On March 2, 1821, Congress voted to admit Missouri on condition that the disputed free-Negro clause "shall never be construed to authorize the passage of any law, and that no law shall be passed in conformity thereto, by which any citizen, of either of the States in this Union, shall be excluded from the enjoyment of any of the privileges and immunities to which such citizen is entitled under the constitution of the United States." The Missouri legislature accepted this vague condition, and subsequent state legislation rendered it ineffective. Congress' action came as no surprise to Representative

[13] *Ibid.*, pp. 48, 96, 108–9, 113, 537, 597, 601, 637–39.

William Plumer, Jr., of New Hampshire. Two months before, he had predicted that Missouri would be admitted "with some declaratory proviso . . . which will in fact amount to nothing, but serve merely as a salve to tender consciences." [14] Determining the legal status of free Negroes remained a matter for local, state, and federal discretion.

After 1821, Congress debated Negro rights with greater regularity and intensity. As abolition sentiment and agitation increased, southern and "Doughface" congressmen seized every opportunity to demonstrate the inconsistency of northern pronouncements on equality and freedom with the treatment accorded free Negroes in the North. In the classic Webster-Hayne debate of 1830, for example, the South Carolina Senator charged that those slaves who escaped to the North found themselves treated as outcasts and assigned to "the dark and narrow lanes, and obscure recesses" of the cities. "Sir," he cried, "there does not exist on the face of the earth, a population so poor, so wretched, so vile, so loathsome, so utterly destitute of all the comforts, conveniences, and decencies of life, as the unfortunate blacks of Philadelphia, and New York, and Boston. Liberty has been to them the greatest of calamities, the heaviest of curses." How, southerners asked, could the North so glibly condemn slavery when it worked free Negroes severely in menial employments, excluded them from the polls, the juries, the churches, and the learned professions, snubbed them in social circles, and finally even barred them from entering some states? Did not northerners place the Negro in a much higher scale by their rhetoric than by their practice? "Go home, and emancipate your free Negroes," a Virginia congressman demanded. "When you do that, we will listen to you with more patience." [15]

[14] Everett S. Brown (ed.), *The Missouri Compromise and Presidential Politics, 1820–1825* (St. Louis, 1926), p. 21.

[15] *Congressional Debates*, 21 Cong., 1 sess., pp. 47, 201, 215; *Congressional Globe*, 30 Cong., 1 sess., pp. 602, 609–10, 612; *Appendix to the Congressional*

The South made its point, found it to be a most effective one, and used it to frustrate abolitionist spokesmen for the remainder of the ante bellum period. Southern travelers in the North buttressed the argument with their own observations. "What's the use to talk about equallity when no such thing exists," a Georgian noted in Philadelphia. "A body sees that in ther churches, and theatres, and courts, and evrywhar else. Nobody here that has any respect for themselves, treats a nigger as ther equal, except a few fannyticks, and they only do it to give the lie to ther own feelins, and to insult the feelins of others." [16] The security of southern society, however, required that its spokesmen in and out of Congress overlook one major fallacy in an otherwise effective indictment of northern racial hypocrisy. The northern Negro admittedly faced political, economic, and social restrictions. Nevertheless, he spoke out freely against his condition; he organized, agitated, penned editorials and pamphlets, and petitioned state and federal bodies to improve his position. Much of this agitation proved legislatively fruitless, but the northern Negro could place his grievances before the public, and few whites challenged his right to do so. Organized slave or even southern free-Negro protests, on the other hand, invited severe repression, punishment, or death.

After 1840, southern congressmen could assert that the federal government itself offered documentary proof of the advantages of slavery over freedom for Negroes. The sixth census of the United States, released in 1841, enumerated for

Globe, 29 Cong., 2 sess., p. 349; 30 Cong., 1 sess., pp. 44–45, 581; 30 Cong., 2 sess., pp. 116–18; 31 Cong., 1 sess., p. 1654.

[16] [William T. Thompson], *Major Jones's Sketches of Travel* (Philadelphia, 1848), pp. 104–5. See also [William Bobo], *Glimpses of New-York City* (Charleston, 1852), pp. 95–97, 125–30; A. A. Lipscomb, *North and South: Impressions of Northern Society Upon a Southerner* (Mobile, 1853), pp. 19–21; J. C. Myers, *Sketches of a Tour through the Northern and Eastern States, the Canadas & Nova Scotia* (Harrisonburg, Va., 1849), pp. 378–79, 381–82.

the first time the mentally diseased and defective — or "insane
and idiots," as they were then officially described — and contained the startling revelation that their prevalence among free
Negroes was about eleven times higher than among slaves. In
the southern states, the ratio of insane or idiotic among Negroes stood at 1 to every 1,558; in the northern states, it was
1 to every 144.5. In fact, the frequency of these afflictions
among Negroes decreased from Maine to Louisiana with virtual mathematical precision. For example, it was found that
in Maine every 14th Negro was either a lunatic or an idiot;
in New Hampshire every 28th; in Massachusetts every 43d;
in Connecticut every 184th; in New York every 257th; and
in New Jersey every 297th. This was in sharp contrast with the
South, where the proportion ranged from 1 in 1,229 in Virginia and 1 in 2,477 in South Carolina to 1 in 4,310 in
Louisiana.[17]

Such statistics not only offered obvious moral lessons but
gave official credence to popular "scientific" ideas about the
peculiar suitability of Negroes for slavery. One northern observer, in a letter to a New York business journal, explained
that the prevalence of insanity among local Negroes resulted
from "the rigors of a northern winter, which have no influence
on the temperament of the whites" but "which affect the cere-
bral organs of the African race." Slavery, he added, apparently helped to lessen such occurrences among southern Negroes.[18] The *Southern Literary Messenger*, however, dismissed

[17] *Compilation of the Enumeration of the Inhabitants and Statistics of the
United States, as Obtained at the Department of State, from the Returns of the
Sixth Census* (Washington, D.C., 1841), pp. 4–104; Albert Deutsch, "The First
U.S. Census of the Insane (1840) and Its Use as Pro-Slavery Propaganda,"
Bulletin of the History of Medicine, XV (1944), 469–82; William R. Stanton,
The Leopard's Spots: Science and the American Idea of Equality, 1815–1860
(Chicago, 1960), pp. 58–59; Edward Jarvis, "Insanity among the Coloured
Population of the Free States," *American Journal of the Medical Sciences*, VII
(1844), 71–83.
[18] "Table of Lunacy in the United States," *Hunt's Merchants' Magazine and
Commercial Review*, VIII (1843), 460–61.

the climatic explanation, attributed the sectional disparity to "moral causes" resulting from the condition of Negroes in the two sections, and concluded that they fared worse in those areas where slavery had been abolished. On the basis of the recent census, the journal warned its readers that the consequences of emancipation might be disastrous. "Let us . . . suppose," it remarked, "a half of a million of free negroes suddenly turned loose in Virginia, whose propensity it is, constantly to grow more vicious in a state of freedom. . . . Where should we find Penitentiaries for the thousands of felons? Where, lunatic asylums for the tens of thousands of maniacs? Would it be possible to live in a country where maniacs and felons met the traveller at every cross-road?" [19] Seizing upon the census for political profit, southern congressmen contrasted "the happy, well-fed, healthy, and moral condition of the southern slaves, with the condition of the miserable victims and degraded free blacks of the North." Such must be the case, a Mississippian declared, for "idiocy and lunacy . . . in the lower classes, had been shown by medical men to be invariably caused by vice and misery." [20]

These remarkable statistics could be used to counter foreign as well as domestic criticism of southern slavery. This was most vividly demonstrated during the diplomatic crisis over Texas. In 1844, the British government, in a communication to Secretary of State Abel Upshur, had expressed a desire to see slavery abolished in Texas and throughout the world. John C. Calhoun, Upshur's successor and a firm defender of the "peculiar institution," replied that slavery in Texas was the concern of neither the British nor the federal government, but was a local matter. Calhoun nevertheless took this opportunity to lecture the British foreign secretary on the relative merits of slavery and freedom for American Negroes, and

[19] "Reflections on the Census of 1840," *Southern Literary Messenger*, IX (1843), 342, 344, 346–47.
[20] *Congressional Globe*, 28 Cong., 1 sess., p. 239.

he used the latest statistics to support his argument. The recent census, Calhoun wrote, demonstrated, on the basis of "unquestionable sources," that "in all instances in which the States have changed the former relation between the two races, the condition of the African, instead of being improved, has become worse. They have invariably sunk into vice and pauperism, accompanied by the bodily and mental inflictions incident thereto — deafness, blindness, insanity, and idiocy — to a degree without example." In the slaveholding states, on the other hand, Negroes have shown marked improvement "in number, comfort, intelligence, and morals." Experience and recent statistical evidence had thus conclusively demonstrated that the subjection of Negroes to whites secured the peace, safety, and progress of both races, while that relation demanded by Great Britain — "under the plausible name of the abolition of slavery" — would either destroy the inferior race or reduce it to "vice and wretchedness." [21]

Calhoun's "unquestionable sources" did not go unchallenged. Dr. Edward Jarvis, Massachusetts-born physician and specialist in mental disorders and one of the founders of the American Statistical Association, delivered the fatal blow.[22] In his first reaction to the census tables on insanity and idiocy, Jarvis agreed that slavery must have "a wonderful influence upon the development of moral faculties and the intellectual powers." Upon more careful investigation, however, he found that the errors in these returns were nearly as startling as the statistics themselves, and in January, 1844 — four months

[21] John C. Calhoun to Lord Richard Pakenham, April 18 and April 27, 1844, in "Proceedings of the Senate and Documents Relative to Texas," *Senate Document*, 28 Cong., 1 sess., No. 341 (1844), pp. 50–53, 65–67.

[22] Jarvis went to Louisville, Kentucky, to practice in 1837, but his antipathy to slavery prompted his return to Massachusetts six years later. He became a leading statistician, served for thirty-one years as president of the American Statistical Association, and helped to prepare the Censuses of 1850, 1860, and 1870. See William R. Leonard, "Edward Jarvis," in Allen Johnson and Dumas Malone (eds.), *Dictionary of American Biography* (22 vols.; New York, 1928–58), IX, 621–22.

prior to Calhoun's letter — Jarvis thoroughly refuted the census findings. Contrasting the population returns with the insanity figures, he found that in many northern towns the census listed insane Negroes where no Negro population existed and that in others the figures exceeded the reported number of Negro residents. Jarvis concluded that the census contributed nothing to the statistical classification of diseases among Negroes but that, instead, it constituted "a bearer of falsehood to confuse and mislead." In the name of the nation's honor, medical science, and truth, he demanded that appropriate steps be taken to correct the census.[23] Hoping to precipitate such action, the American Statistical Association submitted to Congress a memorial which enumerated the errors found in the insanity tables.[24]

Similar objections were raised elsewhere. After carefully examining the returns, a Boston newspaper concluded that the startling prevalence of insanity among northern Negroes existed "only in the error of the census." The *North American Review*, one of the nation's leading journals, regretted that obvious carelessness virtually invalidated the statistics on insanity. Meanwhile, northern Negroes vigorously denied the association of insanity with emancipation. "Freedom has not made us mad," a Negro leader wrote to the New York *Tribune*, "it has strengthened our minds by throwing us upon our own resources, and has bound us to American institutions with a tenacity which nothing but death can overcome." Reinforcing this sentiment, a group of prominent New York Negroes petitioned Congress to re-examine the recent census and make appropriate revisions.[25]

[23] Stanton, *The Leopard's Spots*, pp. 58, 60; Deutsch, "The First U.S. Census of the Insane," pp. 475–76.

[24] "Errors in Sixth Census," *House Report*, 28 Cong., 1 sess., No. 580 (1844), pp. 1–9.

[25] Boston *Daily Advertiser and Patriot*, as quoted in *The Liberator*, August 18, 1843; "What Shall We Do With The Insane?" *North American Review*, LVI

Against this background of growing protest, Representative John Quincy Adams of Massachusetts took the initiative in Congress to call for a thorough investigation and revision of the 1840 census. There existed in that document, Adams declared, gross errors by which "atrocious misrepresentations had been made on a subject of deep importance." Referring to Calhoun's use of the statistics, the former President charged that the United States had nearly found itself at war with Great Britain and Mexico on the basis of those census errors. It was imperative, therefore, that the true state of facts be reported.[26] But census critics faced a formidable obstacle in the person of John C. Calhoun, whose Department of State was responsible for the findings and would have to undertake any revision. On February 26, 1844, the House directed the Secretary of State to investigate and report on the existence of alleged "gross errors" in the census, but Calhoun evaded the inquiry by finding a technical error in the resolution. Adams then called on the Secretary of State, only to be told "that where there were so many errors they balanced one another, and led to the same conclusion as if they were all correct."[27] In June, the House committee to which the memorial of the American Statistical Association had been referred reported that it could find no reason to doubt the validity of the criticism and agreed that this destroyed the utility of the findings on Negro insanity and negated any conclusions that might be based upon them. Apparently aware of the futility of securing a revision, the committee hoped that no such errors would appear in the next census.[28]

(1843), 172n.–73n.; James McCune Smith to the Editor, January 29, 1844, New York *Daily Tribune*, February 1, 1844; *The Liberator*, May 10 and 31, 1844.

[26] *Niles' National Register*, LXVI (May 11, 1844), 175. For a defense of Calhoun's use of the statistics, see *Brownson's Quarterly Review*, I (1844), 404–7.

[27] Adams (ed.), *Memoirs of John Quincy Adams*, XII, 22–23, 29; *Journal of the House*, 28 Cong., 1 sess., pp. 471, 877.

[28] "Errors in Sixth Census," *House Report*, 28 Cong., 1 sess., No. 580 (1844),

Although confronted with hostile House and Senate committee reports, Calhoun adamantly maintained his defense of the census. In response to a new House resolution of inquiry, he stated that his department had given a "full and thorough examination" to the alleged errors and that "the result would seem fully to sustain the correctness of the census." Errors could be expected in such an ambitious undertaking, Calhoun conceded, but they did not alter the conclusion that a far greater prevalence of the diseases of insanity, blindness, deafness, and muteness existed among northern Negroes. This fact "stands unimpeachable." In the face of such evidence, how could one not conclude that the emancipation of southern slaves "would be . . . to them a curse instead of a blessing"? [29]

The Census of 1840 remained unaltered, and for good reason. Its findings provided anti-abolition orators and publicists with "unquestionable" proof of the benign influence of slavery on Negroes. In fact, a Georgia congressman reportedly admitted to Jarvis that the census contained a number of errors. Nevertheless, he added, "it is too good a thing for our politicians to give up. They had prepared speeches based on it, which they could not afford to lose." [30] Although readily used by slavery apologists, the statistics on Negro insanity found little support in the North once they had been refuted. On the eve of the Civil War, a Unitarian clergyman perhaps wrote their proper epitaph: "It was the census that was insane, and not the colored people." [31]

Although northern opposition to the expansion of slavery increased considerably in the 1840's and the 1850's, the free

---

p. 1. A Senate committee reached identical conclusions. *Senate Document*, 28 Cong., 1 sess., No. 146 (1845), pp. 1–2.

[29] John C. Calhoun to the Speaker of the House of Representatives, February 8, 1845, reprinted in *Niles' National Register*, LXVII (June 7, 1845), 218–19.

[30] Deutsch, "The First U.S. Census of the Insane," p. 478.

[31] James Freeman Clarke, "Condition of the Free Colored People of the United States," *The Christian Examiner*, LXVI, Ser. 5, IV (1859), 258.

Negro found little cause for optimism. Most proponents of slavery restriction made it clear that their concern was not for the plight of the black man but for the welfare of the white race. When Representative David Wilmot of Pennsylvania made his historic move to exclude slavery from the territories acquired from Mexico, he carefully explained that he did not propose to interfere with southern institutions and that he possessed "no squeamish sensitiveness upon the subject of slavery, no morbid sympathy for the slave." What he wanted was free states for free white men. "I plead the cause and the rights of white freemen," he told Congress in 1847. "I would preserve to free white labor a fair country, a rich inheritance, where the sons of toil, of my own race and own color, can live without the disgrace which association with negro slavery brings upon free labor." [32]

While challenging the constitutional authority of Congress to check slavery in the territories, opponents of the Wilmot proviso also reiterated the charge that northern treatment of the Negro belied a professed humanitarianism and devotion to liberty. Few northern congressmen challenged the South on this point. Representative Henry C. Murphy of New York, for example, insisted that Congress possessed full power to legislate for the territories but agreed that his state had found it impossible for the two races to live together on equal social or political terms. Nevertheless, Murphy felt some compassion for the Negro. As long as that degraded race remained in the South, it might be happy and contented. Once Negroes entered the free states, however, they would almost certainly "be the objects of contumely and scorn." Under these circumstances, he appealed to the South to retain its Negro population; indeed, he would favor the adoption of severe laws "against any who shall bring the wretched beings to our Free States, there to taint the blood of the whites, or to destroy their

[32] *Appendix to the Congressional Globe*, 29 Cong., 2 sess., p. 317.

own race by vicious courses." [33] Such was undoubtedly the sentiment of a large portion of the North.

During the debates on slavery expansion, another New York representative formally proposed that Congress inquire into the expediency of setting apart a portion of the public domain for the exclusive use and possession of free Negroes. The area would be separately organized, governed by Congress, and eligible for territorial status. In other words, an Ohio representative charged, the Whigs and "negro-loving" New York congressmen proposed to establish a Negro colony which could eventually send blacks to Congress. The author of the resolution replied that he had no such intention, that his plan simply called for ultimate territorial status "and nothing more." The House refused to receive the resolution, and the matter was allowed to die.[34]

If the new territories were to be reserved for whites, as envisioned by Wilmot, Congress would have to bar Negroes from the benefits of federal land policy. The Senate attempted this in 1841 when it voted to confine the privileges of the new pre-emption law to whites. In casting the sole vote against the measure, Augustus Porter of Michigan explained that no previous act had embodied such a clause and that it conflicted with the right of all persons to buy and dispose of property. Although Negroes could neither vote nor hold political office in his state, they could at least enjoy the protection of life, liberty, and property, and this most certainly included the right to hold and dispose of real estate. On reconsideration, the Senate reversed itself and deleted the restriction from the bill. Nevertheless, an opinion from the Attorney General was required to qualify Negroes for the benefits of the act.[35]

[33] Ibid., 30 Cong., 1 sess., pp. 579–81.
[34] Congressional Globe, 30 Cong., 1 sess., p. 778; Appendix to the Congressional Globe, 30 Cong., 1 sess., pp. 727, 730–31.
[35] Congressional Globe, 26 Cong., 2 sess., pp. 77, 114; Appendix to the Congressional Globe, 26 Cong., 2 sess., p. 27; Official Opinions, IV, 147–48.

This proved to be a momentary victory for Negro rights to the public domain. On several occasions, exclusionist sentiment prompted Congress to tack white restrictionist amendments onto land and homestead bills. In organizing the Oregon and New Mexico territories, for example, Congress agreed to limit public land grants to white settlers. "This is surely a novel proposition," Representative Joshua Giddings of Ohio protested. "Will history record this as an exhibition of the narrow, the groveling prejudices which govern the American Congress?" But Giddings' colleagues apparently argued more persuasively that granting public lands to Negroes would only encourage and prolong their co-existence with whites. "I sympathize with them deeply," an Ohio representative exclaimed, "but I have no sympathy for them in a common residence with the white race. God has ordained, and no human law can contravene the ordinance, that the two races shall be separate and distinct. . . . I will vote against any measure that has a tendency to prolong their common residence in this Confederacy, or any portion of it." [36]

Prior to 1857, the federal government still had no consistent policy governing the Negro's rights to the public lands. In fact, the Secretary of the Interior informed a New York Negro that no law barred him from settling upon the public domain or claiming pre-emption rights. But the Dred Scott decision dealt a crushing blow to the Negro's position. Shortly afterwards, the commissioner of the General Land Office announced that since Negroes were not citizens, they could not qualify for pre-emption benefits. [37] Consequently, any Negro who desired to settle on the newly opened western lands now faced not only

[36] 9 U.S. Stat. at Large 497; 10 ibid. 308; Congressional Globe, 31 Cong., 1 sess., pp. 1090-93; 33 Cong., 1 sess., pp. 1057-58, 1071-73; Frederick Douglass' Paper, March 17, 1854.

[37] Annual Reports of the American Anti-Slavery Society . . . for the years ending May 1, 1857, and May 1, 1858 (New York, 1859), p. 130; New York Daily Times, August 21, 1857.

the anti-immigration laws of various territories and states but the open hostility of the federal government as well. Ironically, Taney's decision struck a severe blow at both the proponents of Negro citizenship and free white territories.

Since no federal ruling or act specifically defined the Negro's legal status, each executive department apparently felt free to pursue its own policy. Although this invariably resulted in proscription, the Negro sometimes benefited from the existing confusion and exercised the rights of white citizens. The opinions of the Attorneys General, the passport policy of the State Department, and the exclusion of Negroes from the postal service graphically illustrate a sometimes conflicting and even chaotic federal approach.

The Attorneys General usually agreed that the Constitution did not confer citizenship on Negroes. The first such ruling, handed down by William Wirt in 1821, affected only Virginia free Negroes, but later interpretations extended its meaning. Since the acts regulating foreign and coastal trade limited the command of vessels to citizens, Wirt advised a Norfolk port official that the Negroes of his state could not legally qualify. Virginia laws barred free Negroes from voting, holding political office, testifying against a white man, enrolling in the militia, possessing weapons, raising a hand against a white man, "except in defence against a wanton assault," or marrying a white woman. Consequently, such persons could not be considered as citizens of the United States. How did this opinion affect Negro rights in other states? Inasmuch as the Attorney General's definition of citizenship included "those only who enjoyed the full and equal privileges of white citizens in the State of their residence," this would appear to qualify—at least by implication—Negroes in several northern states. Wirt did not make this clear, however, and subsequent decisions failed to substantiate the implication. In fact, Chief Justice Roger Taney construed the opinion to apply to all free Negroes.[38]

The efforts of a few southern states to control the movements of American and foreign free colored seamen embarrassed diplomatic relations with Great Britain, forced the federal government to call for the Attorney General's opinion on several occasions, and prompted at least one significant though unpublicized attempt to define the constitutional position of free Negroes. Obsessed with the fear that northern or foreign Negroes had helped to instigate a recent slave uprising, the South Carolina legislature, in 1822, provided for the imprisonment of free colored seamen while the vessels on which they were employed remained in any of the state's ports. Unless the ship captains paid the costs of such confinement, the Negro seamen would be sold to recover the charges. Several other southern states adopted almost identical measures.[39] Such legislation prompted some furious protests abroad and in the North. In a direct appeal to Congress, a group of Boston petitioners charged that these regulations materially affected commerce and deprived qualified Negroes of their constitutionally guaranteed rights as citizens. Indorsing this sentiment, a House committee concluded that the acts violated the Constitution and laws of the United States and should therefore be repealed.[40]

After the British government formally denounced the application of these laws against its own seamen, the State Department called upon the Attorney General for a ruling. William

[38] *Official Opinions*, I, 506–9; *Dred Scott* v. *Sanford*, 19 Howard 40.

[39] Charles S. Sydnor, *The Development of Southern Sectionalism, 1819–1848* (Baton Rouge, La., 1948), p. 152; Philip M. Hamer, "Great Britain, the United States and the Negro Seamen Acts, 1822–1848," *Journal of Southern History*, I (1935), 3–28.

[40] "Free Colored Seamen," *House Report*, 27 Cong., 3 sess., No. 80 (1843). A minority report upheld the acts, blamed recent southern disturbances on northern Negro seamen, pointed to racial proscription in Massachusetts, and dismissed the privileges-and-immunities clause of the Constitution as inapplicable to free Negroes. *Ibid.*, pp. 37–42.

Wirt advised the government in 1824 that the acts violated the Constitution, treaties, and statutes, and conflicted with "the rights of all nations in amity with the United States." No mention was made of the constitutional rights of free Negroes; instead, Wirt's opinion stressed South Carolina's interference with foreign and interstate commerce. Ignoring this ruling, the offending states continued to enforce the acts. Seven years later, Attorney General John Berrien confirmed their action and found the legislation to be a lawful exercise of state police powers. "The general right of a State to regulate persons of color within its own limits," Berrien ruled, "is one too clearly recognized by the tenth amendment to the constitution to be drawn into controversy." In this case, the state had simply moved to protect its white and colored citizens from the "moral contagion" of insurrection.[41]

Refusing to accept such an explanation, Great Britain remained adamant in protesting the detention of her free Negro seamen. Upon the receipt of another formal note in 1831, Secretary of State Edward Livingston submitted the question to Andrew Jackson's Attorney General, Roger Taney. Although never completed for publication and little publicized, the reply extended Wirt's earlier opinion, affirmed the legal inferiority of all Negroes in the United States, and clearly anticipated the decision Taney made twenty-five years later. No federal act or treaty, he advised, could prevent a state from taking appropriate steps to insure its internal security. The charge that such steps might violate the constitutional rights of Negroes could easily be dismissed, for those rights simply did not exist. The framers of the Constitution, Taney contended, had not regarded Negroes as citizens, and the present condition of that race warranted no change in their legal status. "The African race in the United States even when free," the Attorney General wrote, "are everywhere a degraded class, and exercise

[41] *Official Opinions*, I, 659–61; II, 426–42.

no political influence. The privileges they are allowed to enjoy, are accorded to them as a matter of kindness and benevolence rather than of right. . . . And where they are nominally admitted by law to the privileges of citizenship, they have no effectual power to defend them, and are permitted to be citizens by the sufferance of the white population and hold whatever rights they enjoy at their mercy." Negroes thus constituted "a separate and degraded people," and each state could grant or withhold such privileges as it deemed proper and expedient.[42]

Had Taney's opinion been published, it might have settled the question of Negro citizenship well in advance of the Dred Scott decision. But such was not the case, and the confused status of the Negro continued to confront various federal agencies. Attorney General Hugh Legare decided in 1843 that free Negroes were neither aliens nor citizens, but occupied an intermediate position. When asked whether Negroes could apply for benefits under the new pre-emption act, Legare replied that no previous law had excluded them and he saw nothing prohibitory in the new statute. The "plain meaning" of the new act was to exclude aliens and to grant pre-emption rights "to all denizens"; any foreigner who filed his intention of citizenship could thus qualify for its benefits. "Now, free people of color are not aliens," Legare advised. "They enjoy universally . . . the rights of denizens. . . . How far a political *status* may be acquired is a different question, but his *civil* status is that of a complete denizenship." This novel legal position had no discernible effect on the Negro's rights or privileges. Attorney General Caleb Cushing summarily dismissed the ruling in 1856 and charged that Legare "had . . . been carried away in argument by a generous disposition to protect . . . the claim of a free African, without admitting him to be a citizen of the United States." To qualify Negroes

[42] Carl Brent Swisher, *Roger B. Taney* (New York, 1935), p. 154.

for pre-emption rights, Cushing advised, the federal government had either to overrule or to ignore Wirt's 1821 opinion.[43] The legal status of ante bellum free Negroes rested there until the Dred Scott decision, which cited the opinions of both Wirt and Cushing and coupled these with other manifestations of federal racial distinctions, including the State Department's passport policy.

In citing the refusal of the Secretaries of State to grant passports to Negroes, Chief Justice Taney conveniently overlooked the fact that departmental policy had been somewhat erratic and inconclusive. Prior to 1855, several Negroes secured passports which certified that they were American citizens and were thus entitled to full diplomatic protection abroad. On the other hand, the Department rejected the application of a Philadelphia Negro in 1839 because the newly revised Pennsylvania constitution, which limited the suffrage to white males, obviously did not recognize Negroes as citizens. The decision as to whether or not a passport should be granted thus appeared to depend on the rights enjoyed by the applicant in his state of residence. In some cases, however, the intercession of an influential white person might have been even more important.[44]

Hoping to clarify departmental policy, Secretary of State James Buchanan explained in 1847 that regular passports certified that the bearer was a citizen of the United States. Consequently, it had been customary to grant free Negroes special certificates "suited to the nature of the case" instead of passports. Two years later, Secretary of State John M. Clayton insisted that no passports had been granted to Negroes and that protection abroad had been granted them only when they were in the service of United States diplomatic agents. "Our

[43] *Official Opinions*, IV, 147–48; VII, 751–73.
[44] *The Liberator*, April 16, 1858; Barnes and Dumond (eds.), *Weld-Grimke Correspondence*, II, 792–93; Arnold Buffum to Roberts Vaux, May 16, 1834, Vaux Papers, Historical Society of Pennsylvania, Philadelphia.

shipwrecked seamen," the New York *Evening Post* protested, "discharged servants, outraged or insulted citizens, who find themselves destitute, in foreign lands, if they are persons of color, are to be thrust from the doors of our foreign ministers and consuls, and to be denied the aid, sympathy and protection which our diplomatic functionaires were sent abroad mainly for the purpose of dispensing." Nevertheless, Clayton defended his ruling as "the settled regulation of the Department."[45]

In the decade preceding the Civil War, a growing number of Negro leaders sought passports to England, where they planned to lecture and raise money for the abolitionist cause. The State Department rejected most of these applications. Although it could not bar them from traveling abroad, the Department undoubtedly had no desire to encourage or protect the criticism of American institutions. The question of Negro citizenship, Assistant Secretary of State J. A. Thomas noted in 1856, had repeatedly arisen in both the federal and state governments. In view of the opinions of Attorneys General Wirt and Cushing and certain state judicial decisions, Negroes could not be regarded as citizens, either at home or beyond the jurisdiction of the federal government. Nevertheless, the State Department was willing to grant to qualified Negroes special forms certifying that they were free and born in the United States. If any of them should be wronged by a foreign government, "while within its jurisdiction for a legal and proper purpose," American diplomatic officials would seek to protect their rights. It remained questionable, however, whether or not attacking Negro slavery or raising money

[45] John Bassett Moore (ed.), *The Works of James Buchanan* (12 vols.; Philadelphia, 1908–11), VII, 236; *North Star*, July 20, August 24, 1849; *The Non-Slaveholder*, IV (1849), 191; John M. Clayton to the Editor of the Salem *Register*, as quoted in *The [10th] Annual Report of the American and Foreign Anti-Slavery Society, presented at New York May 7, 1850. . . .* (New York, 1850), pp. 128–29.

for American abolitionism constituted "a legal and proper purpose." [46]

Following the Dred Scott decision, the State Department relied on Taney's ruling as proper and sufficient grounds for rejecting Negro passport applicants. Secretary of State Lewis Cass, however, refused to admit that any change had taken place but insisted that the court decision merely confirmed previous policy. "A passport being a certificate of citizenship," he wrote, "has never since the foundation of the Government, been granted to persons of color. No change in this respect has taken place in consequence of the decision of the Dred Scott case." [47] Several newspapers thereupon enumerated, for Cass's edification, those passports which had been granted to free Negroes, including one issued as late as 1854 to a Massachusetts "colored citizen." "The record is so clearly against the Secretary and the Administration," the Boston *Daily Bee* concluded, "that it would have been far more decent and respectable in them to have acknowledged the truth, that *they have changed the policy and practice of the government*, and resolved that colored men shall not be recognized in any manner as citizens of the United States, and that they have determined to degrade and oppress colored men in every possible mode." [48]

Correcting the Secretary of State's historical oversights might help to set the record straight, but it could not alter the effect of the Dred Scott decision. The State Department now had a settled and legally defensible position. "My only hope, now," a rejected Negro applicant declared, "is to go to some foreign country, and through the assistance of friends, claim its protection, or else, through their assistance, get permission to travel as an American outlaw! How much farther

---

[46] *The Liberator*, November 28, 1856; *Official Opinions*, X, 404.
[47] New York *Daily Times*, April 12, 1858.
[48] Boston *Daily Bee*, as quoted in *The Liberator*, April 16, 1858.

this nation intends to sink in infamy, God only knows." [49]
Some states, however, moved to soften the blow and afford protection to their own Negro inhabitants. The Massachusetts legislature, for example, protested that Taney's decision had
"virtually denationalized" the state's Negro citizens, and it
authorized its own secretary of state to grant passports to any
citizen of the Commonwealth, "whatever his color may be." [50]
The impact of the Civil War and a new administration made
any further state action unnecessary. In 1861, Secretary of
State William H. Seward, at the request of Senator Charles
Sumner of Massachusetts, granted a passport to a Boston Negro, "Robert Morris, Jr., a citizen of the United States." [51]

Although the absence of any pertinent statute prompted the
State Department to formulate its own racial policy, the Post
Office Department simply enforced an earlier congressional
act which it had helped to conceive. In a confidential letter to
the chairman of a Senate committee, Postmaster General
Gideon Granger explained in 1802 that there existed objections to Negro mail carriers "of a nature too delicate to en-
graft into a report which may become public, yet too important
to be omitted or passed over without full consideration." Such
Negroes constituted a peril to the nation's security, for employment in the postal service afforded them an opportunity
to co-ordinate insurrectionary activities, mix with other people,
and acquire subversive information and ideas. Indeed, in
time they might even learn "that a man's rights do not depend
on his color" and transmit such ideas to their brethren. Congress had to act against such a possibility. "Every thing which
tends to increase their knowledge of natural rights," Granger
warned, "of men and things, or that affords them an opportunity of associating, acquiring, and communicating senti-

[49] Cleveland *Leader*, May 4, 1858.
[50] Massachusetts *Acts and Resolves*, 1857, p. 558; 1858, pp. 170–71.
[51] Charles Sumner, *Works* (15 vols.; Boston, 1870–83), V, 497–98.

ments, and of establishing a chain or line of intelligence"
might excite alarm.[52]

The Postmaster General's warning aroused sufficient alarm
to spur legislative action. In 1810, Congress ruled that "no
other than a free white person shall be employed in conveying
the mail" and provided fines for any offending mail contractors.[53] There might conceivably arise, however, occasions which
would justify the use of Negroes for some of the physical
labor associated with handling the mails. While instruct-
ing his deputies to adhere strictly to the regulations, Postmaster General John McLean thus ruled in 1828 that Negro labor
might be utilized to carry mailbags from stagecoaches into
post offices, providing a responsible white person carefully
supervised the operation.[54]

The restriction remained in effect and went virtually unchallenged during the remainder of the ante bellum period.
Not until 1862 did Congress consider its repeal. In that year
the Senate agreed to Charles Sumner's bill to revoke the bar
on Negro mail carriers. Never before, a Boston newspaper
recollected, had any bill concerning the Negro, either directly
or indirectly, secured the necessary Senate approval without
debate. "What a good time is coming, when the African race
will no longer be a bone of contention in our legislative
halls!" But such optimism was premature. The House agreed
to table the bill after Schuyler Colfax, Republican chairman
of the post office committee, objected to it on the grounds
that no repeal petitions had been received, no public demand existed for such action, that it would qualify blacks,

[52] American State Papers. Documents, Legislative and Executive, of the
Congresses of the United States. . . . (38 vols.; Washington, D.C., 1832–61),
Class VII: Post Office, p. 27.
[53] 2 U.S. Stat. at Large 594. Re-enacted without change in 1825. 4 ibid. 104.
[54] Jay, Miscellaneous Writings on Slavery, p. 233; William C. Nell, The Colored Patriots of the American Revolution, with Sketches of Several Distinguished
Colored Persons: To which is added a Brief Survey of the Condition and Prospects of Colored Americans (Boston, 1855), p. 312.

Indians, and Chinese as mail contractors and postal officers, and that the Postmaster General had not recommended its passage and did not regard it as being in "the best interest of the Department." [55]

Where Congress had explicitly proscribed the rights of Negroes, as in the postal service, no confusion existed. Elsewhere, the individual departments made their own decisions. By 1857, after some fumbling and hesitation, the executive and legislative branches appeared to have worked out a generally consistent position. That it conformed to public prejudices should not be surprising, for no political party could afford to compromise on this issue. Moreover, the supreme judicial body of the United States now moved to translate federal and state policy and public sentiment into a legal language which would permanently define the constitutional status of American Negroes.

In the Dred Scott decision, Negro citizenship and the Missouri Compromise shared a similar fate. Chief Justice Taney found both to be incompatible with the Constitution. If there existed any doubts concerning the legal status of Negroes, these could finally be dispelled. "This confusion is now at an end," one northern Negrophobe wrote, "and the Supreme Court . . . has defined the relations, and fixed the *status* of the subordinate race *forever* — for that decision is in accord with the natural relations of the races, and therefore can never perish. It is based on historical and existing facts, which are indisputable, and it is a necessary, indeed unavoidable inference, from these facts." [56]

Early in the decision, the Chief Justice confronted the crucial problem of Negro citizenship. Can the descendants of Negro slaves, he asked, be admitted into the political commu-

[55] *Congressional Globe*, 37 Cong., 2 sess., pp. 1260, 1390, 1626, 2231–32, 2262–63; Sumner, *Works*, VI, 385–88.

[56] J. H. Van Evrie, *The Dred Scott Decision* (New York, 1860), p. iii.

nity created by the Constitution and thus be entitled to the rights, privileges, and immunities guaranteed to American citizens? Seeking an answer to this question, Taney reviewed the historical status of the Negro population. For more than a century prior to the Constitutional Convention of 1787, he declared, Negroes had "been regarded as beings of an inferior order, and altogether unfit to associate with the white race, either in social or political relations; and so far inferior, that they had no rights which the white man was bound to respect." [57] This constituted at the time a thoroughly "fixed and universal" opinion in the Western world, "an axiom in morals as well as in politics"; men in every class and position, public and private, acted according to it and colonial legislation confirmed it. Under these circumstances, one could hardly suppose that the framers of the Constitution would agree to grant rights and privileges to Negroes that were denied them in the states. Had they done so, "they would have deserved and received universal rebuke and reprobation." The delegates to Philadelphia understood the state of public opinion in relation to the Negro and acted accordingly. Obviously, then, Negroes were "not intended to be included, and formed no part of the people who framed and adopted" the Declaration of Independence and the Constitution.[58]

Only because the climate and economy rendered slave labor unprofitable, Taney asserted, did the northern states decide to abolish the institution. But this did not, he insisted, alter in any way previously existing racial prejudices. Indeed, state legislation demonstrated conclusively that no moral revolution had occurred. For example, Rhode Island and Massachusetts prohibited interracial marriages; Connecticut forbade Negroes from entering the state to be educated unless civil authorities consented; and New Hampshire limited enrollment in the militia to white citizens. If further evidence were needed,

[57] *Dred Scott* v. *Sanford*, 19 Howard 403, 407.
[58] *Ibid.*, 407–10.

Taney could cite the opinion of Chancellor James Kent of New York that in no portion of the country except Maine did the Negro exercise civil and political rights on an equal basis with whites. Was this not substantial proof that Negroes occupied an inferior status in society, one that was hardly commensurate with citizenship and its attendant rights and privileges? [59]

State and federal citizenship must not be confused, Taney warned, for while a state can legally naturalize its own residents and accord them any rights it deems proper, it has no power to secure to them the privileges and immunities of United States citizens. Only Congress, authorized by the Constitution to establish a uniform rule of naturalization, can exercise such a power. Moreover, no state may, by its own action, introduce into that political community created by the Constitution any new members or any persons "who were not intended to be embraced in this new political family, which the Constitution brought into existence, but were intended to be excluded from it." That this applied to Negroes was abundantly clear to the Chief Justice. Not only had Congress restricted naturalization to "free white persons," but subsequent state and federal legislation and "the conduct of the Executive Department" confirmed his conclusion that Negroes "are not included, and were not intended to be included, under the word 'citizens' in the Constitution, and can therefore claim none of the rights and privileges which that instrument provides for and secures to citizens of the United States." [60]

Two justices joined Taney in his opinion on Negro citizenship, four avoided the issue, and two others — John McLean and Benjamin R. Curtis — wrote vigorous dissents. Curtis contended that the right to confer citizenship rested with the states and that the federal government could only specify the manner in which an alien's disabilities might be removed. Free,

[59] *Ibid.*, 412–16.
[60] *Ibid.*, 404–406, 419–22.

native-born citizens of each state were thus citizens of the United States. Moreover, Curtis denied that Negroes played no part in the political community at the time of the Constitutional Convention. In at least five states, they could exercise suffrage on equal terms with whites. The framers of the Articles of Confederation must have known this, for they rejected a move by South Carolina to restrict the privileges and immunities clause to white persons. Thus Negroes, Curtis concluded, had not only helped to make up the political community which established the Constitution but in certain states had undoubtedly voted on the question of ratification. In view of these facts, they quite clearly qualified as citizens of the United States.[61]

Although many northern political leaders and newspaper editors assailed Taney's decision, they indicated much more concern about its repudiation of the Missouri Compromise than about the constitutional rights of Negroes. After all, the Chief Justice had told the Republican party that the major plank of its political platform — resistance to the further expansion of slavery — was unconstitutional. Few Republicans, on the other hand, had ever defended the rights of free Negroes. Had the Chief Justice confined his argument to the question of Negro citizenship, he might have gone virtually unchallenged, for it merely confirmed existing state and federal practices sanctioned by both major political parties. "Now my opinion," Abraham Lincoln observed, "is that the different states have the power to make a negro a citizen under the Constitution of the United States if they choose. The Dred Scott decision decides that they have not that power. If the State of Illinois had that power, I should be opposed to the exercise of it. That is all I have to say about it." [62] Lincoln's colleague, Senator Lyman Trumbull of Illinois, was even more explicit. What prompted him to repudiate the Dred Scott deci-

[61] Ibid., 572–82.
[62] Roy P. Basler (ed.), The Collected Works of Abraham Lincoln (8 vols.; New Brunswick, N.J., 1953), III, 179.

sion, he told the Senate, was its attempt to limit congressional powers over slavery in the territories. As for Negro citizenship, he could by no means agree to the doctrine that the Constitution required the states to place blacks and whites on an equal footing.[63]

Meanwhile, abolitionists and Negro leaders bitterly condemned Taney's decision. One Negro protest rally called it "a palpably vain, arrogant assumption, unsustained by history, justice, reason or common sense." Frederick Douglass predicted that "the National Conscience" would rise to overturn the clearly objectionable and undemocratic ruling. But Robert Purvis, a Negro abolitionist, warned his people not to comfort themselves with the thought that this decision was unconstitutional and that the whites would therefore rush to their assistance. It was, he declared, "in perfect keeping with the treatment of the colored people by the American Government from the beginning to this day." Several other Negro leaders shared this sentiment; they denounced the decision but expressed no great surprise. After all, it merely confirmed "the already well known fact that under the Constitution and Government of the United States, the colored people are nothing, and can be nothing but an alien, disfranchised and degraded class."[64]

The Dred Scott decision had a brief tenure. Several northern states moved at once to condemn and nullify its ruling on Negro citizenship. The Civil War completed its ruin. On November 29, 1862, Attorney General Edward Bates advised the Secretary of the Treasury that the qualifications for citizenship did not depend on color, race, "the degradation of a people," or the legal right to vote and hold office. "Free men of color, if born in the United States, are citizens of the United States."[65] Six years later, the Fourteenth Amendment confirmed this opinion.

[63] *Congressional Globe*, 35 Cong., 1 sess., p. 1965.
[64] *The Liberator*, April 10, 1857, July 9, 1858; Philip S. Foner (ed.), *The Life and Writings of Frederick Douglass* (4 vols.; New York, 1950–55), II, 411.
[65] *Official Opinions*, X, 382–413.

The Politics of
Repression

Legal and extralegal discrimination restricted northern Negroes in virtually every phase of existence. Where laws were lacking or ineffectual, public opinion provided its own remedies. Indeed, few held out any hope for the successful or peaceful integration of the Negro into a white-dominated society. "The policy, and power of the national and state governments, are against them," a Philadelphia Quaker wrote in 1831. "The popular feeling is against them — the interests of our citizens are against them. The small degree of compassion once cherished toward them in the commonwealths which got rid of slavery, or which never were disfigured by it, appears to be exhausted. Their prospects either as free, or bond men, are dreary, and comfortless." [1]

Most northerners, to the extent that they thought about it at all, rebelled at the idea of racial amalgamation or integration. Instead, they favored voluntary colonization, forced expulsion, or legal and social proscription. The young and

[1] Roberts Vaux to Samuel Emlen, May 31, 1831, Vaux Papers, Historical Society of Pennsylvania.

perceptive French nobleman Alexis de Tocqueville, after an extensive tour of the United States in 1831, concluded that Negroes and whites formed separate communities, that they could never live in the same country on an equal footing, and that the oppressed race — the Negro — consequently faced ultimate extinction or expulsion. Having associated the plight of American Negroes with the institution of slavery, Tocqueville expressed his astonishment at conditions in the North. "The prejudice of race," he wrote, "appears to be stronger in the states that have abolished slavery than in those where it still exists; and nowhere is it so intolerant as in those states where servitude has never been known." Where statutes made no racial distinctions, Tocqueville found that custom and popular prejudices exerted a decisive influence. Although Negroes and whites could legally intermarry in most northern states, public opinion would not permit it. Where Negroes possessed the right to vote, they often faced vigorous resistance at the polls. They might seek redress in the courts, but only whites served as judges; although they were legally entitled to sit on juries, the public would not allow it. Segregation confronted them in public places, including churches and cemeteries. "Thus the Negro is free," Tocqueville concluded, "but he can share neither the rights, nor the pleasures, nor the labor, nor the afflictions, nor the tomb of him whose equal he has been declared to be; and he cannot meet him upon fair terms in life or in death." [2]

In the absence of any pertinent federal statutes, the future of the Negro was left to the states and to the dominant race. As a result, in some states Negroes obtained rights and privileges which in other states they found to be illegal or impossible to exercise. The Negroes' numerical strength, the geographic position of the state, political and economic factors, and pub-

[2] Alexis de Tocqueville, *Democracy in America*, ed. by Phillips Bradley (2 vols.; New York, 1945), I, 359–60, 373.

lic opinion combined to fix their status. This was not a static position, however, but one subject to constant change and fluctuation, ranging from the acquisition of full citizenship in Massachusetts to political disfranchisement in Pennsylvania and from quasi-freedom in New York to attempted expulsion in Ohio.

Nearly every northern state considered, and many adopted, measures to prohibit or restrict the further immigration of Negroes. Those people favoring such legislation included self-styled friends of the Negro, as well as avowed racial bigots. In either case, the professed aim of immigration restriction was to settle the problem of racial relations by expelling the Negro or at least by preventing any sizable increase of his numerical strength.

Basing their arguments largely on the alleged mental and physical superiority of the dominant race, restrictionists warned of the dangers inherent in any attempt to integrate the Negro into the political and social community, for "the natural tendency has been proven by experience, not to be elevation of the degraded, but the deterioration, the lowering, of the better class, towards the standard of the inferior class." Moreover, did not the Bible itself demonstrate conclusively that God had marked and condemned the Negro to servility and social leprosy? "The same power that has given him a black skin, with less weight or volume of brain," an Indiana senator argued, "has given us a white skin, with greater volume of brain and intellect; and that we can never live together upon an equality is as certain as that no two antagonistic principles can exist together at the same time." [3]

Under these circumstances, restrictionists argued that exclusion would be both natural and politic. Indeed, several pro-

[3] *Indiana Constitutional Debates of 1850*, I, 248, 251; *Appendix to the Congressional Globe*, 33 Cong., 2 sess., p. 236.

claimed their support for such a move as a natural consequence of their long friendship with the Negro. Separation of the two races would be mutually beneficial. The real enemies of the Negro were those who desired his continued presence in a country which would never afford him adequate opportunities for advancement. Robert Dale Owen, Indiana politician and reformer, advanced this argument to defend restrictive legislation. A proposed bar on Negroes in his state would, he hoped, advance the cause of humanity, not repression. What would be the alternative to exclusion? Would not Negroes "remain, as now, a race legally and socially excommunicated, as the Helots of Sparta — as the Pariahs of India — disfranchised outcasts; a separate and degraded caste, to whom no honorable career is open; hopeless menials; the hewers of wood and drawers of water of those among whom they are tolerated, not received?" Could there be any decent person, Owen asked, who desired "the continuance among us of a race to whom we are not willing to accord the most common protection against outrage and death?" [4]

Immediate and practical considerations also prompted the demand for exclusion or restriction of Negroes. In the absence of adequate legislation, many feared that the northern states would be inundated with emancipated slaves, some of whom would be too old and worn out to be anything but a burden on the community. This fear was particularly strong in those free states which bordered on the slave states, and it prompted most of them to adopt restrictive measures. In defending the Illinois statute, Senator Stephen A. Douglas asserted that his state would not become "an asylum for all the old and decrepit and broken-down negroes that may emigrate or be sent to it."

[4] *Indiana Constitutional Debates of 1850*, II, 1792. The utopian New Harmony, Indiana, settlement, in which Robert Dale Owen assisted his father, barred Negroes except "as helpers." Constitution of the "Preliminary Society of New Harmony," reprinted in George B. Lockwood, *The New Harmony Movement* (New York, 1907), p. 85.

Indiana also indicated its unwillingness to become "the Liberia of the South."[5]

The adoption of restrictions by many of the new western states and territories impelled several of the older states to reconsider their position. Less than four months after Massachusetts' congressional delegation had argued and voted against the Missouri constitution clause prohibiting Negro immigration, the legislature appointed a committee to investigate the expediency of similar legislation. In its report, the committee warned that increasing restrictions elsewhere would drive Negroes to those states which accorded equal rights and privileges and would consequently increase the number of convicts and paupers, drive white men out of many occupations, and disturb "the good order and tranquility" of the cities. The committee recommended the adoption of measures which would respect "humanity and the just rights of all classes of men" but at the same time protect Massachusetts from "the burthen of an expensive and injurious population." However, a new committee appointed at the next legislative session, although agreeing that "the truest precepts of humanity" demanded some restrictive measure, reported that it could not "conscientiously vindicate" any proposed bill. Such legislation, it concluded, would not be consistent with "that love of humanity, that respect for hospitality and for the just rights of all classes of men" which had traditionally characterized the state of Massachusetts. The legislature made no further attempt to exclude Negroes from the state.[6]

[5] *Appendix to the Congressional Globe*, 31 Cong., 1 sess., p. 1664; *Indiana Constitutional Debates of 1850*, I, 446. For other examples of this argument, see Arthur C. Cole (ed.), *The* [Illinois] *Constitutional Debates of 1847* (Springfield, 1919), pp. 208, 217, 224–25, 237; *Official Reports of the Debates and Proceedings of the Ohio State Convention . . . 1850* (Columbus, 1851), p. 983; *Report of the Debates in the Convention of California . . . 1849* (Washington, D.C., 1850), pp. 48–49, 137–38.

[6] *Niles' Weekly Register*, XX (July 14, 1821), 311–12; Massachusetts House of Representatives, *Free Negroes and Mulattoes* (Boston, 1822).

In contrast to Massachusetts, where Negro immigration had been relatively slight, Pennsylvania's geographically strategic position attracted large numbers of emancipated slaves and fugitives. White residents, especially in the southern portion of the state, continually petitioned the legislature to halt further Negro immigration, but bills for this purpose failed to receive the approval of both houses.[7] In 1829, however, the legislature agreed that the removal of the Negro would be "highly auspicious to the best interests of our country," and indorsed the American Colonization Society.[8] In the absence of legislative action, Pennsylvania restrictionists appealed to the constitutional convention of 1837. Representatives from the southern counties expressed great alarm over the steady influx of Negroes and urged the convention to consider an appropriate constitutional amendment. However, delegate Thaddeus Stevens assailed any proposed restriction and managed to have the question indefinitely postponed.[9]

In several of the newly admitted states, whites threatened drastic action if legislative protection were not forthcoming. The people of southern Illinois, a native warned, "would take the matter into their own hands, and commence a war of extermination." An Indianan told a state constitutional convention that "it would be better to kill them off at once, if there is no other way to get rid of them." After all, he added, "we know how the Puritans did with the Indians, who were infinitely more magnanimous and less impudent than the colored race." In southern Ohio, an aroused populace forcibly thwarted an attempt to settle the 518 emancipated slaves of Virginia's John Randolph. Defending that action, an Ohio congressman warned that "if the test must come and they must resort to force to effect their object, the banks of the Ohio

[7] Edward R. Turner, *The Negro in Pennsylvania* (Washington, D.C., 1911), pp. 151–54, 204.
[8] *House Report*, 21 Cong., 1 sess., No. 24 (1829).
[9] *Pennsylvania Constitutional Debates of 1837–38*, I, 191, II, 199–202.

. . . would be lined with men with muskets on their shoulders to keep off the emancipated slaves." [10]

The nature of restrictionist legislation varied from state to state. Several states required from incoming Negroes certificates proving their freedom and attesting to their citizenship in another state.[11] Connecticut forbade, without the approval of civil authorities, the establishment of any educational institution for the instruction of non-resident Negroes.[12] Most of the new states, particularly those carved out of the Northwest Territory, either explicitly barred Negroes or permitted them to enter only after they had produced certified proof of their freedom and had posted a bond, ranging from $500 to $1,000, guaranteeing their good behavior. If enforced, this requirement alone would have amounted to practical exclusion. Violators were subject to expulsion and fine, the non-payment of which could result in their being whipped, hired out, or, under the Illinois statute of 1853, advertised and sold at public auction. Residents, white or Negro, who employed such persons or encouraged them to remain in the state were subject to heavy fines.[13]

Three states — Illinois, Indiana, and Oregon — incorporated anti-immigration provisions into their constitutions.[14]

[10] *Illinois Constitutional Debates of 1847*, p. 860; *Indiana Constitutional Debates of 1850*, I, 574; *Appendix to the Congressional Globe*, 30 Cong., 1 sess., p. 727.

[11] *The Perpetual Laws of the Commonwealth of Massachusetts . . .* [1780–1788] (Worcester, 1788), p. 349; William Paterson, *Laws of the State of New Jersey* (New Brunswick, 1800), pp. 312–13.

[12] *The Public Statute Laws of the State of Connecticut* (Hartford, 1835), pp. 321–22.

[13] Such legislation, varying only slightly in content, was enacted in Illinois in 1819, 1829, and 1853; in Indiana in 1831 and 1852; in Ohio in 1804 and 1807; in Michigan Territory in 1827; in Iowa Territory in 1839; in Iowa in 1851; and in Oregon Territory in 1849. For a convenient summary of this legislation, see Henry W. Farnam, *Chapters in the History of Social Legislation in the United States to 1860* (Washington, D.C., 1938), pp. 219–20.

[14] Constitutions of Illinois, 1848; Indiana, 1851; Oregon, 1857. For a defense of these provisions, see the state constitutional-convention debates; *Congressional Globe*, 35 Cong., 1 sess., pp. 1964–70, 2204, 2207; *Appendix to the Con-*

The electorates, voting on these provisions separately, indicated their overwhelming approval at the polls. Voters indorsed the Illinois constitutional clause barring the further admission of Negroes by a margin of more than two to one, most of the opposition coming from northern counties in which there were few Negroes. Indianans gave a larger majority to the restriction clause than to the constitution itself, and Oregon approved exclusion by an eight-to-one majority.[15] The popular mandate thus seemed clear. "The tendency, strong and irresistible, of the American mind," an Indianan declared, "is finally to accomplish a separation of the two races."[16]

Despite such overwhelming popular approval, legislation implementing the constitutional prohibitions was only sporadically enforced. The Illinois act remained on the statute books until 1865 and was upheld by the state supreme court, but few efforts were made to invoke it, and one Negro called it "a dead letter."[17] Indiana seldom prosecuted violators. In 1856, however, an Indiana court convicted a Negro of violating the law by bringing a Negro woman into the state in order to marry her. The state supreme court upheld the conviction. "The policy of the state," it declared, "is . . . clearly evolved. It is to exclude any further ingress of negroes, and to remove those already among us as speedily as possible." The law specifically voided all contracts made with Negroes entering the state, and this applied to marriage agreements. "A

gressional Globe, 30 Cong., 1 sess., p. 44; 31 Cong., 1 sess., pp. 1654, 1664; 33 Cong., 2 sess., p. 236.
[15] Illinois Constitutional Debates of 1847, p. xxx; Charles Kettleborough, Constitution Making in Indiana (2 vols.; Indianapolis, 1916), II, 617–18; Charles H. Carey (ed.), The Oregon Constitution and Proceedings and Debates of the Constitutional Convention of 1857 (Salem, 1926), p. 27.
[16] Indiana Constitutional Debates of 1850, I, 562.
[17] John Jones, The Black Laws of Illinois, and a Few Reasons Why They Should Be Repealed (Chicago, 1864), p. 13. Sporadic efforts to enforce the law are cited by Norman D. Harris, The History of Negro Servitude in Illinois (Chicago, 1904), p. 237; Arthur C. Cole, The Era of the Civil War, 1848–1870 (Springfield, 1919), p. 226; J. N. Gridley, "A Case under an Illinois Black Law," Illinois State Historical Society Journal, IV (1912), 401–25.

constitutional policy," the court concluded, "so clearly conducive to the separation and ultimate good of both races
should be rigidly enforced." [18]

Although seldom invoked, the anti-immigration laws reminded Negroes of their inferior position in society and provided whites with a convenient excuse for mob violence and
frequent harassment of the Negro population. Perhaps the
authors of such legislation had no more than this in mind. An
Ohio legislative committee reported in 1838 that "it was never
believed that the law would ever be complied with, nor was
it intended by the makers that it ever should be. Its evident
design was to drive this portion of our population into other
states. It was an unrighteous attempt to accomplish, indirectly
and covertly, what they would shrink from doing openly and
frankly." [19]

Ohio provided a classic example of how anti-immigration
legislation could be invoked to harass Negro residents. That
state's restrictive statutes, enacted in 1804 and 1807 as part
of the Black Laws, compelled Negroes entering the state to
post a $500 bond guaranteeing their good behavior and to
produce a court certificate as evidence of their freedom. No
extensive effort was made to enforce the bond requirement
until 1829, when the rapid increase of the Negro population
alarmed Cincinnati. The city authorities announced that the
Black Laws would be enforced and ordered Negroes to comply or leave within thirty days. The local Negro population
promptly obtained a time extension, sent a delegation to
Canada to find a suitable location for resettlement, and petitioned the legislature for repeal of "those obnoxious black
laws." [20]

[18] Catterall (ed.), *Judicial Cases*, V, 40; Emma Lou Thornbrough, *The Negro
in Indiana* (Indianapolis, 1957), pp. 72–73.
[19] *Journal of the Senate of the State of Ohio*, 36 General Assembly, 1 sess.,
p. 562.
[20] Salmon P. Chase (ed.), *The Statutes of Ohio and of the Northwest Territory*

Impatient for results, white mobs roamed through Cincinnati's Negro quarters, spreading terror and destruction. Subsequently, the Negro delegation sent to Canada returned with a cordial invitation from the governor of Upper Canada. "Tell the Republicans on your side of the line," he declared, "that we royalists do not know men by their color. Should you come to us you will be entitled to all the privileges of the rest of His Majesty's subjects." [21] An estimated 1,100 to 2,200 Negroes departed from the city, most of them apparently settling in Canada. [22] By the end of 1829, the citizens of Cincinnati could assess the results of their action. The editor of the Cincinnati *Gazette*, who had earlier favored enforcement of the Black Laws, lamented the consequences. "It has driven away the sober, honest, industrious, and useful portion of the colored population," he wrote. "The effect is to lessen much of the moral restraint, which the presence of respectable persons of their own colour, imposed on the idle and indolent, as well as the profligate." He then assailed the injustices of the Black Laws and concluded that "the rank oppression of a devoted people, may be consummated in the midst of us, without exciting either sympathy, or operative indignation." [23] Two years later, a prominent Cincinnati lawyer explained to Alexis de Tocqueville that the severe restrictions on Negroes constituted an attempt "to discourage them in every possible

(3 vols.; Cincinnati, 1833), I, 393–94, 555–56; Richard C. Wade, "The Negro in Cincinnati, 1800–1830," *Journal of Negro History*, XXXIX (1954), 50–55.

[21] [Ohio Anti-Slavery Society], *Condition of the People of Color in the State of Ohio* (Boston, 1839), p. 7.

[22] Wade, "The Negro in Cincinnati," p. 56; Carter G. Woodson, "The Negroes of Cincinnati Prior to the Civil War," *Journal of Negro History*, I (1916), 7. For the development of the Negro community in Canada, see Fred Landon, "Social Conditions among the Negroes in Upper Canada," Ontario Historical Society, *Papers and Records*, XXII (1925), 144–61, and Samuel Gridley Howe, *The Refugees from Slavery in Canada West* (Boston, 1864).

[23] Cincinnati *Gazette*, August 17, 1829, quoted in Wade, "The Negro in Cincinnati," pp. 56–57.

way." Not only had the laws provided for their expulsion, the lawyer declared, "but we annoy them in a thousand ways."[24] Growing abolitionist sentiment in the Old Northwest prompted organized efforts to repeal the anti-immigration laws. In Ohio, Negroes and white abolitionists organized an extensive petition campaign for repeal, and the Free Soil party inserted a demand for repeal in its state platform, although at the same time it expressed a desire for "a homogenous population" in Ohio and asserted that such would be the case when slavery ceased to force its victims "upon the uncongenial North." For several years, however, the Ohio legislature successfully resisted such agitation; in fact, in 1839, the state house of representatives resolved that repeal was "impolitic and inexpedient" and that Negro residents had no constitutional right to petition the legislature "for any purpose whatsoever." After considerable maneuvering, a Free Soil–Democratic political bargain in 1849 resulted in the partial repeal of the Black Laws, including the statute compelling Negroes to post bond in order to settle in the state.[25] In no other state where such measures had been adopted did similar agitation meet with success.

Negroes did not share in the expansion of political democracy in the first half of the nineteenth century; indeed,

[24] George Wilson Pierson, *Tocqueville and Beaumont in America* (New York, 1938), p. 565. Further attempts to expel Negroes from Ohio are cited in Carter G. Woodson, *A Century of Negro Migration* (Washington, D.C., 1918), pp. 56–57, and Ebenezer Davies, *American Scenes and Christian Slavery* (London, 1849), p. 129.

[25] "Memorial to the Legislature of Ohio by the Anti-Slavery Society in the Western Reserve," *The Liberator*, December 27, 1834; *Memorial of the Ohio Anti-Slavery Society, to the General Assembly of the State of Ohio* (Cincinnati, 1838) ; *The Address and Reply on the Presentation of a Testimonial to Salmon P. Chase, by the Colored People of Cincinnati* (Cincinnati, 1845); *Minutes and Address of the State Convention of the Colored Citizens of Ohio* (Oberlin, 1849), pp. 17–18, 21–25; Frank U. Quillin, *The Color Line in Ohio* (Ann Arbor, 1913), p. 38; *Journal of the House of Representatives of the State of Ohio*, 37 General Assembly, 1 sess., pp. 235–36; 43 General Assembly, 1 sess., pp. 17–35; Theodore

such expansion frequently came at the expense of their rights and privileges. By 1840, some 93 per cent of the northern free Negro population lived in states which completely or practically excluded them from the right to vote. Only in Massachusetts, New Hampshire, Vermont, and Maine could Negroes vote on an equal basis with whites. In New York, they could vote if they first met certain property and residence requirements. In New Jersey, Pennsylvania, and Connecticut, they were completely disfranchised, after having once enjoyed the ballot.

In several states the adoption of white manhood suffrage led directly to the political disfranchisement of the Negro. Those who opposed an expanded electorate — for both whites and Negroes — warned that it would, among other things, grant the Negro political power. Adopt universal manhood suffrage, a Pennsylvania constitutional convention delegate declared in 1837, and "every negro in the State, worthy and worthless — degraded and debased, as nine tenths of them are, will rush to the polls in senseless and unmeaning triumph." Would this not constitute, he asked, "a highly *coloured* illustration of the beauty and perfectability of *universal suffrage?*" In New York, a Federalist opponent of universal manhood suffrage warned that "the whole host of Africans that now deluge our City (already too impertinent to be borne), would be placed upon an equal with the citizens." In the face of increasing demands for a liberalized suffrage, a Rhode Island legislative committee advised against extending the vote in 1829, citing as one of its reasons the addition of Negroes and Indians to the electorate. "We ought to recollect," the committee warned, "that all the evils which may result from the extension of suffrage will be evils beyond our reach. We shall entail them upon our latest posterity without remedy. Open

C. Smith, *The Liberty and Free Soil Parties in the Northwest* (New York, 1897), pp. 162–72.

this door, and the whole frame and character of our institutions are changed forever." [26]

White manhood suffragists shared this overwhelming antipathy toward Negro voting, but they soon discovered a convenient and effective way out of the dilemma: eliminate the
racial issue by denying the vote to all Negroes. Consequently,
most arguments for a liberalized suffrage applied only to
whites, and, in those states where no previous restriction existed, incorporated a demand for Negro disfranchisement. The
expansion of political democracy would thus pose no threat to
white supremacy. Suffragists utilized the standard racial arguments to justify this seemingly inconsistent position: granting Negroes equal political rights would be "inexpedient,
impolitic and unsafe"; the Negroes were "a peculiar people,
incapable . . . of exercising that privilege with any sort of
discretion, prudence, or independence"; God had marked
them "a distinct, inferior caste"; they should thus be given
no reason to suppose "that they are entitled to equal rights and
equal privileges with the white man, when, by our laws of
society, they are not, and cannot be permitted to exercise
them." Moreover, equal rights would invite "black outcasts
and worthless vagrants, of other states, to settle among us,"
and this, in turn, would degrade white labor and discourage
colonization.[27]

Advocates of an expanded electorate also offered practical
political considerations to justify Negro disfranchisement.
They warned that Negro voters would control those political
wards in which they were most heavily concentrated; they
would then distribute offices, hold a potential balance of power
between the two political parties, and, through compromises

[26] *Pennsylvania Constitutional Debates of 1837–38*, II, 541; New York Historical Society, *Collections, John Watts de Peyster Publication Fund Series* (80
vols.; New York, 1869 — 1954), XVIII, 306; *House Report*, 28 Cong., 1 sess.,
No. 546 (1844), p. 401.

[27] Nathaniel H. Carter and William L. Stone, *Reports of the Proceedings and
Debates of the Convention of 1821* (Albany, 1821), p. 180; *Pennsylvania Constitutional Debates of 1837–38*, III, 91; IX, 321, 364–65; X, 24, 104.

and bargains, perhaps secure political appointments. A delegate to the New York constitutional convention of 1821 recalled that at one election the votes of three hundred Negroes in New York City had decided the political character of the state legislature.[28] Moreover, once Negroes had secured the ballot, what would then keep them out of future constitutional conventions, the state legislature, the jury box, or even the United States Congress? Would not the election of a Negro to Congress constitute "a gross insult" to the South and threaten the very existence of the Union? Imagine what the reaction of a "southern gentleman" who had freed his slaves and sent them to Pennsylvania or New York would be if he met them in Congress![29]

In addition to the dictates of political, economic, and social necessity, white manhood suffragists maintained that public opinion demanded color distinctions. A Pennsylvania constitutional convention delegate found, in passing through nearly half his state in 1837, "almost unanimous" opposition to Negro suffrage from members of both political parties. "There can be no mistaking public opinion on this subject," he declared. "The people of this state are for continuing this commonwealth, what it always has been, a political community of white persons." Delegates to New York's constitutional convention of 1821 expressed a similar reaction. They reported overwhelming sentiment against Negro suffrage, especially in those areas where Negroes made up a substantial portion of the population. "If that sentiment should alter," one delegate proposed, "if the time should ever arrive when the African shall be raised to the level of the white man — when the distinctions that now prevail shall be done away — when the colours shall intermarry — when negroes shall be invited to your tables —

[28] Pennsylvania Constitutional Debates of 1837–38, III, 83; IX, 365–66, 383; X, 95; New York Constitutional Debates of 1821, pp. 185–86, 198–99, 212.
[29] New York Constitutional Debates of 1821, p. 181; Pennsylvania Constitutional Debates of 1837–38, II, 478; III, 88; V, 418; IX, 366; X, 95.

to sit in your pew, or ride in your coach, it may then be proper to institute a new Convention, and remodel the constitution so as to conform to that state of society." [30]

Public opinion appeared to be so fixed on this subject that various delegates to the state constitutional conventions warned that violence and bloodshed would inevitably accompany Negro suffrage. The statute books might make the Negro and the white equal, but "you can never force the citizens of this commonwealth to believe or practice it; we can never force our constituents to go peaceably to the polls, side by side with the negro." A Philadelphian "entertained not the slightest doubt" that Negro suffrage would lead to bloody riots. Within twenty-four hours after the first Negro had voted, he warned, "not a negro house in the city or county would be left standing." [31]

In the face of such vigorous opposition, some whites still protested attempts to deny the ballot to the Negro while extending it to more whites, and argued — largely in vain — that Negro voters would not endanger white supremacy and that consistency demanded equal suffrage. Disfranchisement, they contended, would set an "ominous and dangerous precedent" which could be applied to other minority groups, and it would certainly bring forth a well-deserved "shout of triumph and a hiss of scorn" from the slave states. Moreover, Negroes would not abuse the ballot any more than "the many thousands of white fawning, cringing sycophants, who look up to their more wealthy and more ambitious neighbours for direction at the polls, as they look to them for bread." [32]

This was hardly a popular position in those regions which looked with growing fear at the rapid increase of the Negro

[30] *Pennsylvania Constitutional Debates of 1837-38*, IX, 357; *New York Constitutional Debates of 1821*, p. 190.

[31] *Pennsylvania Constitutional Debates of 1837-38*, IX, 328, 393. See also II, 477; III, 696; IX, 350, 365.

[32] *Ibid.*, IX, 333, 375; X, 123; *New York Constitutional Debates of 1821*, pp. 184, 188.

population. But even the friends of equal suffrage had their reservations. One Pennsylvanian, for example, opposed disfranchisement but conceded that Negroes "in their present depressed and uncultivated condition" were not "a desirable species of population," and he "should not prefer them as a matter of choice." [33] Such admissions as these hardly added to the popular acceptance of Negro suffrage, and the advocates of such a dangerous doctrine found themselves labeled as either radical amalgamationists or hypocrites. There could be no middle ground. "Has any gentleman on this floor, the boldest and the warmest advocate for negro equality and suffrage," a Pennsylvania constitutional convention delegate asked, "gone so far as to say — to insinuate that he is willing to extend to the blacks his social equality and rights; to receive him in his family or at his table, on the same footing and terms with his white friends and acquaintances; allow them to marry with his children, male and female? — not a word of the kind. They will give him the rights of the people — of the commonwealth — but not of their own houses and homes." [34]

Utilizing various political, social, economic, and pseudo-anthropological arguments, white suffragists moved to deny the vote to the Negro. From the admission of Maine in 1819 until the end of the Civil War, every new state restricted the suffrage to whites in its constitution. In New Jersey and Connecticut, where no racial distinctions had appeared in the original constitutions, the legislatures limited the suffrage to whites, and subsequent constitutions incorporated the restrictions. The changes occasioned little public debate or opposition. [35] In Rhode Island, a reform party led by Thomas W. Dorr attempted to secure control of the state in 1841 in order

[33] *Pennsylvania Constitutional Debates of 1837–38*, IX, 332.
[34] *Ibid.*, X, 94.
[35] Marion T. Wright, "Negro Suffrage in New Jersey, 1776–1875," *Journal of Negro History*, XXXIII (1948), 172–76; James T. Adams, "Disfranchisement of Negroes in New England," *American Historical Review*, XXX (1925), 545.

to replace the old colonial charter with a constitution providing for a liberalized suffrage. The new "People's Constitution," however, provided for white manhood suffrage. Reminded of this apparent inconsistency, one of Dorr's followers stated that they had originally intended to make no distinctions but that the opposition had utilized this to prejudice the public against them. In any event, the Dorrites went down to defeat, with the partial assistance of Rhode Island Negroes, and the victorious party rewarded its allies by removing the racial restrictions in the 1842 constitution.[36]

In New York and Pennsylvania, which contained the largest number of northern Negroes, disfranchisement faced some vigorous opposition. Abolition societies and Negro organizations had long been active in both states. Moreover, Negroes had previously exercised the right to vote, at least in some regions, and had generally favored certain political parties or factions. Under these circumstances, it was only natural that the favored groups would attempt to retain this segment of political support. Such was the case in New York.

Prior to 1821, property and residence requirements for New York voters applied equally to both races. Those Negroes who were thereby eligible to vote apparently did so in substantial numbers, and there could be no mistaking their strong Federalist sympathies. This support continued until the demise of the Federalists, after which many Negroes switched their allegiance to the National Republicans and the Whigs. To understand these political loyalties, one must remember that many Negroes had been raised as slaves in Federalist households, their emancipation had been advocated by prominent Feder-

[36] William Goodell, *The Rights and Wrongs of Rhode Island* (Oneida Institute, 1842), p. 5; [Frances H. W. Greene], *Might and Right* (Providence, 1844), pp. 291–92; *House Report*, 28 Cong., 1 sess., No. 546 (1844), pp. 110–17; Frederick Douglass, *Life and Times* (Hartford, 1884), pp. 272–75; *The Liberator*, October 29, November 19, December 10, 31, 1841, July 8, August 19, 1842; William Lloyd Garrison to George W. Benson, July 8, 1842, Garrison Papers.

alist leaders (who helped to organize and lead the New York Manumission Society), and the gradual-abolition law had been enacted by a Federalist legislature and signed by a Federalist governor.[37] But this signified more than a sentimental attachment to the party of their old masters. Negroes supported the Federalists because that party demonstrated greater concern than the Republicans for the protection of their rights and privileges. The identification of the Republican party with southern slavery strengthened this conviction. Southerners, a Negro leader asserted in 1809, generally adhered to the Republicans and "are the very people who hold our African brethren in bondage. These people, therefore, are the enemies of our rights." Negro voters would thus be not only "wanting in duty" to their people, but would be "destitute of the *spirit of freemen*," were they not to support the Federalists and revere that "*standard of liberty* which was erected by the IMMORTAL WASHINGTON: and which has been consecrated by the blood of the MARTYRED HAMILTON."[38]

When the Republicans captured control of the New York legislature in 1811, they recognized this sentiment and promptly drafted legislation which would compel Negroes to present certificates of freedom before being permitted to vote. However, the Federalist-dominated Council of Revision vetoed the proposal, saying that it was too vague, and charged that it would force Negroes to the "humiliating degradation of being challenged in consequence of a supposed taint" and would expose them to "wanton insult and contumely, merely on account of their complexion." The legislature sustained the veto but enacted a similar bill later in the year.[39] Meanwhile, Negroes

[37] Dixon Ryan Fox, "The Negro Vote in Old New York," *Political Science Quarterly*, XXXII (1917), 253–56.

[38] Joseph Sidney, *An Oration, Commemorative of the Abolition of the Slave Trade in the United States* (New York, 1809), pp. 10–15.

[39] Lincoln (ed.), *Messages from the Governors*, II, 686; *Public Laws of the State of New York passed at the Thirty-fourth Session of the Legislature* (Albany, 1811), p. 372.

continued to play a prominent role in New York politics and were credited in some instances with holding the balance of power.[40] The Republicans, continually growing in strength, waited for the constitutional convention of 1821 to make their next move.

The "Reform Convention" of 1821 has come to symbolize the expanded democracy which made possible the triumph of Andrew Jackson seven years later. Martin Van Buren, a rising Republican politician and a prominent figure in the convention, later wrote that the new constitution provided for "increased action on the part of the People themselves in the management of public affairs" and elevated New York's political institutions "to the standard required by the advance made by public opinion in that direction." [41] The report of the committee on suffrage reflected this sentiment and sounded the keynote of the convention. It expressed the hope that the only qualification for voting would be "the virtue and morality of the people," and it proclaimed that the national trend "is for the extension, and not the restriction of popular rights." At the same time, and without explanation, the report recommended that the suffrage henceforth be restricted to "every white male citizen." [42] With one blow, then, the Republican-dominated convention intended to remove not only a bloc of Federalist voters but also any objection that might be raised against an expanded suffrage on the grounds that it would admit degraded Negroes.

With only a few exceptions, the Republicans favored virtual universal white manhood suffrage, while the Federalists supported a continued property qualification for both races and

[40] Fox, "The Negro Vote in Old New York," pp. 257–58, 263 n.; *New York Constitutional Debates of 1821*, p. 212.

[41] John C. Fitzpatrick (ed.), *The Autobiography of Martin Van Buren* (Washington, D.C., 1920), p. 112.

[42] *New York Constitutional Debates of 1821*, pp. 178–79.

vigorously opposed Negro disfranchisement.[43] Despite the eloquent plea of Federalist Chancellor James Kent that the delegates had not gathered "to *disfranchise* any portion of the community or to take away their rights," the convention voted practically to disfranchise the Negro. In future elections, Negroes would be entitled to vote if they could meet the age and residence requirements and if they possessed a freehold estate worth $250.[44] Van Buren and others supported the "compromise" proviso on the grounds that it would not close the door on Negro suffrage but would, instead, encourage the Negro's economic improvement. One delegate, however, more appropriately called it "an attempt to do a thing indirectly which we appeared either to be ashamed of doing, or for some reason chose not to do directly, a course . . . every way unworthy of us."[45]

The delegates had correctly gauged public opinion. New York voters accorded the new constitution their overwhelming approval. Five years later, a Republican legislature abolished the few remaining restrictions on white voters while retaining the property proviso for Negroes.[46] The triumph of white democracy was now complete. After visiting New York in 1832, an English traveler assessed the Negro's position and concluded: "To be worth two hundred and fifty dollars is not a trifle for a man doomed to toil in the lowest stations; few

[43] Jabez D. Hammond, *History of Political Parties in the State of New York* (2 vols.; Cooperstown, 1846), II, 21.
[44] *New York Constitutional Debates of 1821*, p. 190; *The Revised Statutes of the State of New York* (3 vols.; Albany, 1836), I, 38–40.
[45] *New York Constitutional Debates of 1821*, pp. 364, 369, 376. Van Buren had previously voted against total disfranchisement "for he would not draw a revenue from them, and yet deny to them the right of suffrage." During the presidential election of 1840, a young Illinois Whig, Abraham Lincoln, assailed Van Buren for "his votes in the New York Convention in allowing Free Negroes the right of suffrage . . . ." Basler (ed.), *Collected Works of Abraham Lincoln*, I, 210. At the same time, a New York Negro newspaper refused to endorse Van Buren because of his "objectionable" conduct during the 1821 convention. *Colored American*, October 3, 1840.
[46] *Revised Statutes*, I, 50.

Negroes are in consequence competent to vote. They are in fact very little better than slaves, although called free." [47]

Against a background of increasingly explosive racial bitterness, marked by a series of riots, the Pennsylvania constitutional convention of 1837 debated white manhood suffrage and Negro disfranchisement. "I should rejoice," a Democratic party leader declared, "to see adopted in this commonwealth a constitution which would give to every citizen — I use the word citizen as not embracing the coloured population, — whether in poverty or affluence, that right, sacred and dear to every American citizen — the right of suffrage." [48] To the Negro, this was by now a familiar cry — free votes for all free white men.

Neither the 1776 nor 1790 state constitutions had explicitly excluded Negroes from the suffrage. Indeed, those opposing the abolition of slavery in Pennsylvania had warned that Negroes would henceforth be allowed to vote and to hold office. By 1837, Negroes still voted in some counties, though barred by public opinion in others. A Philadelphian told Alexis de Tocqueville in 1831 that Negroes could not appear at the polls without being mistreated. "And what becomes of the reign of law in this case?" the French traveler asked. "The law with us is nothing," the Philadelphian replied, "if it is not supported by public opinion." Six years later, an English visitor asked why Negroes did not vote, since no law specifically barred them. "Just let them try!" he was told. [49]

Although at first the delegates refused to disfranchise the

[47] Carl D. Arfwedson, *The United States and Canada, in 1832, 1833, and 1834* (2 vols.; London, 1834), I, 239.

[48] *Pennsylvania Constitutional Debates of 1837–38*, IX, 324.

[49] *Ibid.*, I, 149; II, 478, 541; III, 83, 89–90, 695; V, 414; IX, 380; X, 21, 50, 63; Turner, *Negro in Pennsylvania*, pp. 178–87; Pierson, *Tocqueville and Beaumont in America*, p. 514; Andrew Bell, *Men and Things in America* (London, 1838), p. 179; Adlard Welby, *A Visit to North America and the English Settlements in Illinois with a Winter Residence at Philadelphia* (London, 1821), in Reuben G. Thwaites (ed.), *Early Western Travels, 1748–1846* (32 vols.; Cleveland, 1904–7), XII, 319.

Negro, there transpired outside the convention hall events which led to a reversal of the earlier vote. In July, 1837, the Pennsylvania Supreme Court ruled that Negroes could not legally exercise the right to vote. The chief justice cited a 1795 court decision excluding Negroes from the suffrage, and although no record of this case existed, he declared that the memory of a good friend and Philadelphia lawyer was "perfect and entitled to full confidence." Besides, as he proceeded to demonstrate, the decision had been based on "the true principles of the constitution." [50]

Three months later, the Democratic candidates in a Bucks County election attributed their defeat to the margin of Negro votes. In addition to arousing public excitement over this alleged injustice, the incident prompted Democratic meetings to petition the legislature and the constitutional convention for an alteration of the existing electoral laws. One newspaper warned that the Negroes' claim to voting rights had been inspired by unscrupulous abolitionists. "Thaddeus Stevens!" it charged, "a man who has taught the NEGROES to contend for the rights of a white man at the polls! by his zealous support of the accursed doctrines of ABOLITION." [51] Meanwhile, the defeated candidates appealed to the courts and secured a favorable opinion. Judge John Fox of the Bucks County Court ruled that Negroes did not have the right to vote. The framers of the state constitution, he declared, "were a political community of white men exclusively," and Negroes were not even contemplated by that document, for they were then, as now, a degraded and inferior race. "What white man," Judge Fox asked, "would not feel himself insulted by a serious imputation that he was a negro, and who, having believed himself

[50] Catterall (ed.), *Judicial Cases*, IV, 288–89. See also Frederick Marryat, *A Diary in America* (3 vols.; London, 1839), I, 296–315.

[51] *Niles' National Register*, LIII (November 11, 1837), 162, (February 10, 1838), 382; *The Liberator*, November 10, 17, 1837; Turner, *Negro in Pennsylvania*, pp. 170–71.

to be of the white race, if he should be found to be strongly
tainted with black blood, would not feel and experience that
he had fallen greatly in the social scale?" Judge Fox claimed,
moreover, that Negroes had never voted in the city or county
of Philadelphia, where most of them lived, or in the greater
portion of the state.[52]

Such pronouncements had the desired effect on the constitutional convention. To remove all doubts concerning Negro
suffrage, the delegates voted overwhelmingly to restrict the vote
to white men.[53] Meeting shortly afterwards, Philadelphia Negroes appealed to the electorate to reject the white suffrage
proviso on grounds that it divided "what our fathers bled to
unite, to wit, TAXATION and REPRESENTATION." Denying any intention to seek amalgamation or "social favors,"
they warned Pennsylvania voters that disfranchisement would
destroy the state's "foundation principle of equal rights" and
convert forty thousand friends into enemies. Meanwhile, white
abolitionists appealed to William Lloyd Garrison to publish
some "trumpet calls" in The Liberator in order to arouse Negroes and sympathetic whites to defeat the new constitution.[54]
In October, 1838, however, the electorate, as expected, gave
the new document a decisive vote of approval.

Neither complete disfranchisement in Pennsylvania nor
practical disfranchisement in New York eliminated the Negro
from politics. Pennsylvania Negroes continued to remonstrate
for equal suffrage rights and blamed their increasing degradation and repression on disfranchisement. Finally, in 1855,

[52] Opinion of the Hon. John Fox, President Judge of the Judicial District Composed of the Counties of Bucks and Montgomery, against the Exercise of Negro
Suffrage in Pennsylvania (Harrisburg, 1838). See also Pennsylvania Constitutional Debates of 1837–38, X, 48, 87.

[53] Pennsylvania Constitutional Debates of 1837–38, X, 106.

[54] Appeal of Forty Thousand Citizens, Threatened with Disfranchisement, to
the People of Pennsylvania (Philadelphia, 1838). Reprinted in The Liberator,
April 13, 1838, and The Colored American, May 3, June 2, 1838. Elizur Wright, Jr.,
to William Lloyd Garrison, October 9, 1838, Wright Papers, Library of Congress.

they appealed directly to Congress. After seventeen years of disfranchisement, they complained that their position had become "one of mere toleration and sufferance," that they had memorialized and petitioned without success, and that they had waited patiently but in vain for an aroused public conscience to accord them equal rights. Under these circumstances, they turned to the national legislature for assistance.[55] Fourteen years later — in 1869 — Congress submitted the Fifteenth Amendment to the states for ratification.

In New York, the propertied Negro remained a factor in state politics. To the dismay of local Democrats, Whig candidates carried those New York City wards in which Negroes were most numerous, and an English visitor to that city in 1833 remarked that he never met a Negro who was not "an anti-Jackson man."[56] Meanwhile, Negroes organized and petitioned for equal suffrage rights. "Foreigners and aliens to the government and laws," they complained, "strangers to our institutions, are permitted to flock to this land and in a few years are endowed with all the privileges of citizens; but we, *native born Americans, the children of the soil,* are most of us shut out."[57]

In their efforts to achieve an unrestricted suffrage, New York Negroes encountered vigorous Democratic opposition and Whig apathy. In the 1838 election, for example, the Democratic gubernatorial candidate expressed his opposition to any move to grant Negroes equal suffrage rights. His Whig opponent, William H. Seward, objected to any property qualification for voting, but, at the same time, he was "not prepared

[55] *Memorial of Thirty Thousand Disfranchised Citizens of Philadelphia to the Honorable Senate and House of Representatives* (Philadelphia, 1855).

[56] Fox, "The Negro Vote in Old New York," p. 264; Edward S. Abdy, *Journal of a Residence and Tour in the United States of North America, from April, 1833, to October, 1834* (3 vols.; London, 1835), II, 9.

[57] *The Weekly Advocate*, February 22, 1837. (Changed its name to the *Colored American* on March 4, 1837.)

to say, having in view the actual condition of that race, that no test ought to exist." The Whig candidate for lieutenant governor, on the other hand, assailed the restriction as "an anomaly entirely at war with democratic principles." [58] The election results, in which Seward was elected and his running mate defeated, appeared to vindicate the Whigs' non committal attitude. Five years later, in a reflective mood, Seward recalled that "prejudice, interest, and passion" sometimes counseled him to overlook "without compromise of principle, and even with personal advantage" what appeared to be the rights of Negroes. Nevertheless, Seward explained, he had always adhered to a philosophy of equality and had condemned those practices and institutions which deprived men of their just rights. [59]

Against this background of legislative inaction and Whig double talk, some Negroes turned to the newly organized Liberty party, which pledged itself to secure equal suffrage rights. Several Negro leaders, on the other hand, warned that alignment with the new party would incur the opposition of both Whigs and Democrats and thus destroy whatever political effectiveness the Negro possessed. [60] Moreover, Whig leaders — including Seward, Horace Greeley, and Thurlow Weed — finally announced their support of unrestricted Negro suffrage and prepared to back this stand at the forthcoming constitutional convention of 1846. The Democratic press, including William Cullen Bryant's New York *Evening Post*, warned that such a move would dangerously increase Whig power in the

[58] *Niles' National Register*, LV (November 3, 1838), 155–58, and (November 24, 1838), 206.

[59] George E. Baker (ed.), *The Works of William H. Seward* (5 vols.; Boston, 1884), III, 438. For a Virginia congressman's discussion of Seward's position on Negro suffrage, see *Congressional Globe*, 36 Cong., 1 sess., pp. 238–39.

[60] Charles H. Wesley, "The Participation of Negroes in Anti-Slavery Political Parties," *Journal of Negro History*, XXIX (1944), 39–48. The Liberty party national convention of 1843 included Negro delegates, speakers, and officials, marking the first time that Negroes had participated actively in the leadership of an American political party.

state and might even lead to a dissolution of the Union.[61] Three months before the convention, a New York Democrat wrote John C. Calhoun that the attempt to remove the property restriction on Negro voting constituted "the most dangerous movement that has ever occurred in this country." Its immediate effect, he declared, would be to give the Whig party political control of the state and the Presidency.[62] The Democratic-controlled convention, however, after extensive and heated debates, voted to retain the property proviso for Negroes but agreed to submit a proposal for equal suffrage to the voters at the next election. The proposal was decisively defeated.[63]

In 1848, several Negro leaders turned enthusiastically and hopefully to the new Free Soil party, but their enthusiasm was not shared by many New York Negroes. Had not Samuel J. Tilden, a prominent state Free Soil leader, voted against Negro suffrage — even the property proviso — at the recent constitutional convention? Had not the Free Soil candidate for governor been noted for his opposition, as a senator, to antislavery petitions, to the abolition of slavery in the District of Columbia, and for his frequent avowals that the Negro was an inferior being? Was it not "well known" that Van Buren and nine-tenths of the prominent "Barnburners" opposed equal suffrage rights for Negroes? Although the national Free Soil convention had welcomed and applauded Negro delegates, it would take more than fancy slogans and an ovation for Frederick Douglass to convince Negroes that their political savior had arrived.[64]

[61] Fox, "The Negro Vote in Old New York," pp. 265–67. For various newspaper reactions, see The Liberator, November 14, 1845, January 23, April 10, 17, 1846.

[62] Chauncey S. Boucher and Robert P. Brooks (eds.), Correspondence Addressed to John C. Calhoun, 1837–1849 (Washington, D.C., 1930), pp. 327–29.

[63] For the debates on Negro suffrage, most of which repeated the arguments of the 1821 convention, see William G. Bishop and William H. Attree, Report of the Debates and Proceedings of the Convention for the Revision of the Constitution of the State of New York (Albany, 1846), especially pp. 1014–20, 1026–36, 1042–48, 1065, and 1078–79.

[64] North Star, August 18, September 1, 22, November 24, 1848, January 5, 12, May 25, 1849.

In view of the distrust of Free Soilism and growing disillusionment with Whiggism, New York Negroes assumed an
increasingly cynical attitude toward the existing political
parties. Assessing the political scene in 1851, a Negro convention concluded that support of either of the two major political parties was "gratuitous on our part" and that in the
future Negroes should be prepared to indorse "any design
which may be deemed necessary to defeat either of the two, if
their principles should be considered at war with our interest."
In view of the convention claim that five thousand Negro voters
held the balance of power in New York State, such political
tactics seem plausible.[65]

The organization, program, and successes of the Republican
party raised Negro hopes for an improvement of their political
position. But in New York, as elsewhere, Republican victories
resulted in no legislative improvements. Republican newspapers courted the Negro with liberal advice and some indorsed equal suffrage rights. Nevertheless, they added little
to the popular acceptance of such rights. Greeley's *Tribune*, for
example, campaigned for equal suffrage, but, at the same time,
it admitted that Negroes were hardly "an attractive" or "a
favorite class" and that they possessed many faults, as did "all
degraded, downtrodden tribes or races." Moreover, it called
on Negroes to turn their efforts from "the sterile path of political agitation" to economic improvement. In their present "indolent, improvident, servile and licentious" condition, they
could hardly convince the public of their ability to become
useful members of society.[66] Meanwhile, the Republican New
York *World* made no pretenses but openly rejected Negro
suffrage and called on Republicans to demonstrate "moral

[65] *Ibid.*, April 10, 1851.
[66] New York *Tribune*, September 22, 1855, and reply by Douglass in *Frederick Douglass' Paper*, September 28, October 5, 1855; Horace Greeley, "Christianity and Color," as reprinted in *Douglass' Monthly*, November, 1860.

courage and political independence" and to defeat any proposed changes in the existing voting provisions.[67]

In 1860, the state legislature submitted the suffrage question
to the voters, but the sectional crisis and the dramatic presidential election pushed the matter into the background. Frederick Douglass, while touring the state on behalf of equal
suffrage, reported that "neither Republicans nor Abolitionists
seem to care much for it." The election results appeared to confirm Douglass' discouragement. Although New York helped to
elect Abraham Lincoln to the Presidency, it overwhelmingly
rejected the proposal for equal suffrage. "We were," Douglass
concluded, "over shadowed and smothered by the Presidential
struggle — over laid by Abraham Lincoln and Hannibal Ham-
lin. The black baby of Negro Suffrage was thought too ugly to
exhibit on so grand an occasion. The Negro was stowed away
like some people put out of sight their deformed children when
company comes."[68] As late as 1869, New York voters defeated
proposals to grant equal suffrage rights to Negroes, thus post-
poning complete enfranchisement until the ratification of the
Fifteenth Amendment.

By 1860, five states — Massachusetts, Rhode Island, Maine,
New Hampshire, and Vermont — in which dwelled 6 per cent
of the total northern Negro population, had provided for equal
suffrage rights. Doubts still lingered, however, concerning the
practical exercise of political rights in these states. For example, a Boston newspaper claimed in 1830 that the state
constitution excluded Negroes from "places of emolument and
trust." As late as 1850, a skeptical southern senator charged
that the aversion to Negro suffrage was so great in Massachusetts that "the voters absolutely drive them from the polls at an
election, and scorn and spit upon them." Five years later, a
French traveler observed that the Negroes of Massachusetts

[67] *Douglass' Monthly*, October, 1860, with editorial comment by Douglass.
[68] *Ibid.*, November, December, 1860.

and other New England states, although qualified, were frequently "designedly omitted" from the tax lists and thus
blocked from voting.[69] These reports, however, do not accord
with overwhelming evidence that Negroes voted, held the balance of power in some locations, acted as election officials, and
were sometimes elected to local offices.[70]

Elsewhere, the general pattern of disfranchisement prevailed until the adoption of the Fifteenth Amendment. Several
states submitted the question to the voters, but only in Wisconsin did Negro suffrage meet with popular approval.[71] The
issue usually transcended party lines. Republican apathy in
New York accorded with the party's attitude in other states.
"The controlling idea of the one-horse politicians," Horace
Greeley concluded in 1859, "is that the republicans must not
let their adversaries have a chance to raise the cry of 'nigger'
against them — that hence they must be as harsh, and cruel,
and tyrannical, toward the unfortunate blacks as possible, in
order to prove themselves 'the white man's party,' or else all
the mean, low, ignorant, drunken, brutish whites will go against
them from horror of 'negro equality.' "[72] In the era of Jacksonian democracy, Negro disfranchisement had been adopted
in order to advance universal manhood suffrage and maintain
white supremacy; on the eve of the Civil War, it still accorded
with popular sentiment and party policy; in 1870, idealism,

[69] Boston *Evening Transcript*, September 28, 1830; *Appendix to the Congressional Globe*, 31 Cong., 1 sess., p. 1654; Michael Chevalier, *Society, Manners,
and Politics in the United States* (Boston, 1839), p. 361 n.

[70] John R. Godley, *Letters from America* (2 vols.; London, 1844), II, 70;
Congressional Globe, 30 Cong., 1 sess., p. 609; Nell, *Colored Patriots*, p. 112;
North Star, November 24, 1848.

[71] Wisconsin voters approved a Negro-suffrage amendment in 1849, but a state
supreme court decision was required in 1866 to uphold the validity of the vote. In
the meantime, Negroes had not been permitted to vote, and the state's electorate
had twice — in 1857 and 1865 — defeated suffrage extension. See John G. Gregory,
"Negro Suffrage in Wisconsin," *Transactions of the Wisconsin Academy of
Sciences, Arts, and Letters*, XI (1898), 94–101.

[72] Horace Greeley, *An Overland Journey from New York to San Francisco, in
the Summer of 1859* (New York, 1860), p. 37.

political expediency, and a gradually aroused public conscience forced its abandonment.

Racial discrimination extended from the polls to the courtroom. No state questioned a Negro's right to legal protection and a redress of injuries, but some added significant qualifications. Five states — Illinois, Ohio, Indiana, Iowa, and California — prohibited Negro testimony in cases where a white man was a party, and Oregon forbade Negroes to hold real estate, make contracts, or maintain lawsuits. Under these circumstances, an Oregonian protested, the colored man "is cast upon the world with no defense; his life, liberty, his property, his all, are dependent on the caprice, the passion, and the inveterate prejudices of not only the community at large but of every felon who may happen to cover an inhuman heart with a white face." [73] But this, nevertheless, was the Negro's judicial plight in a large part of the North and West.

Although rigidly enforced, restrictions on Negro testimony were subject to varying court interpretations. When a lower Indiana court, for example, rejected such testimony in a case involving a Negro charged with the attempted murder of a white man, the state supreme court ordered that the witness be admitted, since the state was not "contemplated as a person of any particular color." The California Supreme Court, on the other hand, ruled that in a criminal action against a white man, a Negro, even if he were the injured party, could not testify. [74]

Where courts refused to admit Negro testimony, legal protection obviously had its limits. A white man could assault, rob, or even murder a Negro in the midst of a number of Negro witnesses and escape prosecution unless another white man had been present and had agreed to testify. Such laws scarcely

[73] *Oregon Constitutional Debates of 1857*, p. 385.
[74] Catterall (ed.), *Judicial Cases*, V, 39, 336.

secured a Negro's life and property; indeed, a prominent Cincinnati lawyer told Alexis de Tocqueville that it often resulted in "the most revolting injustices." [75] After dismissing a case because Negro testimony had been admitted, an Ohio judge angrily protested from the bench that in all of his judicial experience he could not recall a single instance where the law had served the purposes of justice. "The white man may now plunder the Negro," he declared, "he may abuse his person; he may take his life: He may do this in open daylight . . . and he must go acquitted, unless . . . there . . . be some white man present." [76] In 1849, after many years of agitation, Ohio finally abrogated the ban on Negro testimony, but in the southern portion of the state, where the Negro population was heaviest, observers admitted that the repealed law would still be practically enforced. [77]

In most of the North, custom and prejudice, in the absence of any appropriate statute, combined to exclude Negroes from jury service. [78] Only in Massachusetts, where the Negro advanced more rapidly toward equal rights than in any other state, were Negroes admitted as jurors prior to the Civil War. As late as 1855, a Boston Negro leader had protested the absence of colored jurors and had called upon his people to agitate relentlessly for equal judicial rights. Five years later, two Negroes were named as jurymen in Worcester, and they were called "the first of such instances" in the state's history. [79]

The absence of Negro jurors, judges, and witnesses, when added to the general economic degradation of the colored people, largely explains the disproportionate number of Ne-

[75] Pierson, *Tocqueville and Beaumont in America*, p. 565.

[76] Catterall (ed.), *Judicial Cases*, V, 11.

[77] Ohio *State Journal*, February 24, 1849.

[78] [Isaac Candler], *A Summary View of America* (London, 1824), p. 291.

[79] *Triumph of Equal School Rights in Boston. Proceedings of the Presentation Meeting held in Boston, December 17, 1855* (Boston, 1856), p. 21; *The Liberator*, April 1, 1859, June 15, 1860; C. J. Furness, "Walt Whitman Looks at Boston," *New England Quarterly*, I (1928), 356; *Appendix to the Congressional Globe*, 36 Cong., 1 sess., p. 284.

groes in northern jails, prisons, and penitentiaries. Contemporary statistical studies demonstrated convincingly that Negroes made up a startling percentage of convicted offenders. One such study, published in 1826, revealed that Massachusetts Negroes comprised one seventy-fourth of the population but contributed one-sixth of the state's prisoners; New York Negroes constituted one thirty-fifth of the population but contributed one-fourth of the state's convicts; and Pennsylvania Negroes made up one thirty-fourth of the population but supplied one-third of the prisoners.[80] "Already are our prisons and poor houses crowded with the blacks," a Pennsylvania state senate committee reported in 1836. "The disparity of crime between the whites and the blacks, which is at present so distressing to every friend of humanity and virtue, and so burdensome to the community, will become absolutely intolerable in a few years: and the danger to be apprehended is, that if not removed, they will be exterminated." [81] While northern legislatures and governors expressed alarm over the situation, southern observers smugly concluded that this was simply an inevitable product of emancipation.[82]

Statistics, however, ignored the two-sided nature of northern justice. In some states or cities, authorities arrested Negroes for various minor offenses, such as vagrancy, while ignoring similar infractions committed by whites; Negroes often found it difficult to obtain competent legal counsel and witnesses on their behalf; judges sometimes sentenced Negroes for longer terms than whites although both were convicted of the same

[80] First Annual Report of the Board of Managers of the Boston Prison Discipline Society (6th ed.; Boston, 1830), pp. 23–25; Free Negroism: or, Results of Emancipation in the North and the West India Islands (New York, 1862), pp. 2–3, 6; J. S. Buckingham, The Eastern and Western States of America (3 vols.; London, 1842), II, 26.

[81] Journal of the Senate of Pennsylvania, 1836–37 sess., I, 680. See also Pennsylvania Archives (Ser. 4, 12 vols.; Harrisburg, 1900–1902), V, 386–87.

[82] Congressional Debates, 21 Cong., 1 sess., p. 201; E. N. Elliott, Cotton Is King, and Pro-Slavery Arguments (Augusta, Ga., 1860), pp. 37–40; "Reflections on the Census of 1840," Southern Literary Messenger, IX (1843), 345–47.

crime; and Negroes found it much more difficult to secure
pardons than whites or to pay fines imposed on them.[83]

Had racial prejudice not permeated both bench and jury, it
would have been remarkable. "It is hardly possible," a New
Yorker told the 1846 constitutional convention, "that persons
in their condition [Negroes] should have an impartial trial.
Hated, trodden down, and despised, they had not the means to
procure counsel to defend themselves against false and ma-
licious charges, and false witnesses; and too often, an accu-
sation against them was equivalent to conviction."[84] After
inspecting several northern prisons, speaking with their
colored inmates, and surveying the general condition of the
Negro in the North, English traveler Edward Abdy concluded
that when a crime was committed, public opinion almost invariably turned upon the Negro. Moreover, he added, "want
of work, ignorance, and the difficulty of finding unprejudiced
witnesses and juries . . . have led too many of this unfortunate race to the prisons and penitentiaries of the country."[85]

Improvement did not come easily. When Worcester admitted Negroes to the jury box, for example, some northerners
viewed it as a frightening spectacle and a dangerous precedent.
"Republicanism . . . in Massachusetts," an irate Indiana
congressman warned, "would allow a white man to be accused of crime by a negro; to be arrested on the affidavit of a
negro, by a negro officer; to be prosecuted by a negro lawyer;
testified against by a negro witness; tried before a negro judge;
convicted before a negro jury; and executed by a negro execu-
tioner; and either one of these negroes might become the hus-

[83] *A Statistical Inquiry into the Condition of the People of Colour, of the City
and Districts of Philadelphia* (Philadelphia, 1849), p. 27; *The Present State and
Condition of the Free People of Colour, of the City of Philadelphia and Adjoining
Districts* (Philadelphia, 1838), pp. 15–17; *A Review of a Pamphlet, entitled an
Appeal to the Public on Behalf of a House of Refuge for Colored Juvenile De-
linquents* (Philadelphia, 1847), pp. 8–10.
[84] *New York Constitutional Debates of 1846*, p. 1030.
[85] Abdy, *Journal of a Residence and Tour*, I, 46–47, 95, III, 151.

band of his widow or his daughter !" [86] Although this statement
exaggerated the consequences, it correctly reflected the improved legal position of Massachusetts Negroes. However, this
was not the general northern pattern. By 1860, most Negroes
still found severe limitations placed upon the protection of
their life, liberty, and property.

While statutes and customs circumscribed the Negro's
political and judicial rights, extralegal codes — enforced by
public opinion — relegated him to a position of social inferiority and divided northern society into "Brahmins and Pariahs." [87] In virtually every phase of existence, Negroes found
themselves systematically separated from whites. They were
either excluded from railway cars, omnibuses, stagecoaches,
and steamboats or assigned to special "Jim Crow" sections;
they sat, when permitted, in secluded and remote corners of
theaters and lecture halls; they could not enter most hotels,
restaurants, and resorts, except as servants; they prayed in
"Negro pews" in the white churches, and if partaking of the
sacrament of the Lord's Supper, they waited until the whites
had been served the bread and wine. Moreover, they were
often educated in segregated schools, punished in segregated
prisons, nursed in segregated hospitals, and buried in segregated cemeteries. Thus, one observer concluded, racial prejudice "haunts its victim wherever he goes, — in the hospitals
where humanity suffers, — in the churches where it kneels to
God, — in the prisons where it expiates its offences, — in the
graveyards where it sleeps the last sleep." [88]

[86] *Appendix to the Congressional Globe*, 36 Cong., 1 sess., p. 285.
[87] Abdy, *Journal of a Residence and Tour*, I, 44; Chambers, *Things as They Are in America*, pp. 354–58; Henry B. Fearon, *Sketches of America* (London, 1818), pp. 60–61, 168–69.
[88] Gustave De Beaumont, *Marie, or Slavery in the United States* (tr. by Barbara Chapman, Stanford, 1958), pp. 66, 75–76; Bell, *Men and Things in America*, pp. 179–81; [James Boardman], *America, and the Americans* (London, 1833), p. 311; Chambers, *American Slavery and Colour*, pp. 131–35; Francis J. Grund, *Aris·*

To most northerners, segregation constituted not a departure from democratic principles, as certain foreign critics
alleged, but simply the working out of natural laws, the inevitable consequence of the racial inferiority of the Negro. God
and Nature had condemned the blacks to perpetual subordination. Within the context of ante bellum northern thought
and "science," this was not an absurd or hypocritical position.
Integration, it was believed, would result in a disastrous mixing of the races. "We were taught by our mothers," a New
York congressman explained, "to avoid all communications
with them" so that "the theorists and utopians never would
be able to bring about an amalgamation." [89]

The education of northern youths — at home and in school
— helped to perpetuate popular racial prejudices and stereotypes and to confirm the Negro in his caste position. In 1837,
for example, a Boston Negro minister discussed the origins
of racial attitudes in the younger generation. As children,
whites were warned to behave or "the old nigger will carry
you off," and they were reprimanded as being "worse than
a little *nigger*." Later, parents encouraged their children to
improve themselves, lest they "be poor or ignorant as a *nigger*" or "have no more credit than a *nigger*." Finally, teachers
frequently punished their students by sending them to the
"nigger-seat" or by threatening to put them in a Negro class.
Such training, the Negro minister concluded, had been "most
disastrous upon the mind of the community; having been instructed from youth to look upon a black man in no other light
than a slave." [90] Under such circumstances, white adults could

tocracy in America (2 vols.; London, 1839), I, 177–78; [Thomas Hamilton], *Men
and Manners in America* (2 vols.; London, 1834), I, 93–99; Charles Mackay, *Life
and Liberty in America* (2 vols.; London, 1859), II, 41–42; Edward Sullivan,
Rambles and Scrambles in North and South America (London, 1852), pp. 203–4.
    [89] *Appendix to the Congressional Globe*, 30 Cong., 1 sess. p. 581.
    [90] Hosea Easton, *A Treatise on the Intellectual Character, and Civil and Politi-
cal Condition of the Colored People of the United States; and the Prejudice
Exercised Towards Them* (Boston, 1837), pp. 40–41, 43.

hardly be expected to afford Negroes equal political and social rights.

Northerners drew the Negro stereotype in the image of his political, economic, and social degradation and constantly reminded him of his inferiority. Newspapers and public places prominently displayed cartoons and posters depicting his alleged physical deformities and poking fun at his manners and customs. The minstrel shows, a popular form of entertainment in the ante bellum North, helped to fix a public impression of the clownish, childish, carefree, and irresponsible Negro and prompted one Negro newspaper to label these black-face imitators as "the filthy scum of white society, who have stolen from us a complexion denied to them by nature, in which to make money, and pander to the corrupt taste of their fellow-citizens." [91] Nevertheless, the minstrel shows, newspapers, and magazines combined to produce a Negro stereotype that hardly induced northerners to accord this clownish race equal political and social rights. As late as 1860, a group of New York Negroes, in an appeal for equal suffrage, complained bitterly that every facet of northern opinion had been turned against them. "What American artist has not caricatured us?" they asked. "What wit has not laughed at us in our wretchedness? has not ridiculed and condemned us? Few, few, very few." [92]

In addition to persistent public reminders of their physical and mental inferiority, Negroes frequently complained that they had to endure "abusive epithets" and harassment when walking through white areas or shopping in white stores. In passing a group of white men, "ten chances to one" there would be a "sneer or snigger, with characteristic accompanying remarks." Children often tormented them in the streets and hurled insulting language and objects at them. [93] "There

[91] *North Star*, October 27, 1848.
[92] Aptheker (ed.), *Documentary History*, p. 456.
[93] Easton, *A Treatise*, p. 41; *North Star*, March 30, 1849; Abdy, *Journal of a*

appears to be a fixed determination on the part of our oppressors in this country," a Negro wrote in 1849, "to destroy every vestige of self-respect, self-possession, and manly independence left in the colored people; and when all things else have failed, or may be inconvenient, a resort to brow-beating, bully-ragging, and ridicule is at once and at all times had." [94]

Anti-Negro sentiment did not confine itself to popular ridicule and petty harassment. It frequently took the forms of mob action and violence, especially in the large centers of Negro population. In 1829, Cincinnati mobs helped to convince more than half of the Negro inhabitants of that city that flight was preferable to violence and enforcement of the "Black Codes." Twelve years later, a mob descended on the Negro section and prompted its inhabitants to seek protection from city officials. Agreeing to disarm, Negro men found themselves placed in the city jail in order to avoid further violence. The mob then turned on their women and children. "Think, for one moment," the Cincinnati *Gazette* reported, "of a band calling themselves men, disarming, carrying away and securing in prison, the male negroes, promising security and protection to their women and children — and while they were confidently reposing in that security, returning with hellish shouts, to attack these helpless and unprotected persons!" [95]

Sporadic outbreaks, preludes to the disastrous Draft Riots of 1863, occurred in New York City, but violence flared even more frequently in Philadelphia. Between 1832 and 1849, Philadelphia mobs set off five major anti-Negro riots. In July, 1834, a white mob stormed through the Negro section, clubbed and stoned its victims, destroyed homes, churches, and meeting halls, forced hundreds to flee the city, and left many others

Residence and Tour, III, 206–7; Mrs. Felton, *American Life: A Narrative of Two Years' City and Country Residence in the United States* (London, 1842), p. 58.
[94] *North Star*, March 30, 1849.
[95] *Tenth Annual Report of the Board of Managers of the Massachusetts Anti-Slavery Society* (Boston, 1842), pp. 99–102; J. Reuben Sheeler, "The Struggle of the Negro in Ohio for Freedom," *Journal of Negro History*, XXXI (1946), 213–14.

homeless. In assessing the causes of the riot, a citizens' committee cited the frequent hiring of Negroes during periods of depression and white unemployment and the tendency of Negroes to protect, and even forcibly rescue, their brethren when the latter were arrested as fugitive slaves. To prevent further violence, the committee called upon influential Negroes to impress upon their people "the necessity, as well as the propriety, of behaving themselves inoffensively and with civility at all times and upon all occasions; taking care, as they pass along the streets, or assemble together, not to be obtrusive." [96]

Perhaps influenced by the Philadelphia outbreak, anti-Negro violence erupted in other parts of the state. In August, 1834, a Columbia mob invaded the Negro section of that city, destroyed homes, and forced many of its victims to hide in nearby woods until order was restored. A meeting of "the working men and others favorable to their cause" blamed the riots on abolitionist attempts to amalgamate the two races, agreed to boycott merchants who hired Negroes "to do that species of labor white men have been accustomed to perform," and declared its support of the American Colonization Society. Subsequently, white leaders met with Negro property-holders to discuss the disposition of their property at "a fair valuation" and to advise them not to receive any Negro residents from other areas. Few of these property-holders, the committee reported, indicated any reluctance to "sell as fast as funds could be raised." A new meeting then called upon local "capitalists" to give serious consideration to this "very profitable investment of their funds." Meanwhile, mob violence continued and finally prompted one wealthy Negro coal and lumber dealer to offer his entire stock at a reduced price in order to close his business. [97]

[96] Turner, *Negro in Pennsylvania*, pp. 160–65; Abdy, *Journal of a Residence and Tour*, III, 316–33; Joseph Sturge, *A Visit to the United States in 1841* (London, 1842), p. 46; Bell, *Men and Things in America*, pp. 178–79.

[97] *The Liberator*, September 20, 1834; William F. Worner, "The Columbia Race Riots," *Lancaster County Historical Society Papers*, XXVI (1922), 175–87.

Political disfranchisement did not, as some of its backers
had promised, eliminate racial tensions. Violence broke out
in New York City in 1834, and on August 1, 1842, Philadelphia mobs attacked a Negro parade commemorating the abolition of slavery in the West Indies. This touched off a riot
which ended only after whites had beaten many Negroes, destroyed several homes, and burned the new African Hall and
the Colored Presbyterian Church. A grand jury subsequently
placed the blame on the provocative nature of the Negro
processions, but others charged that the attack had been pre-
meditated and strengthened by unemployed white workers.
Economic depression still prevailed in a large part of the country, and, according to one observer, the whites felt that the destruction or expulsion of the Negroes would open up job opportunities.[98] Robert Purvis, a Philadelphia Negro leader, called
it "one of the most ferocious and bloody spirited mobs, that
ever cursed a Christian (?) community" and charged city
officials with apathy and negligence. "Press, Church, Magis-
trates, Clergymen and Devils are against us," Purvis wrote.
"The measure of our suffering is full. . . . From the most
painful and minute investigation, in the feelings, views and
acts of this community — in regard to us — I am convinced
of our utter and complete nothingness in public estimation."
Only a year before, an English Quaker visiting Philadelphia
remarked that probably no city exists "where dislike, amount-
ing to hatred of the coloured population, prevails more than
in the city of brotherly love!" When new riots broke out in
1849, Frederick Douglass concluded: "No man is safe — his
life — his property — and all that he holds dear, are in the
hands of a mob, which may come upon him at any moment —
at midnight or mid-day, and deprive him of his all." [99]

[98] Abdy, *Journal of a Residence and Tour*, III, 115–25; Beaumont, *Marie*, pp.
243–52; Samuel D. Hastings to Lewis Tappan, August 19, 1842, Tappan Papers,
Library of Congress; *The Liberator*, August 12, 19, 26, September 2, 9, 16, 1842.
[99] Robert Purvis to Henry C. Wright, August 22, 1842, Weston Papers, Boston
Public Library; Sturge, *Visit to the United States*, p. 40; *North Star*, October 19,
1849.

In explaining the need for a segregated society, whites usually referred to the economic degradation of the northern Negro and his inability to rise above the menial employments. However, those Negroes who managed to accumulate property and advance their economic position generally achieved a greater respectability only among their own people and found no escape from the scorn and ridicule of white society. "The worst are treated with contempt," an English observer noted, "while the better portion are spoken of with a degree of bitterness, that indicates a disposition to be more angry with their virtues than their vices." [100] Indeed, economic improvement might incur even greater hostility and suspicion. Northern whites had come to accept irresponsibility, ignorance, and submissiveness as peculiar Negro characteristics, as natural products of the Negroes' racial inferiority. Consequently, those who rose above depravity failed to fit the stereotype and somehow seemed abnormal, even menacing. The "drunken, idle, ignorant, and vicious" Negro, Frederick Douglass explained, was the proper butt of the white man's humor; he was termed "a good-natured fellow" and was always the first to be asked to hold the horse or shine the boots of the white man. As long as he catered to white wishes and pride, as long as "he consents to play the buffoon for their support," he would be tolerated. But if he rejected this servile position, educated himself, and improved his economic position, he aroused white prejudice and jealousy for attempting to leave his "place" in society.[101]

By the 1840's, an increasing number of northern Negroes refused to accept passively their assigned place in society. In addition to agitating for equal suffrage, judicial, and educational rights, they sought to break down those barriers which excluded them from public places and vehicles or which seg-

[100] Abdy, *Journal of a Residence and Tour*, I, 117.
[101] *North Star*, June 13, 1850.

regated them in Jim Crow sections. Experience had taught the
Negro that only constant pressure for immediate changes,
rather than a passive trust in gradualism, would produce results. Accordingly, Negroes secured the assistance of white
abolitionists, formed independent organizations, published
several newspapers, and achieved some remarkable progress
toward racial equality. The success of their agitation varied
from state to state, but nowhere was it more vividly demonstrated than in Massachusetts.

After 1821, the political position of the Massachusetts Negro gradually and perceptibly improved. His right to vote and
hold office had been generally acknowledged, but such progress had not been made in the economic and social spheres,
where Negroes competed with new immigrants for the menial
employments and encountered the familiar pattern of segregation, extending from public transportation to the theater.
In 1831, Boston's mayor, Harrison Gray Otis, described the
Negro inhabitants as "a quiet, inoffensive, and in many re-
spects a useful race," but the "repugnance to intimate social
relations with them is insurmountable." Fifteen years later,
the state statistician reported that racial prejudice doomed
Massachusetts Negroes to economic and social inferiority and
accounted for the decrease of their numerical strength in proportion to the whites. On the eve of the Civil War, abolitionist
Senator Henry Wilson admitted in Congress that powerful
prejudices still existed and that Negroes "with the same intellectual qualities, the same moral qualities, are not in Massachusetts regarded as they would be if they were white men." [102]

Possession of the suffrage, then, did not automatically open
the doors of white society. Statutes barred Massachusetts Negroes from intermarrying with whites, and extralegal restrictions segregated them in public places and vehicles. In 1841,

[102] *Niles' Weekly Register,* XLV (September 14, 1833), 43; Jesse Chickering,
A Statistical View of the Population of Massachusetts, from 1765 to 1840 (Boston,
1846), pp. 155–60; *Congressional Globe,* 35 Cong., 1 sess., p. 1966.

the fear of possible mob violence even prompted Boston authorities to place Negro participants in the rear of President William Henry Harrison's funeral procession.[103] Any attempt to secure equal rights for Negroes would first have to arouse public opinion to the undemocratic nature of such distinctions. With this in mind, Massachusetts abolitionists — Negro and white — set out to convince an apathetic and frequently hostile public that a consistent stand against southern slavery involved the full recognition of the rights of local Negroes.

In one of the first issues of *The Liberator*, William Lloyd Garrison launched a campaign to repeal the law barring marriages between Negroes and whites.[104] Abolitionists accompanied an incessant editorial barrage with a continuous flow of petitions to the legislature and placed particular emphasis on the inconsistency of such a statute with the state's traditional hostility to slavery. "So long as Southerners can point to it on her Statute Book," John Greenleaf Whittier declared, "the anti-slavery testimony of Massachusetts is shorn of half its strength."[105] Agreeing with this sentiment, a legislative committee concluded that the existence of such a law belied "sentiments which we have heretofore expressed to Congress and to the world on the subject of slavery, for by denying to our colored fellow-citizens any of the privileges and immunities of freemen, we virtually assert their inequality, and justify that theory of negro slavery which represents it as a state of necessary tutelage and guardianship."[106]

The possibility that Massachusetts might actually repeal its ban on interracial marriages drew some bitter comments from both northern and southern newspapers, including a warning

[103] *National Anti-Slavery Standard*, May 20, 1841.
[104] *The Liberator*, January 8, 1831. See also May 7, 1831, January 28, February 11, March 31, 1832, February 5, 1841, February 24, 1843.
[105] *Ibid.*, February 22, 1839.
[106] *Massachusetts House of Representatives, House Report*, No. 46 (March 6, 1840), pp. 7–8; No. 7 (January 19, 1841).

that "such alliances will never be tolerated in New England." [107] Some legislators defended the law on grounds that it was not discriminatory because it applied equally to both races; moreover, it recognized certain natural distinctions, "which nothing but the insanity of fanaticism dares to arraign," and prevented a deterioration of the white race.[108] Nevertheless, after more than a decade of agitation, the legislature voted, on February 24, 1843, to repeal the act. Abolitionists hailed the successful campaign as "another staggering blow . . . to the monster prejudice," and Garrison reassured an English correspondent that their object was not to promote amalgamation but "to establish justice, and vindicate the equality of the human race." [109]

Simultaneously with their attack on the intermarriage ban, abolitionists moved to abolish the Jim Crow railroad cars. Precedents already established in stagecoaches and steamships, as well as the existing state of public opinion, accounted for the assignment of Negroes to special coaches.[110] Josiah Quincy, Jr., president of the Boston and Providence Railroad, recalled that when the Providence road opened the shortest route to New York, "it was found that an appreciable number of the despised race demanded transportation. Scenes of riot and violence took place, and in the then existing state of

[107] Editorial comment reprinted in *The Liberator*, April 2, May 21, June 11, 1831, February 8, 1839, and in *National Anti-Slavery Standard*, April 1, 1841. For the critical reaction of a Hallowell, Maine, town meeting, see Charles L. Remond to Elizabeth Pease, May 5, 1841, Garrison Papers, Boston Public Library.

[108] *Massachusetts House of Representatives, House Report*, No. 28 (February 25, 1839), p. 10; No. 74 (April 3, 1839).

[109] William Lloyd Garrison to Richard D. Webb, February 28, 1843, Garrison Papers.

[110] For origins of the term "Jim Crow" as applied to separate railroad accommodations, apparently first used in Massachusetts, see Mitford M. Mathews (ed.), *A Dictionary of Americanisms* (2 vols.; Chicago, 1951), I, 906–7. Some examples of stagecoach and steamboat segregation may be found in *Freedom's Journal*, March 23, 1827; *The Liberator*, January 15, December 10, 1831, July 7, August 11, 1832, December 28, 1833, November 30, 1838, September 17, 1841; Abdy, *Journal of a Residence and Tour*, II, 48–49.

opinion, it seemed to me that the difficulty could best be met by assigning a special car to our colored citizens." [111] As early as 1838 — only a few years after railroads first came into public use in Massachusetts — Negroes demanded an end to segregation on trains, steamboats, and stagecoaches. By the 1840's, the newspapers frequently reported cases of Negroes' being forcibly removed from railroad cars for refusing to sit in the Jim Crow sections. [112]

The failure to secure a court injunction against such practices prompted Negroes to turn to the legislature for relief. Meanwhile, abolitionists urged their followers to boycott companies which sanctioned segregation and to flood the legislature with petitions. In an effort to arouse public indignation, they pointed out that southern slaveholders, when traveling through the state, were allowed to keep their Negro bondsmen with them in cars which excluded native free Negroes. Therefore, "it is *not* color alone which excluded a man from the best car. The colored person to be excluded must also be *free*!!" [113]

Abolitionist agitation produced the desired effect. In 1842, a joint legislative committee, after conducting hearings, reported that the railroad restrictions violated the Negro's rights as a citizen, conflicted with the state constitution, and "would be an insult to any white man." Since the railroad companies derived corporate privileges from the legislature, the committee recommended a bill which would prohibit any distinctions in accommodations because of descent, sect, or color. [114]

[111] Josiah Quincy, Jr., *Figures of the Past* (Boston, 1883), pp. 340–41.

[112] August W. Hanson to Frances Jackson, October 22, 1838, Garrison Papers; *The Liberator*, October 18, 1839, July 2, 9, 23, August 27, October 1, 8, 15, November 5, 12, 1841; *Colored American*, September 25, October 30, 1841.

[113] *The Liberator*, October 1, November 5, 1841. Two unsuccessful attempts to obtain court action against the railroads are described in *ibid.*, August 6, November 5, 1841.

[114] *Massachusetts Senate, Senate Report*, No. 63 (February 22, 1842). For the testimony of Wendell Phillips and Charles L. Remond before the legislative committee, see *The Liberator*, February 18, 25, 1842.

Governor Marcus Morton suggested, in the following year, that
if any citizens, in railroad cars or elsewhere, sustained injuries because of their descent or color for which no legal
redress was available, they should be provided with "remedies adequate to their protection in the enjoyment of their just
and equal rights." [115]

Such sentiment was not unanimous. The railroad directors
argued that all Massachusetts corporations had been granted
the power to make "reasonable and proper" by-laws for the
management of their business, and "the established usage
and the public sentiment of this community authorize a separation of the blacks from the whites in public places." A Boston newspaper charged that recent legislative proposals,
designed to make Massachusetts a "paradise of colored
people," had resulted in a sizable increase in Negro immigration. The effect of the proposed railroad bill, the newspaper
pointed out, would be to subject passengers "to the hazard of
being compelled to sit cheek by jowl with any colored person
who may chance to seize upon the adjoining seat." Moreover,
a state senator warned, such legislation would not stop at
forcing the mixture of Negroes and whites in railroad cars
but would subsequently be applied to hotels, religious societies, "and through all the ramifications of society." [116]

The legislature refused to adopt the proposed act. Nevertheless, constant abolitionist pressure, the growing impact of
public opinion, and the threat of legislative action prompted
the railroad companies to abandon segregation, and only a
few cases were reported after 1842. Frederick Douglass, who
had frequently been a victim of these restrictions, noted in
1849 that "not a single railroad can be found in any part of
Massachusetts, where a colored man is treated and esteemed

[115] Marcus Morton to Henry I. Bowditch, October 2, 1843, Garrison Papers.
[116] *The Liberator*, November 5, 1841, February 10, 17, 1843.

in any other light than that of a man and a traveler." The abolitionists had scored a significant triumph.[117]

Although so often rebuked for their ignorance, Negroes frequently found it difficult to take advantage of the increasing opportunities for adult education, particularly the popular lecture presentations of the Lyceum. Lecture-hall managers either refused them admittance or consigned them to remote corners, usually in the balcony. In Boston, where this was apparently not the practice, one Lyceum subscriber protested in the local press that he refused to "carry a lady to a lecture, and compel her to do the pennance of sitting cheek by jowl with a negro." In the absence of any restrictions, he warned that the Boston Lyceum, among the first to be established in the United States, would "become nothing more than the patron and upholder of abolition orgies; the auditory consisting of the same class usually found in the third tier and gallery of the theatres."[118] The Boston Lyceum apparently withstood such attacks and managed to survive.

In nearby New Bedford, however, Lyceum authorities in 1845 excluded Negroes from membership and assigned them to gallery seats — after they had once enjoyed the same privileges as whites. This precipitated an immediate reaction. In addition to abolitionist threats to boycott the Lyceum, three prominent lecturers — Ralph Waldo Emerson, Charles Sumner, and Theodore Parker — refused to appear there until the restrictions had been rescinded. Emerson told a Concord abolitionist "that the Lyceum being a popular thing designed for the benefit of all, *particularly* for the most ignorant . . . he should not know how to address an assembly where this class was excluded, and if any were excluded, it should be the cultivated classes."[119] When the Lyceum remained ada-

---

[117] *Ibid.*, April 28, 1843, June 8, 1849.

[118] *Ibid.*, January 13, 1843.

[119] Mary Brooks to Caroline Weston, March 19, November 24, 1845, Weston Papers; Deborah Weston to Anne Warren Weston, October 1845, *ibid.*; Sumner,

mant in its refusal to admit Negroes to membership, abolitionists organized a rival association.[120]

By 1859, a Boston Negro leader could point not only to the
frequent presence of his people at popular lectures but also
to the actual appearance of Frederick Douglass and other
prominent Negro abolitionists on Lyceum platforms. Exclusion and segregation, however, still confronted Negroes in
several Boston theaters, and legal action to abolish these restrictions proved largely unsuccessful.[121]

By the eve of the Civil War, Massachusetts Negroes had
made considerable progress toward the attainment of full
civil rights, but much remained to be done. "Some persons
think," a Boston Negro leader remarked in 1860, "that because we have the right to vote, and enjoy the privilege of
being squeezed up in an omnibus, and stared out of a seat in
a horse-car, that there is less prejudice here than there is farther South." This was only partially true, he continued, for
"it is five times as hard to get a house in a good location in
Boston as it is in Philadelphia, and it is ten times as difficult
for a colored mechanic to get work here as it is in Charleston."
Moreover, local restaurants, hotels, and theaters continued to
exclude the Negro, while at least two amusement places helped
to perpetuate existing prejudices through constant caricature
and ridicule.[122]

Few could deny, however, that in several areas the Negro
had at least ceased to be a second-class citizen. He could now
vote, hold public office, testify in court, sit as a juror, ride

Works, I, 160–62; Zephaniah W. Pease (ed.), *The Diary of Samuel Rodman: A
New Bedford Chronicle of Thirty-Seven Years, 1821–1859* (New Bedford, 1927),
pp. 269–70; *The Liberator*, October 31, November 28, 1845.

[120] Maria (Weston) Chapman, "An Incident of Anti-Slavery Reform," n.d.,
Weston Papers; *The Liberator*, December 5, 19, 1845.

[121] Catterall (ed.), *Judicial Cases*, IV, 524, 527–28; Mary C. Crawford, *Romantic Days in Old Boston* (Boston, 1922), p. 249; *The Liberator*, October 30,
1857.

[122] *The Liberator*, March 16, 1860.

public vehicles, and intermarry with whites. To many observers, especially those from outside the state, it was a rather frightening spectacle: amalgamation had run amuck in the Puritan Commonwealth.[123]

Elsewhere in the North, Negroes met with little success in their efforts to break down segregation. Rather than submit to further harassment on New York City public conveyances, Negroes formed the "Legal Rights Association," deliberately violated company segregation rules, and employed, among others, Chester A. Arthur as legal counsel.[124] The railroad directors replied, however, that public sentiment required separate cars for Negroes and pointed out that Negroes could stand on the front platforms of any cars. In a case involving the expulsion of a Negro woman from a segregated car, the presiding judge instructed the jury that Negroes, "if sober, well behaved, and free from disease," possessed the same rights as whites and could not be excluded by force or violence from public conveyances. The jury convicted the railroad company of negligence and ordered damages paid to the plaintiff.[125] However, one year later — in 1856 — a jury refused to convict a railroad company for ejecting a Negro minister from one of its cars. In a lengthy instruction to the jury, the presiding judge pointed out that common carriers had the right to prescribe reasonable rules and regulations, that they were not obligated to carry particular persons when such action might adversely affect their interests, and that consideration had to be given to "the probable effect upon the capital, business and interests of admitting blacks into their cars indiscriminately with the whites." Moreover, the principles in-

[123] *Appendix to the Congressional Globe*, 36 Cong., 1 sess., pp. 284–85.
[124] New York *Daily Times*, August 27, 1855; *Frederick Douglass' Paper*, May 11, September 7, 1855; Leo H. Hirsch, Jr., "The Negro and New York, 1783 to 1865," *Journal of Negro History*, XVI (1931), 426.
[125] New York *Daily Times*, May 29, 1855; *Frederick Douglass' Paper*, July 28, 1854, March 2, 1855.

volved in this case could readily be applied to hotel owners, omnibus proprietors "and all others of that description." [126]

When Philadelphia streetcars went into operation in 1858, Negroes could ride only on the front platform. Protesting this practice, one local newspaper charged that Philadelphia was the only northern city which barred Negroes from the public conveyances and that this prevented them from moving to outlying areas where they could secure cleaner and more comfortable homes at cheaper rates. The Philadelphia District Court, however, upheld the restriction as a consequence of the different treatment accorded Negroes and whites, particularly since 1838. Finally, in 1867, a legislative act forbade segregation in public conveyances. [127]

Although the Negro made substantial gains in Massachusetts and scored sporadic successes elsewhere, his general political and social position remained unaltered. By 1860, the North had clearly defined its position on racial relations: white supremacy and social peace required a vigorous separation of blacks and whites and the concentration of political and judicial power in the hands of the superior race — the Caucasian. "The result," an English traveler observed, "is a singular social phenomenon. We see, in effect, two nations — one white and another black — growing up together within the same political circle, but never mingling on a principle of equality." [128]

[126] New York *Daily Times*, December 18, 20, 1856.

[127] *The Liberator*, September 21, 1860; Turner, *Negro in Pennsylvania*, pp. 197–98; *A Brief Narrative of the Struggle for the Rights of the Colored People of Philadelphia in the City Railway Cars* (Philadelphia, 1867).

[128] Chambers, *Things as They Are in America*, p. 357.

Education:
Separate and
Unequal

Education was one of the foremost aspirations of the northern Negro. "If we ever expect to see the influence of prejudice decrease and ourselves respected," a Negro national convention resolved in 1832, "it must be by the blessings of an enlightened education." [1] This sentiment was repeated throughout the ante bellum period. Through education, the Negro hoped to improve his economic status, produce his own literary and scientific figures, and break down the barriers of discrimination. However, the Negro's quest for educational opportunities, partly because he hoped to accomplish such goals, prompted some strong and frequently violent protests in the North. The possibility that Negro children would be mixed with white chil-

[1] *Minutes and Proceedings of the Second Annual Convention, for the Improvement of the Free People of Color in these United States* (Philadelphia, 1832), p. 34.

113

dren in the same classroom aroused even greater fears and prejudices than those which consigned the Negro to an inferior place in the church, the theater, and the railroad car. This, indeed, constituted virtual amalgamation.

Although some white schools admitted Negroes, especially before 1820, most northern states either excluded them altogether or established separate schools for them. As early as 1787, Boston Negroes petitioned the legislature to grant them educational facilities, since they "now receive no benefit from the free schools." Forty years later, the first Negro newspaper repeated this complaint. "While the benevolence of the age has founded and endowed seminaries of Learning for all other classes and nations," it declared, "we have to lament, that as yet, no door is open to receive the degraded children of Africa. Alone they have stood — alone they remain stationary; while charity extends the hands to all others." [2]

The means employed to exclude Negroes from the public schools varied only slightly from state to state. In New England, local school committees usually assigned Negro children to separate institutions, regardless of the district in which they resided. Pennsylvania and Ohio, although extending their public school privileges to all children, required district school directors to establish separate facilities for Negro students whenever twenty or more could be accommodated. The New York legislature authorized any school district, upon the approval of a town's school commissioners, to provide for segregation. The newer states frequently excluded Negroes from all public education, but by 1850, most of them had consented to separate instruction. [3] In the absence of legal restrictions,

[2] Aptheker (ed.), *Documentary History*, pp. 19–20; *Freedom's Journal*, May 18, 1827.

[3] For a general survey of state policies concerning Negro education, see U.S. Commissioner of Education, *Special Report . . . on the Condition and Improvement of Public Schools in the District of Columbia, submitted to the Senate June, 1868, and to the House, with additions, June 13, 1870* (Washing-

115

custom and popular prejudice often excluded Negro children
from the schools. For example, an Indianan noted in 1850 that
the laws provided no racial distinctions in the state school system, but "the whites rose *en-masse*, and said your children
shall not go to schools with our children, and they were consequently expelled. Thus, then, we see that in this respect, there
is a higher law than the Constitutional law." [4] By the 1830's,
statute or custom placed Negro children in separate schools
in nearly every northern community.

Proposals to educate Negroes invariably aroused bitter controversy, particularly in the new western states. The admission
of Negroes to white schools, opponents maintained, would result in violence and prove fatal to public education. Moreover,
some contended that Negroes, "after a certain age, did not cor-
respondingly advance in learning — their intellect being apparently incapable of being cultured beyond a particular
point." [5] When an Ohio legislative committee rejected a petition to grant Negroes a share of the education fund, it conceded
that this might "at first appear unnatural, and unbecoming a
charitable, high-minded, and intelligent community," but the
security of the government depended upon "the morality, virtue, and wisdom" of its white citizens and the school fund
should thus not be confused with charity. [6] Opponents also
warned that equal educational privileges would encourage
Negro immigration and antagonize southern-born residents.
On the basis of such a pretext, a California mayor vetoed
appropriations for Negro schools as "particularly obnoxious
to those of our citizens who have immigrated from Southern
States." The city aldermen defended his action with a warning

ton, D.C., 1871), Part II, *Legal Status of the Colored Population in Respect to
Schools and Education in the Different States*, pp. 301–400, and Carter G. Woodson, *The Education of the Negro prior to 1861* (New York, 1915), pp. 307–35.
[4] *Indiana Constitutional Debates of 1850*, I, 573.
[5] Chambers, *Things as They Are in America*, p. 357.
[6] Abdy, *Journal of a Residence and Tour*, II, 394.

against placing the two races on an equal basis, "not withstanding the distinction stamped by Divinity between them." [7]

Delegates to the state constitutional conventions debated various proposals to exclude Negroes from the schools. Westerners, fearing an increase in Negro immigration, voiced some especially vehement objections. "They are not by nature equal to the whites," an Iowan declared, "and their children cannot be made equal to my children, or those of my constituents." In 1850, an Ohio convention delegate opposed any measure, including education, which would tend to encourage Negro immigration or impede colonization. Nine years later, a Kansas Republican warned that he would immediately object to any Negro's attending school with white children. However, he opposed any legal bars, claiming that the "neighborhood could protect itself." Other Kansas convention delegates predicted that voters would reject the proposed constitution unless it explicitly prohibited racial mixing in the schools. As late as 1860, an Iowa congressman warned that no northwestern state would countenance biracial education. [8] Ante bellum constitutional provisions and legislation confirmed his prediction.

Southern representatives denounced congressional efforts to provide for Negro education in Washington, D.C. White parents would allow their children to remain in ignorance, opponents contended, rather than send them to school with Negroes. Moreover, integrated schools would conflict with the established policy of the southern and many northern states. Senator Jefferson Davis of Mississippi opposed any appropriations for Negro schools and charged that, aside from some

[7] Sacramento *Daily Union*, as quoted in *The Liberator*, December 14, 1855; J. Holland Townsend, "American Caste and Common Schools," *Anglo-African Magazine*, I (March, 1859), 81–82.

[8] *The Debates of the Constitutional Convention; of the State of Iowa* (2 vols.; Davenport, 1857), II, 826; *Ohio Constitutional Debates of 1850*, p. 683; *Kansas Constitutional Convention . . . 1859* (Topeka, 1920), pp. 175–83, 193–95; *Congressional Globe*, 36 Cong., 1 sess., p. 1680.

men "led away by a sickly sentimentality," northern whites rejected any racial mixing.[9]

The objections to classroom integration extended beyond the public schools to private academies and colleges. The admission of Negroes into two New England schools — Wesleyan University in Middletown, Connecticut, and the Noyes Academy in Canaan, New Hampshire — vividly demonstrated this sentiment.

When Charles B. Ray, later a prominent Negro leader, entered Wesleyan in 1832, both southern and northern students voiced objections. His decision to board at the campus aroused even more vigorous opposition. Several students protested Ray's presence to the college president, threatened to leave school, and called a meeting at the chapel to propose to the trustees that he be removed. A resolution adopted at the meeting called Ray's presence on the campus "inexpedient" and provided for a special fund to defray any expenses he incurred in coming to the university. Although the president promised him protection, Ray agreed to leave. His campus "friends" thereupon declared that he had taken "the wisest course" since "our Institution is in its infancy" and had to rely on both southern and northern support. They hoped, however, that time would eventually eradicate these odious racial barriers.[10]

The Canaan episode involved the hostility of a community rather than a group of students. In March, 1835, twenty-eight whites and fourteen Negroes commenced classes at newly established Noyes Academy. The school, which had several abolitionists on its board of trustees, admitted all qualified applicants, regardless of race or color. In announcing this liberal policy, the trustees cited the exclusion of Negroes from

[9] *Congressional Globe*, 36 Cong., 1 sess., pp. 1678–83; *Appendix to the Congressional Globe*, 35 Cong., 1 sess., pp. 371–72.
[10] *The Liberator*, January 12, 1833.

educational institutions in the free states and proposed "to afford colored youth a fair opportunity to show that they are capable, equally with the whites, of improving themselves in every scientific attainment, every social virtue, and every Christian ornament." [11] Abolitionists enthusiastically indorsed the academy and appealed for further support. The Massachusetts Anti-Slavery Society praised the town of Canaan and concluded optimistically that her example would soon induce other academies to admit Negroes.[12] Even an English visitor to Canaan commented on the "spirit of liberality unknown, or at least unheard of, in any other part of the Union" which "had inspired the townsmen of this sequestered spot" to open such a school. Although he had heard of some threats to the institution while in Concord, he found that few opponents remained and that the inhabitants were "hospitable, intelligent, and disinterested; simple in their habits, and frank in their manners." [13]

The new school attracted Negroes from other states, including several who later became important leaders in the struggle for civil rights. From New York, Henry H. Garnet, Thomas S. Sidney, and Alexander Crummell traveled by Jim Crow steamboats and stagecoaches to attend the academy. Thomas Paul, son of a prominent Negro minister, arrived from Boston and wrote two weeks later that the townsmen of Canaan "will occupy a conspicuous station among those who have been foremost in pleading for the slave." [14]

The New Hampshire village was destined for a far different

[11] *Ibid.*, October 25, 1834.
[12] *Proceedings of the New Hampshire Anti-Slavery Convention, held in Concord, on the 11th and 12th of November, 1834* (Concord, 1834), p. 11; Minutes of a Special Meeting of the Board of Managers of the Massachusetts Anti-Slavery Society, June 15, 1835, Weston Papers.
[13] Abdy, *Journal of a Residence and Tour*, III, 265–69.
[14] Alexander Crummell, *Africa and America* (Springfield, Mass., 1891), pp. 278–79; William M. Brewer, "Henry Highland Garnet," *Journal of Negro History*, XII (1928), 41–42; *The Liberator*, May 2, 16, 1835.

fame, however. The mixing of Negro and white youths set off a series of rumors through the town. Negroes would overrun Canaan; fugitive slaves would line the streets with their huts and burden the town with paupers and vagabonds; the school would become a public nuisance. "Fourteen black boys with books in their hands," Crummell wrote, "set the entire Granite State crazy!" [15]

Objecting to reports that they supported the biracial academy, some of Canaan's residents met to denounce such stories as false. Moreover, they announced that more than four-fifths of the townspeople opposed the school "and are determined to take effectual measures to remove it." On July 4, 1835, a mob approached the academy, but the local magistrate dispersed them. Later that month, "a legal Town Meeting" appointed a committee to abolish the school in "the *interest* of the town, the *honor* of the State, and the *good* of the whole community, (both black and white)." On August 10, the committee proceeded with its assigned task, enlisted the assistance of men from neighboring towns and nearly one hundred yoke of oxen, and removed the school building from its foundations to "the common near the Baptist meeting-house." There it stands, the Concord *Patriot* reported, "not like the monument on 'Bunker's Heights,' erected in memory of those departed spirits, which fought and fell, struggling for Liberty, — but as the monument of the folly of those living spirits, who are struggling to destroy what our fathers have gained." After completing its job, the committee met briefly to condemn abolitionism and to praise the Constitution and the Revolutionary patriots. "So ended the day," the *Patriot* remarked, "joyful to the friend of his country, but sorrowful to the Abolitionists." [16]

[15] *Human Rights* (American Anti-Slavery Society), October, 1835; *The Liberator*, October 3, 1835; Crummell, *Africa and America*, p. 280.

[16] *The Liberator*, August 8, September 5, October 3, 1835; *Fourth Annual Report of the Board of Managers of the Massachusetts Anti-Slavery Society* (Boston, 1836), pp. 27–29. On March 22, 1839, *The Liberator* reported that a fire had destroyed the building formerly occupied by the Noyes Academy.

Defending the conduct of his constituents, Senator Isaac Hill told Congress that the people of Canaan had simply thwarted an invidious abolitionist scheme to mingle Negro and white children. Since "they could rid themselves of the nuisance in no other way," the townsmen had removed the building "to a place where it could not be used for that purpose." This demonstrated, Hill declared, "the deep feeling that pervades New Hampshire, indeed . . . the whole of New England, on the subject of slave agitation," and should fully satisfy the South with regard to "the present disposition of the North." [17]

Wesleyan and Canaan illustrated two methods of opposition to integrated schools. Since white schools generally excluded Negroes, such cases occurred infrequently. Most Negro youths continued to attend segregated institutions or secured no education at all. White political leaders, including those who bitterly opposed Negro education, could thus contend that widespread illiteracy in the Negro population prevented any extension of the suffrage or other civil rights. "The colored people are . . . charged with want of desire for education and improvement," a Negro remarked in 1839, "yet, if a colored man comes to the door of our institutions of learning, with desires ever so strong, the lords of these institutions rise up and shut the door; and then you say we have not the desire nor the ability to acquire education. Thus, while the white youths enjoy all these advantages, we are excluded and shut out, and must remain ignorant." [18]

Excluded from white schools, Negroes moved to establish

[17] *Appendix to the Congressional Globe*, 24 Cong., 1 sess., p. 91. A Negro journal later reported that the people of Canaan had repented of their conduct, "and being determined to redeem what they had lost by imprudence, sought out the only colored man in the town and made him justice of the peace." *Anglo-African Magazine*, I (March, 1859), 81.

[18] *Sixth Annual Report of the Executive Committee of the American Anti-Slavery Society* (New York, 1839), p. 11.

their own educational institutions and enlisted the support of abolitionists, some white philanthropists, and several state legislatures. By 1860, a number of private ventures had been attempted, with varying success, and nearly every northern state had provided for a Negro public school system.

The early antislavery societies, especially those in Pennsylvania and New York, placed particular stress on the education of the emancipated slave. As early as 1790, the Pennsylvania Society appointed a committee to supervise the instruction of free Negro youths and to encourage their attendance at some school. Five years later, the committee asked the legislature to establish "Free Schools, without Discrimination of Colour, and in populous Towns to promote particular Institutions for the Education of Blacks." By 1820, the legislature granted Pennsylvania Negroes a share of the state school fund to support separate instruction. In New York, the Manumission Society organized the African Free Schools in 1787 and eventually transferred them to city authorities. Negroes took the initiative in Massachusetts to establish a school in 1789 and subsequently secured the assistance of white philanthropy and state appropriations. In Ohio, Negroes organized the School Fund Society and established some educational centers.[19] Such efforts, however, provided educational opportunities for only a small fraction of Negro youth.

After 1831, the revived abolitionist movement gave substantial support and encouragement to Negro education. The constitution of the American Anti-Slavery Society cited the importance of the "intellectual, moral, and religious improve-

[19] Minutes of the Committee for Improving the Condition of Free Blacks, Pennsylvania Abolition Society, 1790–1803, Historical Society of Pennsylvania, pp. 1–2, 113, 219–20; *ibid.*, 1837–1853, pp. 29–33; Needles, *Historical Memoir*, pp. 40, 43, 68, 69–70, 104–5; Charles C. Andrews, *The History of the New-York African Free-Schools* (New York, 1830); U.S. Commissioner of Education, *Special Report, 1871*, p. 357; Sheeler, "The Struggle of the Negro in Ohio for Freedom," pp. 215–17; Charles Hickok, *The Negro in Ohio, 1802–1870* (Cleveland, 1896), pp. 82–83, 88.

ment" of Negroes, and William Lloyd Garrison praised Negro efforts to obtain adequate educational facilities.[20] Convinced "that faith without *works* is death," Cincinnati abolitionists, prompted by Theodore Weld, provided instruction for the Negro community through the establishment of a regular adult school, Sabbath and evening schools, Lyceum lectures, and Bible classes. "Everything goes on here as we could wish," a Cincinnati abolitionist wrote in 1834. "Our colored brethren are animated with hope. A calm determination to alter their condition is firmly fixed in every breast. Elevation, moral, political and religious, fires their mind." The schools, he added, had aroused no overt opposition.[21] Other communities attempted to duplicate the work of the Cincinnati abolitionists but were less successful.

Exclusively Negro schools did not necessarily meet with popular favor. The identification of abolitionism with the cause of Negro education provided whites with a convenient excuse for resisting such institutions. In Ohio, for example, whites demonstrated their hostility in some instances by destroying newly established Negro schools and exposing their teachers to insults and violence. When a young woman opened such a school in Zanesville, whites entered the building, destroyed the books and furnishings, and finally drove the institution from the town. In 1840, an Ohio newspaper reported that in the town of Troy, residents had virtually demolished a school "all because a white man had undertaken to keep a school for the black children in the neighborhood." [22] Some states very reluctantly agreed to the establishment of Negro

[20] *The Declaration of Sentiments and Constitution of the American Anti-Slavery Society* (New York, 1835), p. 8; *First Annual Report of the Board of Managers of the New-England Anti-Slavery Society* (Boston, 1833), p. 7.

[21] Barnes and Dumond (eds.), *Weld-Grimke Correspondence*, I, 132–35, 178–80, 211–18.

[22] *Fourth Annual Report of the American Anti-Slavery Society* (New York, 1837), p. 109; Hickok, *Negro in Ohio*, pp. 89–90; Elyria (Ohio) *Advertiser*, as quoted in *National Anti-Slavery Standard*, December 24, 1840.

schools. The Michigan legislature, for example, approved the incorporation of such a school only after some vigorous protests and the adoption of an amendment expressly prohibiting the admission of whites.[23]

Two classic incidents in the Negro's struggle for education involved attempts to institute schools for their benefit in New Haven and Canterbury, Connecticut. In both cases, townspeople vigorously protested the establishment of any school which might attract Negroes from other states or threaten the property values and peace of the town. The participation of prominent abolitionists in these projects further enabled the opposition to hide its racial prejudices behind slogans of patriotism, racial purity, and national unity.

The attempt to establish a Negro college in New Haven coincided with the advent of Garrisonian abolitionism. In June, 1831, three antislavery leaders — Simeon S. Jocelyn, a Yale graduate and white minister in a New Haven Negro church; Arthur Tappan, a New York merchant and philanthropist; and Garrison — proposed such a school to a Negro national convention. It would be self supporting and based on the manual-labor system, "so that the student may cultivate habits of industry and obtain a useful mechanical or agricultural profession, while pursuing classical studies." Moreover, the success of such an enterprise would demonstrate the Negro's capabilities, advance the abolitionist cause, and "produce a band of educated men to take up the pen" for Negro rights. New Haven appeared to be an ideal site for such a college because of its literary and scientific fame, its central location, the relative liberality of state laws, and the "friendly, pious, generous, and humane" character of the city's residents. Since New Haven traded extensively with the West Indies, backers of the college hoped that many of the Islands' Negro inhabitants would send their sons to be educated at

[23] *The Liberator*, April 4, 1845.

New Haven and thus establish "a fresh tie of friendship." The Negro convention enthusiastically indorsed the proposed college, organized an extensive fund-raising campaign, and resolved that the trustees of the new institution should include a majority of Negroes.[24]

New Haven, however, did not share this enthusiasm. One month after the convention, a local journal warned that any attempt to bind Negroes to this country and raise them to an equal level with whites, "whether by founding colleges, or in any other way," tended "to counteract and thwart the whole plan of colonization."[25] In August, 1831, Nat Turner's Insurrection broke out in Virginia, inducing the southern states to add further restrictions on slaves and free Negroes and increasing apprehension in New Haven over the proposed college. One month later, a crowded New Haven town meeting, called by the mayor and aldermen, accused the abolitionists of conspiring to use Negro colleges to propagate antislavery sentiments. The gathering then proceeded to denounce the proposed college as incompatible with the existence and prosperity of Yale and other notable local institutions and "destructive to the best interests of this city," and it concluded that no such school should be imposed on any community without that community's consent. Only Jocelyn raised his voice in protest as the meeting formally approved these sentiments by approximately seven hundred to four.[26] New Haven had taken its stand.

"Our beautiful city is clothed in sackcloth," Jocelyn wrote. "Our proud elms hang their heads. The temples of God, our

[24] *Minutes and Proceedings of the First Annual Convention of the People of Colour* (Philadelphia, 1831), pp. 5–7.

[25] New Haven *Religious Intelligencer*, July, 1831, as quoted in Jay, *Inquiry into the Character and Tendency of the American Colonization, and American Anti-Slavery Societies*, p. 26.

[26] *College for Colored Youth: An Account of the New-Haven City Meeting and Resolutions* (New York, 1831), pp. 4–5; Robert A. Warner, *New Haven Negroes* (New Haven, 1940), pp. 55–56; James Forten to William Lloyd Garrison, October 20, 1831, Garrison Papers.

halls of justice and our seats of learning break forth because of oppression." The establishment of an ordinary Negro school, Jocelyn contended, had aroused no open opposition, but the proposal to found a college had caused great alarm. It must have been the name "college" that frightened them, he wrote to Garrison, for "it carries the assurance of equality with it." [27] Several newspapers joined Jocelyn in reprimanding the city for its "disgraceful" conduct. "Men complain of the ignorance and vice of the colored population," the New York *Journal of Commerce* remarked, "and yet when a project is presented to rescue them, or a part of them, from their deep degradation, the same men are round at once to the highest pitch of opposition." A Massachusetts newspaper assailed the town-meeting proceedings and hoped that Boston might now have "the glory of the first establishment of a seminary for the instruction of a much wronged race of men." The major objection to the Negro college, the Boston *Courier* claimed, was that it would offend the southern patrons of Yale.[28]

Local opinion, however, supported the town meeting. The establishment of a Negro college would threaten the prosperity of the city; it would add to an "unwholesome colored population," lower moral standards, and frighten away summer visitors and students for Yale and the girls' schools.[29] Besides, a New York newspaper asked, "what possible good can arise from giving them a collegiate education— the highest classical honors and attainments? . . . Will it give to them that equality which exists among white men? Certainly not. The very leaders who open their purses for such objects will not allow a

[27] *The Liberator*, September 24, 1831; *College for Colored Youth*, p. 11; Francis and Wendell P. Garrison, *William Lloyd Garrison*, I, 260 n.

[28] New York *Journal of Commerce*, September 15, 1831, *Massachusetts Journal*, September 17, 1831, and Boston *Courier*, September 20, 1831, as quoted in *College for Colored Youth*, pp. 17–18, 20.

[29] Warner, *New Haven Negroes*, pp. 56–59; *Niles' Weekly Register*, XLI (October 1, 1831), 88.

learned Negro to sit at their table or marry their daughter."
Exposing Negroes to a higher education would only increase
their discontent, for "what benefit can it be to a waiter or coachman to read Horace, or be a profound mathematician?" Some
elementary schools admitted Negroes, "and beyond this their
wants cannot lead them." [30] A Philadelphia pro-colonization
meeting echoed this sentiment in congratulating the citizens of
New Haven "on their escape from the monstrous evil" of a
Negro college.[31]

The abolitionists accepted defeat and abandoned the project. The next annual Negro convention denounced the conduct
of the town and expressed the hope that a new and more favorable location could be found.[32] New Haven could now
breathe more easily. In 1834, some Connecticut citizens met
to discuss the increase of the Negro population and recalled
the three-year-old New Haven incident. "Not satisfied with
depriving us of our labor, they are determined to become our
Lawyers, Physicians, Divines and Statesmen. The first attempt
of this kind miscarried." [33]

It was but a short distance from New Haven to Windham
County. There, in the quiet and picturesque Connecticut coun-
tryside, stood the village of Canterbury. In 1831, Prudence
Crandall, a young Quaker schoolmistress, established in Canterbury a successful and popular girls' boarding school. Miss
Crandall's welcome proved to be short lived, however, for one
year later, she agreed to admit a Negro. This immediately
aroused the town, brought protests from the white parents, and
resulted in the withdrawal of most of the students. The schoolmistress thereupon made a hasty trip to Boston and New York,
where she consulted with William Lloyd Garrison and other
leading abolitionists about the expediency of opening her

[30] New York *Courier & Enquirer*, as quoted in *The Liberator*, December 3, 1831.
[31] *The Liberator*, December 10, 1831.
[32] *Minutes and Proceedings of the Second Annual Convention*, p. 34.
[33] *The Liberator*, February 15, 1834.

school exclusively to Negro girls.[34] On March 2, 1833, *The Liberator* announced the establishment of "a High School for young colored Ladies and Misses" and published a list of "sponsors" which included virtually every prominent Negro and white abolitionist leader in the North. Garrison praised the projected school but warned Miss Crandall that she now faced possible "reproach and persecution." For once, at least, Garrison had understated the case.

Canterbury responded to news of the proposed school with meetings, delegations of protest, bitter attacks on abolitionism, and warnings that terrible consequences might follow. Such a school would depreciate property values; local Negroes would claim an equality with the new arrivals, and these, in turn, would demand equality with the whites; the town had to resist this obvious abolitionist plot, this invidious attempt "to foist upon the community a new species of gentility, in the shape of sable belles." [35] The town's elected officials reiterated these charges in a letter to the American Colonization Society: "We might ask the citizens of any town in New-England, wherever situated, would it be well for that town to admit the blacks from Slave States, or other States, to an unlimited extent? Once open this door, and New-England will become the Liberia of America." [36]

Against a background of increasing tension, a Canterbury town meeting convened on March 9, voiced its "unqualified disapprobation" of the proposed school, and appointed a com-

[34] Samuel J. May, *Some Recollections of Our Anti-slavery Conflict* (Boston, 1869), pp. 40–42. See also Francis and Wendell P. Garrison, *William Lloyd Garrison*, I, 315–16.

[35] *A Statement of Facts, Respecting the School for Colored Females, in Canterbury, Ct.* (Brooklyn, Conn., 1833), p. 7; Prudence Crandall to Simeon S. Jocelyn, February 26, 1833, in "Abolition Letters Collected by Captain Arthur B. Spingarn," *Journal of Negro History*, XVII (1933), 80–81; Crandall to William Lloyd Garrison, March 19, 1833, and George Benson to Garrison, March 5, 1833, Garrison Papers; *The Liberator*, April 6, 1833.

[36] Reprinted in *The Liberator*, April 6, 1833. See also *The Colonizationist and Journal of Freedom*, May, 1833, pp. 59–60.

mittee to persuade Miss Crandall to abandon her project in view of "the injurious effects, and incalculable evils" that would follow. At the same time, certain "responsible" towns-people offered to purchase her newly acquired house upon condition that the school be discontinued. Two of Miss Cran-dall's friends appeared at the meeting on her behalf, but the chairman refused to recognize them.[37] Afterwards, Andrew T. Judson, town selectman, Democratic politician, and an officer of the local colonization society, explained that Negroes could never rise above their menial condition and proposed that they be colonized in Africa, where they could civilize and Chris-tianize the natives. In the meantime, he asserted, "that nigger school shall never be allowed in Canterbury, nor in any town in this State." [38]

The Quaker schoolmistress and her abolitionist backers re-fused to abandon the school. "I have put my hand to the plough," she declared, "and I will *never no never* look back." She hoped that public sentiment might change, and, in the meantime, cautioned the temperamental Garrison to handle the prejudices of Canterbury "with all the mildness possible" since severe attacks would only further inflame the inhabi-tants.[39] The abolitionists, however, spared few words in rush-ing to Miss Crandall's defense. This had become not only a moral issue but a test of strength; defeat would create a dan-gerous precedent and prove a major setback to the entire abolitionist movement. She "must be sustained at all hazards," Garrison wrote. "If we suffer the school to be put down in Canterbury, other places will partake of this panic, and also prevent its introduction in their vicinity. We may as well,

[37] *A Statement of Facts*, pp. 7–8; May, *Recollections*, pp. 44–46; Samuel J. May, *The Right of Colored People to Education, Vindicated* (Brooklyn, Conn., 1833), pp. 7–10; *The Liberator*, March 16, 1833.

[38] May, *Recollections*, pp. 47–49.

[39] Prudence Crandall to Simeon S. Jocelyn, April 17, 1833, in "Abolition Letters Collected by Captain Arthur B. Spingarn," p. 83; Crandall to William Lloyd Gar-rison, March 19, 1833, Garrison Papers.

'first as last,' meet this proscriptive spirit, *and conquer it*." [40]
The school opened in April and attracted students from
Philadelphia, New York, Providence, and Boston. Meanwhile,
the town adopted a new form of opposition—harassment.
Stores denied necessary provisions to the school; townspeople
insulted the students in the streets and filled the school's well
with manure, forcing Miss Crandall to import water from
her father's farm two miles away; the village physician refused to treat the pupils; the churches admitted them only
under degrading circumstances; civil authorities threatened to
invoke an old vagrancy law against them; and another town
meeting appealed to the state legislature for appropriate
measures.[41]

Connecticut's legislators, responsible only to a white electorate, acted quickly. On May 24, they formally agreed that
an increase of the Negro population would not serve the best
interests of the state and thus adopted a law which prohibited
the establishment of "any school, academy, or literary institution, for the instruction or education of colored persons who
are not inhabitants of this state" and which forbade anyone
to instruct, harbor, or board such persons without the approval
of local authorities.[42] The state had dealt a mortal blow to
Miss Crandall's school for Negro girls. Indeed, the town bells

[40] Francis and Wendell P. Garrison, *William Lloyd Garrison*, I, 320. For additional abolitionist and Negro support, see *Proceedings of the Anti-Slavery Convention, assembled at Philadelphia, December 4, 5, and 6, 1833* (New York, 1833),
p. 18, and *Minutes and Proceedings of the Fourth Annual Convention for the
Improvement of the Free People of Colour, in the United States* (New York,
1834), p. 18.

[41] May, *Recollections*, pp. 50–51; Francis and Wendell P. Garrison, *William
Lloyd Garrison*, I, 317 n., 321; Abdy, *Journal of a Residence and Tour*, I, 199–203;
Prudence Crandall to Simeon S. Jocelyn, April 9 and 17, 1833, in "Abolition
Letters Collected by Captain Arthur B. Spingarn," pp. 81–84; George Benson to
William Lloyd Garrison, March 5, 1833, Henry E. Benson to Samuel J. May, March
31, 1833, Almira Crandall to Henry E. Benson, April 30, 1833, Garrison Papers;
The Liberator, May 18, 1833; *A Statement of Facts*, pp. 8–10.

[42] John C. Hurd, *Law of Freedom and Bondage in the United States* (2 vols.;
Boston, 1858), II, 45–46.

and cannon greeted the news in Canterbury. "In the midst of all this," a student wrote the next day, "Miss Crandall is unmoved. When we walk out, horns are blown and pistols fired. . . . The place is delightful; all that is wanting to complete the scene is *civilized* men." In Boston, *The Liberator* cried: "GEORGIA OUTDONE!!" [43]

In the face of this overwhelming legal and extralegal pressure, Miss Crandall refused to close her school. Local authorities thereupon arrested her on charges of violating the new law. The controversy had thus been transferred to the courts. "Consider me your banker," Arthur Tappan wrote from New York. "Command the services of the ablest lawyers. See to it that this great case shall be thoroughly tried, cost what it may." [44] On August 23, the schoolmistress stood before the Windham County Court. Although the judge instructed the jury that "the law was constitutional and obligatory on the people of the State," it failed to agree on a verdict and was discharged. [45] Two months later, Chief Justice David Daggett presided at a second trial. His charge to the jury anticipated much of the Dred Scott decision. First, he dismissed the defense's contention that the law violated the privileges-and-immunities clause of the federal constitution. The "plain and obvious" meaning of that provision, he declared, was "to secure to the *citizens* of all States, the same privileges as are secured to our own, by our own State laws." Second, he ruled that Negroes were not citizens. "God forbid," the Chief Justice declared, "that I should add to the degradation of this race of men; but I am bound, by my duty, to say, they are not citizens." This time, the jury found Miss Crandall guilty, but an appellate

[43] *The Liberator*, June 1, 22, 1833.
[44] May, *Recollections*, p. 58.
[45] *Report of the Trial of Miss Prudence Crandall. Before the County Court for Windham County, August Term 1833. On an Information Charging Her with Teaching Colored Persons Not Inhabitants of this State* (Brooklyn, Conn., 1833).

court reversed the conviction on a technical defect in the information.[46]

Meanwhile, the villagers subjected the school to continuous harassment. Visiting Canterbury in August, 1834, an English traveler remarked that the school "had become more odious to its enemies in proportion to their failure in trying to put it down with or without law." It had been frequently stoned, and an unsuccessful attempt had been made to burn it down. Finally, on September 10, 1834, the siege ended. Miss Crandall abandoned the school and departed for Illinois.[47]

Three years later, Theodore Weld met the chairman of the legislative committee responsible for the "Black Law" of 1833. "I could weep tears of blood for the part I took in that matter," he told Weld. "I now regard that law as utterly abominable," but at the time, "my prejudices . . . were so violent as to blind me to the dictates of common humanity and justice." Consequently, he headed a repeal petition to the legislature which charged that the law was impolitic, unjust, and unconstitutional. In May, 1838, the state senate repealed the law by a unanimous vote, and the house concurred with only four dissents.[48]

Despite abolitionist fears, the New Haven and Canterbury defeats failed to establish any real precedent. Most communities consented, some reluctantly, to the establishment of Ne-

[46] Catterall (ed.), *Judicial Cases*, IV, 415–16, 430–33; *The Liberator*, October 26, 1833, August 2, 9, September 27, October 11, 1834; May, *Recollections*, pp. 66–70. See also E. L. Pierce, *Memoir and Letters of Charles Sumner* (4 vols.; Boston, 1877–93), II, 257.

[47] Abdy, *Journal of a Residence and Tour*, III, 208–13, 303–7; May, *Recollections*, pp. 70–71; Almira Crandall to George Benson, July 9, 1833, Garrison Papers; *The Liberator*, September 21, November 2, December 21, 1833.

[48] Barnes and Dumond (eds.), *Weld-Grimke Correspondence*, I, 397–98; Hurd, *Law of Freedom and Bondage*, II, 46; *The Liberator*, June 8, 1838. In 1886, four years prior to Miss Crandall's death, the Connecticut legislature voted her an annuity of $400.

gro schools. But this did not necessarily advance the cause of education. Segregated schools afforded Negro children a poor educational environment; such schools invariably resulted in inferior facilities and instruction and prompted frequent protests from both Negroes and white school officials. "What are the advantages to be derived from an instruction in these schools," a Negro newspaper asked in 1827, "compared to those of a higher and more elevated nature? What are the incentives held out to a lad of colour? Are there higher schools to stimulate him to greater exertions? Is he placed, and considered, an equal with other boys in schools of the same rank?" Trustees expected little from Negro students, the newspaper found, for their color alone usually elicited praise from school visitors, when the same performance from white youths "would pass unnoticed, and be considered as a thing of course." [49]

Negro classes frequently met in ill-equipped and poorly ventilated buildings. Rhode Island Negroes complained of "indifferent school houses, with but partial accommodations." New Haven school officials described the buildings housing Negro students as "all excessively crowded and destitute of some of the first requisites." Confirming this report, Daniel Coit Gilman, the school visitor and later president of Johns Hopkins University, noted that the buildings were "far behind what the District should be willing to own." As late as 1857, a New York education society contrasted white children in "splendid, almost palatial edifices" with Negro students "pent up in filthy neighborhoods, in old and dilapidated buildings" and "held down to low associations and gloomy surroundings." It attributed this injustice to the disproportionate allocation of school funds. Although a one to forty ratio existed in the number of Negro and white children, expenditures on education amounted to the extraordinary ratio of one to sixteen

[49] *Freedom's Journal*, June 1, 1827.

hundred![50] In Rochester, New York, where Frederick Douglass led the attack on separate schools, a committee appointed by the board of education noted that although the city taxed both Negro and white property "to build commodious school houses," Negro children found themselves excluded and "grouped together in some 'Rented Rooms,' in darkness and ignorance, there to seek education with all the attending disadvantages."[51]

Negro schools also encountered difficulties in securing competent teachers. An official committee visiting New Haven's Negro schools attributed student disinterest to a lack of "fitness both in respect of tact and of acquired information on the part of their teachers" and suggested that more competent instruction would increase both attendance and the progress of the students.[52] In the absence of trained Negro instructors, school boards frequently hired whites. Such teachers, however, not only received relatively meager salaries but in some communities faced insults and social ostracism. In Providence, a white teacher threatened to punish any of his Negro students who dared to greet him in public.[53] Where Negro instructors could be obtained, school boards frequently granted them lower salaries than whites, without reference to qualifications or the size of classes. In the New York African Schools, for example, an English observer noticed that the trustees "have made a distinction between the white and black teachers, that is consistent neither with justice nor good policy."[54] Rhode Island Negroes protested that the school board paid one white

[50] George T. Downing and others, *Will the General Assembly Put Down Caste Schools?* (Providence, 1857), pp. 1, 6–7; Warner, *New Haven Negroes*, pp. 74–75; *Anglo-African Magazine*, I (July, 1859), 222–24; Hirsch, "The Negro and New York," pp. 427–28.

[51] *North Star*, August 17, November 2, 1849.

[52] Warner, *New Haven Negroes*, p. 76.

[53] Julian S. Rammelkamp, "The Providence Negro Community, 1820–1842," *Rhode Island History*, VII (1948), 26.

[54] Abdy, *Journal of a Residence and Tour*, I, 8.

instructor in Providence's Negro grammar school as much as all the Negro teachers of Providence, Newport, and Bristol and that the board generally hired "indifferent teachers" for the Negro school, paying them not more than half the salary granted to teachers in white schools.[55]

In addition to sub-standard teaching conditions, Negro schools generally provided only the most elementary curriculum. To a large extent, this limitation reflected the exclusion of Negroes from most professional pursuits and the prevailing belief that the average Negro's intellectual capacity debarred him from advanced studies. The trustees of the New York African Schools, for example, discouraged higher education for Negroes by informing parents that there was "no disgrace incurred by the pursuit of any honest calling however humble" and that it was "the duty of everyone to do all the good in his sphere in which Providence has placed him." [56] Too many Negro parents, David Walker argued in 1829, evaluated their son's education in terms of a neat handwriting and considered spelling and grammar immaterial: "If it only looks beautiful, they say he has as good an education as any white man — he can write as well as any white man, etc." Most of the blame, however, could be placed on the schools. For example, Walker continued, a Negro student had told him that the white instructor forbade his class to study grammar and explained that the school committee permitted such training only in the white schools.[57] The New Haven Board of Education admitted in 1860 that few Negroes graduated with a sufficient knowledge of arithmetic to enable them to be clerks or to conduct independent businesses.[58] In summing up the state of Negro edu-

[55] Downing and others, *Will the General Assembly Put Down Caste Schools?* p. 6.

[56] Enid V. Barnett, "Educational Activities by and in Behalf of the Negroes in New York, 1800–1830," *Negro History Bulletin*, XIV (February, 1951), 102.

[57] David Walker, *Walker's Appeal, in Four Articles* (3rd ed.; Boston, 1830), pp. 35–39.

[58] Warner, *New Haven Negroes*, p. 77.

cation, a Negro national convention charged in 1847 that the instruction of Negro youth "has been shamefully limited," consisting only of "rudimental notings, and superficial glancings. . . . In comprehensiveness it has never yet made any pretensions, to profundity not the most distant approach. . . . In very deed it has not reached the dignitary, and the elevation of education."[59]

In the face of a growing demand for integrated schools, northern boards of education finally took steps to improve the existing separate institutions. By the 1850's, considerable progress had been made in the quality of both the instruction and the classrooms. But the Negro, too, had advanced, and his fight for equal rights could no longer countenance the existence of segregated schools.

Although Negroes hoped for eventual integration, many of them agreed, in the meantime, to send their children to separate schools. Seizing upon such support, segregationists charged that Negroes originated these distinctions and desired their maintenance. Boston school officials, for example, pointed out that separate schools had been established "at the urgent and repeated requests of the colored people themselves" and that Negroes regarded such schools "as a great privilege, and the only means by which their children could receive the benefits of education." In nearby Providence, the president of Brown University noted that segregated education "works well" and that the Negro residents preferred it to integration.[60]

[59] *Proceedings of the National Convention of Colored People and Their Friends, held in Troy, N.Y., on the 6th, 7th, 8th, and 9th October, 1847* (Troy, 1847), p. 34. Cited hereafter as *National Colored Convention, Troy, 1847.*

[60] City of Boston, *Report of the Primary School Committee, June 15, 1846, on the Petition of Sundry Colored Persons, for the Abolition of the Schools for Colored Children* (Boston, 1846), pp. 15, 20; City of Boston, *Report of a Special Committee of the Grammar School Board, presented August 29, 1849, on the Petition of Sundry Colored Persons, Praying for the Abolition of the Smith School* (Boston, 1849), p. 40.

Some Negroes defended segregation. During the attack on Boston's Negro school, an officer of that institution justified it as "the greatest advantage to the colored people" and declared that its abolition would be "unjust, inexpedient and injurious." Separate schools, he asserted, afforded Negroes the opportunity to refute charges of inferiority by producing scholars superior to those of the best white schools. The abolition of such schools would lead whites to infer "that when equally taught and equally comfortable, we are ashamed of ourselves, and feel disgraced by being together." [61] In Hartford and Providence, Negroes petitioned for separate schools after once enjoying "equal" advantages with whites. [62] In New York, however, Negroes simply preferred segregated education to no education whatsoever. "The choice of the least between two evils," a prominent New York Negro leader, school director, and teacher wrote, prompted him "to improve the colored schools in this city — believing them to be only better than no schools at all." [63]

In many cases, antipathy toward biracial education and the mistreatment of Negroes, where admitted with whites, required or encouraged the establishment of separate schools. For example, Negro petitioners in Rochester, New York, asked for a separate school on grounds that "the literary and moral interests of the coloured scholar can scarcely prosper" in the present integrated system. The Negro student found himself "reproached with his colour; he is taunted with his origin; and if permitted to mingle with others in the joyous pastimes of youth, it is of favour, not by right." In 1807, a Salem, Massachusetts, minister declared that "pride" prevented the presence of Negroes in the existing school for poor children,

[61] Thomas P. Smith, *An Address Delivered before the Colored Citizens of Boston in Opposition to the Abolition of Colored Schools* (Boston, 1850), pp. 4–6.
[62] U.S. Commissioner of Education, *Special Report*, 1871, pp. 334, 383.
[63] James McCune Smith to Charles L. Reason, December 21, 1849, in *The Liberator*, January 4, 1850.

and called for separate instruction. In Connecticut, both races once attended the same schools but frequent insults and humiliations prompted Hartford Negroes to ask for separation. School authorities admitted similar problems in other areas. "To escape intolerable persecution and contempt," two Boston school officials observed, Negroes "were once glad to be herded together by themselves." [64]

Increasingly after 1830, Negro spokesmen denounced segregated schools as unequal and inferior and demanded integration. The Colored American charged in 1837 that separate schools "so shackled the intellect of colored youth, that an education acquired under such circumstances, was, comparatively, of little advantage." Frederick Douglass dismissed pro-segregation Negroes as unworthy of equality with the whites and demanded court action to open all schools without discrimination. In 1850, a convention of fugitive slaves advised recent arrivals in the North not to send their children to any school "which the malignant and murderous prejudice of white people has gotten up exclusively for colored people." Despite the value of education, they declared, "it is too costly, if it is acquired at the expense of such self-degradation." [65]

The growing demand for integration prompted abolitionists to reconsider their own efforts to establish an exclusively Negro manual-labor college. In view of the willingness of more white colleges to admit Negroes, an abolitionist leader asked William Lloyd Garrison in 1834 if it would not be preferable to patronize those institutions rather than build new ones, since

[64] Assembly Document, New York State Assembly, 55 sess., No. 77 (1832); William Bentley, Diary (4 vols.; Salem, 1905–14), III, 273; Warner, New Haven Negroes, pp. 71–72; City of Boston, Report of the Minority of the Committee of the Primary School Board, on the Caste Schools of the City of Boston (Boston, 1846), p. 17.

[65] Colored American, April 22, 1837; Frederick Douglass' Paper, August 25, 1854; Aptheker (ed.), Documentary History, p. 303. See also Freedom's Journal, February 15, 1828; Colored American, August 4, 1838; Proceedings of the State Convention of Colored People, held at Albany, New York (Albany, 1851), pp. 8, 33; Ohio Colored Convention of 1849, p. 18.

"the object we aim at, the destruction of caste, will be the sooner gained." [66] Two years later, an abolitionist convention resolved not to countenance the establishment of separate schools. "When a school is established," Lewis Tappan advised the delegates, "notify the colored people of it. Get some colored teachers who are well qualified for the work. There will then be no difficulty, as some have feared, that white people will come to the exclusion of the colored." Negro schools, added delegate Henry C. Wright, helped to sustain racial prejudices. For this reason, the convention should not regret the recent demise of abolitionist Gerrit Smith's Negro school at Peterboro, New York. "It made a distinction that God never made. I believe that every such colored school will go down, and ought to go down." [67]

In the light of these developments, Harriet Beecher Stowe's plan to use proceeds from the sale of *Uncle Tom's Cabin* to establish a Negro school aroused considerable discussion in abolitionist circles. Although even Frederick Douglass advised her to found a Negro manual-labor college, Mrs. Stowe finally decided to oppose any exclusive institution. "Indeed she distinctly deprecated all separate instruction of the coloured children," a friend wrote. "She wished to promote their education, but would have it conducted in mixed schools." By the 1850's, however, abolitionists appeared to be less interested in the education of the northern Negro than in the impending crisis over slavery. Mrs. Stowe's plan to found an academy open to both races thus met with little enthusiasm. "This, she thinks, will be Uncle Tom's last Monument," Samuel May, Jr., wrote. "Mr. G[arrison] thought favourably of it, but suggested that it was of the first and highest importance to appropriate it [the money] in such a way as would make it tell most powerfully against the System itself of Slavery."

[66] Elizur Wright, Jr., to William Lloyd Garrison, June 30, 1834, Wright Papers, Library of Congress.
[67] *The Liberator*, November 19, 1836.

Mrs. Stowe finally abandoned the project, and abolitionists turned to more pressing matters.[68]

Although confined nearly everywhere to separate public schools, Negroes gradually gained admittance to white colleges. The first Negro college graduate, John Russwurm, attended Bowdoin College, Maine, and subsequently helped to edit the first Negro newspaper. By 1860, twenty-eight Negroes had earned degrees from recognized colleges, and many others had been admitted.[69]

In most cases, the opening of colleges to Negroes occasioned little controversy. Dartmouth College at first denied entrance to a Negro applicant, but student petitions helped to reverse the trustees' decision in 1824 and thereby established a permanent school policy.[70] Harvard's president, Edward Everett, announced in 1848 that a Negro applicant would be judged solely by his qualifying examinations, "and if the white students choose to withdraw, all the income of the College will be devoted to his education."[71] The admission of Negroes to these two leading institutions undoubtedly influenced others to follow suit.

In the 1830's, two Ohio colleges — Western Reserve and Oberlin — opened their doors to Negroes. The Oberlin decision, however, evoked some furious protests. Indeed, at the

[68] Eliza Lee (Cabot) Follen to Maria (Weston) Chapman, March 12, 1853, Eliza Wigham to Mary A. Estlin, April 28, 1853, Weston Papers; Samuel May, Jr., to Richard Davis Webb, March 31, 1853, May Papers, Boston Public Library.

[69] Charles S. Johnson, *The Negro College Graduate* (Chapel Hill, N.C., 1938), p. 7; Bowdoin College, *General Catalogue . . . 1794–1950* (Brunswick, Maine, 1950), 58; William M. Brewer, "John B. Russwurm," *Journal of Negro History*, XIII (1928), 413–22.

[70] George F. Bragg to Carter G. Woodson, n.d., Woodson Papers, Library of Congress; Leon B. Richardson, *History of Dartmouth College* (2 vols.; Hanover, 1932), I, 381; *The Liberator*, September 3, 1841.

[71] Paul Revere Frothingham, *Edward Everett* (Boston, 1925), p. 299; John P. Marquand, "New Bottle: Old Wine," in Brooks Atkinson (ed.), *College in a Yard: Minutes by Thirty-nine Harvard Men* (Cambridge, Mass., 1957), p. 179; *Congressional Globe*, 30 Cong., 1 sess., p. 610.

first suggestion of such a move, "a General panic and despair seized the Officers, Students and Colonists." John Jay Shipherd, Oberlin's general agent and the proponent of the biracial plan, found it necessary to disclaim any intention "to hang out an abolition flag, or fill up with filthy stupid negroes." Student opinion, as reflected by a campus poll, divided almost evenly. The board of trustees voted to table the suggestion, but this aroused the protests of abolitionists and the threatened resignation of one of the school's newly appointed professors. In February, 1835, the trustees finally decided to permit the faculty to rule on entrance requirements and thus assured the admission of qualified Negroes.[72]

This action did not squelch all opposition. Oberlin's financial agent in New England wrote that that section had only reluctantly agreed to the admission of both men and women into the same college. However, New England would most certainly not consent to the admission of Negroes, "and if not here then not in this country." Such a move might result in the rapid demise of Oberlin College. "For as soon as your darkies begin to come in in any considerable numbers," he warned, "unless they are completely separated . . . the whites will begin to leave — and at length your Institute will change colour. Why not have a black Institution, Dyed in the wool — and let Oberlin be?"[73]

Prior to 1860, relatively few Negroes entered Oberlin. In some quarters, nevertheless, it had already become a Negro haven. One Massachusetts woman student thus felt it necessary to reassure her family in 1852 "that we don't have to kiss the Niggars nor to speak to them"; moreover, only about six "pure Niggars" could be found at the school, for most of them appeared to be "part white" and, in any case, they

[72] Robert Samuel Fletcher, *A History of Oberlin College* (2 vols.; Oberlin, 1943), I, 169–72, 175–78; Barnes and Dumond (eds.), *Weld-Grimke Correspondence*, I, 194, 197–98.

[73] Fletcher, *History of Oberlin College*, II, 523.

dressed better than most white students. The college permitted both races to eat and room in the same boarding-houses and to attend classes and religious exercises together. "Almost every fifth one at the table is a darky," a student wrote home in 1846. "And the best appearing chap I have seen here is black." By 1860, Negroes comprised 4 per cent of the total student body.[74]

Perhaps the most interesting experiment in biracial education was performed in McGrawville, New York. Founded in 1849 by the American Baptist Free Mission Society, New York Central College admitted both races and sexes, appointed a Negro to the faculty, adopted the manual-labor system of education, and abjured the use of tea, coffee, alcohol, and tobacco. The school's partial dependence on state support occasioned some bitter protests and legislative debates, including the charge that it promoted a "mottled conglomerate of insanities" — miscegenation, women's rights, abolitionism, and socialism. "This is not a negro, but a black and white college," the Albany *State Register* protested, "where the sable African, the white Caucasian, and the yellow mulatto, are indiscriminately mingled together. . . . The white sister is there taught the moral, intellectual and social equality of her Ethiopian brother; the white boy that he is in no respect superior to the negress who is his daily companion." Moreover, the newspaper charged, New York taxpayers helped to support such instruction. Confirming the worst fears of the opposition, the Negro faculty member, William G. Allen, announced his engagement to a prospective white student. Enraged at this alleged indiscretion, the townspeople forced him to flee or be mobbed. The girl, however, soon joined him in New York, where they resolved to marry and establish residence in England. By 1858, the college was bankrupt. After its sale to abo-

[74] *Ibid.*, II, 535–36.

litionist Gerrit Smith, the school reopened briefly in 1860
but finally closed the next year.[75]

By the eve of the Civil War, several other colleges had
agreed to the admission of Negroes. Among them were Am-
herst, Rutland, Oneida Institute, Union College, Princeton,
and various medical colleges and theological seminaries.[76]
This did not necessarily indicate the existence of exclusion
policies at the remaining institutions. The inferiority of Negro
education on the lower levels seriously hampered preparation
for college instruction and limited the number of qualified
applicants. This fact convinced Negro leaders that they had
to press even harder for improved elementary and secondary
education. "The colleges of New England and the West, which
are opened to us, do not meet the needs of our people," a
Negro convention complained in 1847, "because . . . there
is no previous opportunity offered for that early, almost childish culture, which is absolutely necessary to the formation of
true high scholarship; and for which white children possess
superabundant faculties." [77] By 1850, many Negro leaders
concluded that only integrated schools could afford this necessary preparation.

Through convention appeals, petitions, court suits, and editorial campaigns, Negroes maintained a constant agitation in
the 1840's and 1850's for the abolition of school segregation.
"The point which we must aim at," Frederick Douglass wrote,
"is, to obtain admission for our children into the nearest

[75] Ralph V. Harlow, *Gerrit Smith* (New York, 1939), pp. 231–32; *New York
Colored Convention of 1851*, p. 33; *The Liberator*, July 18, 1851; William G.
Allen, *A Refugee from American Despotism: The American Prejudice against
Color* (London, 1853).

[76] Woodson, *Education of the Negro*, pp. 276–77; Martin R. Delany, *The Con-
dition, Elevation, Emigration, and Destiny of the Colored People of the United
States* (Philadelphia, 1852), pp. 110–33, 134–37; William J. Simmons, *Men of
Mark* (Cleveland, 1887).

[77] *National Colored Convention, Troy, 1847*, p. 36.

school house, and the best school house in our respective neighborhoods." Integrated schools would not only afford Negro children a better education; they would strike a fatal blow at racial segregation and create an atmosphere in which Negroes could work more effectively for equal political and social rights. Indeed, Douglass told New York Negroes that the attainment of equal school privileges should take precedence over immediate political demands, such as the suffrage. "Contact on equal terms is the best means to abolish caste," he wrote. "*It is caste abolished.* With Equal Suffrage, 13,675 black men come into contact on equal terms, for ten minutes once a year, at the polls; with equal school rights, 15,778 colored children and youth come in contact on equal terms with white children and youth, three hundred days in the year, and from six to ten hours each day. And these children, in a few years, become the people of the State." [78]

The Negro-abolitionist attack on segregated schools achieved its greatest success in Boston. By 1845, Massachusetts Negroes had won virtual political and legal equality, and they could send their children, without discrimination, to the public schools in Salem, New Bedford, Nantucket, Worcester, and Lowell. [79] Only Boston maintained segregation, and there, Negroes launched the most concerted attack on northern "caste" schools. White abolitionists, convinced that segregation impaired the effectiveness of their antislavery pleas, joined the campaign. "It is useless for us to prate of the conduct of South Carolina," a segregation foe declared in 1845, "so long as we maintain — *illegally* maintain — a

[78] *Douglass' Monthly*, March, 1859.
[79] City of Boston, *Minority Report of the Primary School Committee, 1846*, pp. 14–15, 21–27; City of Boston, *Report of the Minority of the Committee upon the Petition of John T. Hilton and others, Colored Citizens of Boston, Praying for the Abolition of the Smith School, and that Colored Children May Be Permitted to Attend the Other Schools of the City* (Boston, 1849), p. 11; Massachusetts House of Representatives, *House Report*, No. 167 (March 17, 1855), pp. 11–14; *The Liberator*, December 24, 1847.

practice here which at least incidentally sanctions it." Indorsing this sentiment, the Massachusetts Anti-Slavery Society
resolved in the following year that "the friends of the cause"
residing in communities which still practiced educational segregation should immediately inform Negroes of their legal
rights and "afford them all possible aid in securing the full
and equal enjoyment of the public schools." [80]

Negroes and abolitionists directed their attack at Boston's
Primary School Committee, since it assumed responsibility
for the classification and distribution of students. In petitions
to that body, Negroes charged that school segregation injured
the best interests of the community and resulted in needless
expense, neglect, and low standards of scholarship and instruction. [81] Replying to these charges, the Committee issued
lengthy reports in 1846 and 1849, both of which condoned
segregation on grounds that varied from the degrading aspects
of racial mixing to the observation that the Pilgrim Fathers
had not been depressed by their separation from the Indians,
"in whose country they were but strangers and sojourners."
Distinctions established by "the All-Wise Creator," the Committee charged, separated the two races, negated any legislation, and rendered "a promiscuous intermingling in the public
schools disadvantageous" to both Negroes and whites. To substantiate its arguments, the Committee claimed that integration had failed in several Massachusetts communities, while
separate schools had already demonstrated their superiority
in Philadelphia, New York, and Providence. Where attempts
had been made to mix the two races, teachers reported that
Negro children kept pace with the whites in instruction involv-

[80] *The Liberator*, June 27, 1845; *Fourteenth Annual Report Presented to the
Massachusetts Anti-Slavery Society, by its Board of Managers* (Boston, 1846),
pp. 91–92.

[81] City of Boston, *Report of the Primary School Committee, 1846*, p. 2; City of
Boston, *Report of a Special Committee of the Grammar School Board, 1849*,
pp. 4–5.

ing "imitative faculties" but quickly fell behind when progress depended on "the faculties of invention, compassion, and reasoning." In any case, the Committee asked, why should Negroes object to school segregation when they themselves always met together in separate churches and social affairs. "It is as though they thought that a white skin was really better than a dark one; and that the society of all who wear it was more reputable, more to be coveted, than they of a sable tint. In a word, it is as if they were ashamed of themselves."

Even assuming the correctness of integration, the Committee felt that any attempt to implement it would be disastrous "under the present state of public feeling and sentiment." White children would refuse to associate with Negroes; conflicts and disagreement would arouse tempers and lead to possible violence; white parents would withdraw their children rather than permit them to mix with Negroes; and Negro parents would refuse to send their "ill clad" children to a school "where not only color, but dress and station, would be so strongly contrasted." The Committee cited the testimony of a local Negro that integration would bring "poor and ill-educated colored children . . . into disadvantageous competition and association with the more advanced and wealthy white children." This, he warned, would result in "sneers, insults, assaults, jeers, etc."; the Negro children would be set off by themselves, "and what is the difference between an exclusive class and an exclusive school?" Finally, the Committee concluded, legislation could neither regulate social customs nor force children, Negro or white, "to associate with, or be 'crumbled up' among, any class of people, except those to whom it may be mutually agreeable." [82]

Vigorous dissents accompanied each of the Committee's

[82] City of Boston, *Report of a Special Committee of the Grammar School Board, 1849*, pp. 33, 40–42, 53–55, 57–61, 67; City of Boston, *Report of the Primary School Committee, 1846*, pp. 7–8, 10–11, 13–14, 29.

reports, and they included favorable testimony from integrated school officials and teachers. Referring to the anticipated parental opposition, the Committee's minority members
felt that it would probably be less than that being exerted
against the admission of the more numerous Irish children.
In any event, the mingling of white and Negro children could
hardly be more objectionable than the usual meeting of their
parents at the polls, in the courts of justice, and in the daily
pursuits of labor. Segregated schools not only required additional and needless expense; they exercised a damaging effect on white youths. "We deem it morally injurious to the
white children, inasmuch as it tends to create in most, and
foster in all, feelings of repugnance and contempt for the colored race as degraded inferiors, whom they may, or must,
treat as such. This is the standard of morals and humanity
which these schools teach our children, who are thus led to
attach to color alone, sentiments and emotions, which should
arise, if at all, only in view of character." Integration, on
the other hand, could help to destroy racial prejudice, for
where Negro and white children shared "the same bench and
sports, there can hardly arise a manhood of aristocratic prejudice, or separate castes and classes." [83]

While *The Liberator* assailed the majority reports as
"flimsy yet venomous sophistries," Boston Negroes denounced
the Primary School Committee's decision and prepared new
appeals and methods of attack.[84] Some local newspapers, in
the meantime, predicted violence in the wake of any attempt
to integrate the public schools. "Law or no law," the Boston
Post warned, "our citizens of the west end will not suffer the
infusion of forty or fifty colored boys and girls among their

[83] City of Boston, *Minority Report of the Primary School Committee, 1846*,
pp. 12–13, 15–16, 21–27; City of Boston, *Minority Report of the Committee upon
the Petition of John T. Hilton and others, 1849*, p. 8.
[84] *The Liberator*, August 21, 1846, August 10, September 7, November 9, December 14, 1849, February 8, 1850.

own children." Constant harassment faced any integrated
school; whites would abandon "the finest edifices in the city"
and permit them to become Negro schools rather than integrate them; all this because a few "rabid enthusiasts" were
not satisfied with "a system which was working prosperously,
in all love and harmony." [85]

After nearly four years of agitation, Benjamin Roberts, a
Boston Negro, decided to test the legality of the Primary
School Committee's power to enforce segregation. In 1849, he
brought suit in the name of his daughter under a statute which
allowed any person illegally excluded from the public schools
to recover damages from the city. Four times a white primary
school had refused to admit his daughter; consequently, she
now passed five such schools on her way to the Negro primary
school. Charles Sumner, subsequently an antislavery leader
in the United States Senate, took the case of the five-year-old
plaintiff. Peleg W. Chandler, a recognized authority on municipal law, appeared for the city of Boston, and Chief Justice
Lemuel Shaw presided. The stage was thus set for an eloquent
and crucial legal debate. "On the one side is the city of Boston," Sumner declared, "strong in its wealth, in its influence,
in its character; on the other side is a little child, of a degraded
color, of humble parents, still within the period of natural
infancy, but strong from her very weakness, and from the
irresponsible sympathies of good men. . . . This little child
asks at your hands her *personal rights*." [86]

Sumner turned to history, political theory, philosophy,
literature, and legal precedents to demonstrate that the state
constitution, legislature, and courts, as well as "the spirit of
American institutions," recognized no racial distinctions.
Segregated schools violated the principle of equality by rec-

[85] *Ibid.*, November 16, 1849.

[86] Charles Sumner, *Argument . . . against the Constitutionality of Separate
Colored Schools, in the Case of Sarah C. Roberts vs. the City of Boston. Before the
Supreme Court of Mass., Dec. 4, 1849* (Boston, 1849), p. 3.

ognizing "a nobility of the skin" and "hereditary distinctions." Efforts to justify such schools as affording separate but equal facilities constituted "a mockery." Although the quality of instruction might not differ in some cases, "a school, exclusively devoted to one class, must differ essentially, in its spirit and character, from that public school . . . where all classes meet together in equality." Segregation injured both races; it instilled the sentiment of caste in the minds of white youths while it discouraged the aspiring Negro and widened his separation from the rest of the community. "The Helots of Sparta were obliged to intoxicate themselves," Sumner remarked, "that they might teach to the children of their masters the deformity of intemperance. In thus sacrificing one class to the other, both were degraded — the imperious Spartan and the abased Helot." Racial prejudice, Sumner concluded, had found its last refuge in the segregated school. On behalf of a Negro child and the "civilization of the age," he appealed to the court to abolish it.[87]

The city's attorney declined to discuss the merits of segregation but confined his argument largely to a legal defense of the powers of the Primary School Committee.[88] Chief Justice Shaw, delivering a unanimous decision, upheld the Committee's power to enforce segregation. Since Boston provided for the instruction of Negro children, it had discharged its duty. As for the contention that separate schools perpetuated caste distinctions, Shaw replied that the law had not created and could not alter the deep-rooted prejudice which sanctioned segregation. The importance of the decision transcended the local struggle for integration. Shaw's legal defense of segregated schools on the basis of the "separate but equal" doctrine established a controversial precedent in American law.[89]

[87] *Ibid.*, pp. 4–16, 20, 24–25, 28–29, 31–32.
[88] Boston *Courier*, December 5, 1849, quoted in *The Liberator*, December 14, 1849.
[89] Catterall (ed.), *Judicial Cases*, IV, 513–14; Leonard W. Levy and Harlan B.

Rejected by the Primary School Committee and the courts, Boston Negroes turned to legislative appeals and formed the Equal School Rights Committee. Five years after the Roberts case, they won their initial success when the city's committee on public instruction recommended to the mayor and aldermen that separate schools be abolished. In view of the favorable action of other Massachusetts communities, the committee hoped that Boston would at least be the first large American city to integrate its public schools. On March 17, 1855, a legislative committee submitted a bill to prohibit racial or religious distinctions in admitting students to any public school. The legislature approved the bill, and the governor signed it on April 28.[90]

Negroes and white abolitionists held a mass rally to celebrate their triumph. "The best thing learned by these struggles is, how to prepare for another," Wendell Phillips declared. "He should never think Mass. a State fit to live in, until he saw one man, at least, as black as the ace of spades, a graduate of Harvard College. (Cheers) . . . When they had high schools and colleges to which all classes and colors were admitted on equal terms, then he should think Mass. was indeed the noblest representative of the principles that planted her."[91] While integrationists hailed their legislative victory, segregationists in Boston and elsewhere expressed deep concern over this possible precedent. "Now the blood of the Winthrops, the Otises, the Lymans, the Endicotts, and the

---

Phillips, "The Roberts Case: Source of the 'Separate But Equal' Doctrine," *American Historical Review*, LVI (1951), 510–18.

[90] *Report of the Colored People of the City of Boston on the Subject of Exclusive Schools. Submitted by Benjamin F. Roberts, to the Boston Equal School Rights Committee* (Boston, 1850) ; *The Liberator*, April 26, 1850, April 4, 1851, August 18, 1854; Petitions to the State Legislature for "Equal School Rights," Boston Public Library; Massachusetts House of Representatives, *House Report*, No. 167 (March 17, 1855) ; Massachusetts General Court, *Acts and Resolves* (Boston, 1855), pp. 674–75.

[91] *Triumph of Equal School Rights in Boston: Proceedings of the Presentation Meeting held in Boston, December 17, 1855*, p. 15.

Eliots, is in a fair way to be amalgamated with the Sambos, the Catos, and the Pompeys," the New York *Herald* declared. "The North is to be Africanized. Amalgamation has commenced. New England heads the column. God save the Commonwealth of Massachusetts!" [92]

Despite considerable apprehension, violence failed to materialize. In September, 1855, Negro children entered Boston's white schools with little difficulty. The appearance of Negroes in the "heretofore by them unfrequented" streets leading to the school buildings reportedly "created a 'sensation' among the neighbors, who filled the windows, probably in anticipation of trouble," but none occurred. The Boston *Evening Telegraph* concluded that integration had met "with general good feeling on the part of both teachers and white children." Subsequent testimony by Boston school officials and teachers praised its results. Although a few white parents withdrew their children and some Negroes suffered insults, integrated schools resulted in neither race violence nor amalgamation. [93]

The Boston victory encouraged Negroes and abolitionists in other states to step up their agitation. Rhode Island Negroes secured a favorable legislative-committee recommendation in 1859, but the proposed bill lost by two votes. [94] In Philadelphia, Negro leader Robert Purvis protested "the proscription

[92] *The Liberator*, May 4, 1855.
[93] *Frederick Douglass' Paper*, September 14, 1855; Boston *Evening Telegraph*, September 3, 1855; Louis Ruchames, "Race and Education in Massachusetts," *Negro History Bulletin*, XIII (December, 1949), 58, 71; *The Anti-Slavery History of the John Brown Year; being the Twenty-Seventh Annual Report of the American Anti-Slavery Society* (New York, 1861), p. 224; George T. Downing and others, *To the Friends of Equal Rights in Rhode Island* (Providence, 1859), p. 8; Downing and others, *Will the General Assembly Put Down Caste Schools?* pp. 9–11; *The Liberator*, April 17, 1857, January 29, 1858.
[94] Downing and others, *To the Friends of Equal Rights in Rhode Island*, and *Will the General Assembly Put Down Caste Schools? The Liberator*, February 20, April 17, 1857, January 29, 1858, June 10, 1859, February 24, 1860; Irving H. Bartlett, *From Slave to Citizen: The Story of the Negro in Rhode Island* (Providence, 1954), pp. 50–59.

and exclusion of my children from the Public School" by refusing to pay his school tax, but integration efforts failed.[95]
In some states, Negroes appealed directly to the judiciary.
The Ohio courts, however, ruled in 1850 and 1859 that public policy required segregated schools, for, "whether consistent with true philanthropy or not . . . there . . . still is an
almost invincible repugnance to such communion and fellowship." An Indiana court upheld segregation in 1850 "because
black children were deemed unfit associates of whites, as
school companions."[96] By 1860, some small and scattered
communities agreed to integration, but the larger cities, including New York, Philadelphia, Cincinnati, Providence, and
New Haven, hoped to stem increasing agitation by correcting
existing abuses and making the Negro schools equal to those
of the whites.

The growing admission of Negroes into white schools and
colleges did not immediately eradicate old prejudices. The
life of a Negro in an overwhelmingly white school was not
always pleasant. Some communities admitted Negroes to the
public schools but seated them separately and frequently
punished white offenders by forcing them to sit with the Negroes.[97] A Negro attending a Massachusetts private academy,
where "a majority" claimed to be abolitionists, reported that
he could neither live in the same house with the whites nor be
admitted to the dinner table until they had been served.[98]
When Frederick Douglass' daughter entered Seward Seminary
in Rochester, school authorities assigned her to a room separate from the whites and appointed a teacher to instruct her.
Douglass protested the school's action and withdrew his daughter. The principal told him that perhaps prejudice would sub-
side after a few terms and she could then be accorded equal

[95] Woodson (ed.), *Mind of the Negro*, pp. 177–79.
[96] Catterall (ed.), *Judicial Cases*, V, 14, 25, 38.
[97] Francis and Wendell P. Garrison, *William Lloyd Garrison*, I, 253.
[98] Woodson (ed.), *Mind of the Negro*, p. 262.

privileges.[99] College life, a Negro convention reported, frequently imposed "peculiar restraints" on Negroes, for it placed them in the midst of many hostile and few sympathetic colleagues. Social pressures prompted some students to be friendly with Negroes on campus but ignore them elsewhere. A Salem, Massachusetts, Negro thus testified that although white children treated him well in school and even invited him to some of their parties, "they did not seem to know him" on the street. Confirming this reaction, Charlotte Forten, later a prominent Negro abolitionist and teacher, recorded in her diary (kept when she was a student at a New England school) that her white colleagues treated her cordially in the classroom but feared to recognize her in public.[100]

For many Negro students, campus and off-campus life constituted two separate worlds. Although northern whites finally recognized the Negro's right to an adequate education, they maintained, outside the classroom, racial barriers which virtually nullified the benefits of that education. "To what end are these poor creatures taught knowledge, from the exercise of which they are destined to be debarred?" asked an instructor in a New York Negro school. "It is surely but a cruel mockery to cultivate talents, when in the present state of public feeling, there is no field open for their useful employment. Be his acquirements what they may, a Negro is still a Negro, or, in other words, a creature marked out for degradation, and exclusion from those objects which stimulate the hopes and powers of other men." [101]

Educated or not, northern Negroes still faced severely limited opportunities and a prolonged struggle to escape the degradation of menial labor.

   [99] North Star, September 22, 1848; Douglass, Life and Times, pp. 331–32.
   [100] National Colored Convention, Troy, 1847, p. 36; Report of the Primary School Committee, 1846, pp. 11–12; Ray Allen Billington (ed.), The Journal of Charlotte L. Forten (New York, 1953), p. 63.
   [101] Hamilton, Men and Manners in America, I, 89–90.

The Economics of
Repression

In an era of expanding opportunities and social mobility, northern Negroes faced economic discrimination and exploitation. For the greater portion of the black labor force, racial prejudice meant much more than restrictions at the polls, in the theaters, or on public conveyances; it manifested itself in the daily struggle for existence, in the problems of subsistence living, employment in the lowest-paid unskilled jobs, hostile native and immigrant white workers, exclusionist trade unions, and deplorable housing in the "Negro section" of town. This was the Negro's "place" in a white-dominated society. Economic necessity demanded acquiescence, but it could neither motivate Negro youths nor make them optimistic about the future. "Why should I strive hard and acquire all the constituents of a man," the valedictorian of a Negro school asked in 1819, "if the prevailing genius of the land admit me not as such, or but in an inferior degree! Pardon me if I feel

153

insignificant and weak. . . . What are my prospects? To what shall I turn my hand? Shall I be a mechanic? No one will employ me; white boys won't work with me. Shall I be a merchant? No one will have me in his office; white clerks won't associate with me. Drudgery and servitude, then, are my prospective portion. Can you be surprised at my discouragement?" [1]

Although they had been recently employed under slavery in a variety of skilled as well as unskilled occupations, emancipated Negroes found their economic opportunities limited largely to jobs as servants, seamen, or common laborers. [2] "Some of the men follow Mechanick trades," the Pennsylvania Abolition Society reported in 1795, "and a number of them are mariners, but the greatest part are employed as Day labourers. The Women generally, both married and single, wash clothes for a livelihood." Were such employments, the Society asked five years later, conducive to the Negro's "regularity and industry" or to his "natural propensity to thoughtlessness and amusements"? [3] In 1788, a French traveler noted that most northern free Negroes worked as servants, kept small shops, cultivated land, or found jobs on the coasting vessels. This seemed to constitute the extent of their economic opportunity. "The reason is obvious," he concluded. "The Whites, though they treat them with humanity, like not to give them credit to enable them to undertake any extensive commerce, nor even to give them the means of a common education, by receiving them into their counting-houses. If, then, the Blacks are confined to the retails of trade, let us not accuse their

[1] Andrews, *History of the New-York African Free-Schools*, p. 132.

[2] Jacques P. Brissot de Warville, *New Travels in the United States of America* (Dublin, 1792), pp. 282–83; Duke de la Rochefoucault Liancourt, *Travels through the United States of North America* (2 vols.; London, 1799), I, 531–32, II, 166–67; *Mass. Hist. Soc. Colls.*, Ser. 5, III, 400.

[3] Minutes of the Committee for Improving the Condition of Free Blacks, Pennsylvania Abolition Society, 1790–1803, Historical Society of Pennsylvania, pp. 112, 220.

capacity, but the prejudices of the Whites, which lay obstacles in their way."[4]

The situation had not changed materially by 1860. Although some Negroes could be found in the skilled trades and professions, most of them continued to labor in the service and menial occupations. In New York, Philadelphia, and Boston, the men worked largely as laborers, mariners, servants, waiters, barbers, coachmen, bootblacks, porters, second-hand-clothing dealers, and hod carriers, while the women worked as washerwomen, dressmakers, seamstresses, and cooks. Only a few Negroes managed to obtain the financial and educational prerequisites for entrance into business or the professions. As late as 1855, some 87 per cent of the gainfully employed Negroes of New York City worked in menial or unskilled jobs, and this appears to represent their economic condition in other northern cities.[5]

The absence of Negroes from the skilled and professional occupations allegedly confirmed their inferiority. "We see them engaged in no business that requires even ordinary capacity," a Pennsylvanian observed, "in no enterprizes requiring talents to conduct them. The mass are improvident, and seek the lowest avocations, and most menial stations."[6] Fortified with an elaborate set of racial beliefs, whites argued that this situation indicated racial adjustment rather than economic exploitation. The Negro was simply unfit — physically and mentally — to perform skilled labor or enter the professions;

[4] Brissot de Warville, *New Travels in the United States*, pp. 282–83.

[5] Charles H. Wesley, *Negro Labor in the United States, 1850–1925* (New York, 1927), pp. 30–32, 37–39, 42–50; *Proceedings of the Colored National Convention . . . Philadelphia, October 16th, 17th and 18th, 1855* (Salem, N. J., 1856), pp. 19–24; *Stimpson's Boston Directory* (Boston, 1840), pp. 445–51; *Register of the Trades of the Colored People in the City of Philadelphia and Districts* (Philadelphia, 1838), pp. 3–8; *Statistics of the Colored People of Philadelphia* (Philadelphia, 1856), pp. 13–15; *Douglass' Monthly*, March, 1859; Robert Ernst, "The Economic Status of New York City Negroes, 1850–1863," *Negro History Bulletin*, XII (March, 1949), 139–41, 142 n., 143 n.

[6] *Pennsylvania Constitutional Debates of 1837–38*, IX, 364.

he was naturally shifty and lazy, childlike and immature, untrustworthy, irresponsible, unable to handle complicated machines or run business establishments, and seriously lacking in initiative and ingenuity. Recognizing these qualities, a New York merchant insisted that Negro laborers must be treated as children requiring adult white guardianship.[7] Under these circumstances, how could Negroes qualify for anything but simple, unskilled labor? Such a lowly economic status, however, allegedly imposed no real hardships on the Negro, for he possessed little motivation for economic advancement and demanded only the satisfaction of immediate needs and desires. "He can supply all his physical wants without industry," the Connecticut Colonization Society contended, "and beyond the supply of his immediate physical wants, he has little inducement to look."[8] Such racial stereotypes as these reinforced the determination to keep Negro labor in its proper place; they both explained and justified the economic plight of northern Negroes.

In filling the menial occupations, Negroes not only acted "naturally" but performed, at the same time, a valuable economic and psychological service for white society. "They submit themselves to do menial service, and we get the profit," a Pennsylvanian declared. "If they would not do this, we ourselves would be compelled to do it." For this very reason, the Senate Foreign Relations Committee, in 1828, objected to the colonization of the American Negro in Africa. Since the blacks performed "various necessary menial duties," the Committee concluded, colonization would create a vacuum in the seaboard cities, increase the price of labor, and attract rural Negroes and fugitive slaves to the urban centers.[9] Just as

[7] A New York Merchant, *The Negro Labor Question* (New York, 1858), pp. 5–6, 21–22.
[8] *African Repository*, IV (1828), 118.
[9] *Pennsylvania Constitutional Debates of 1837–38*, V, 457; Senate Document, 20 Cong., 1 sess., No. 178 (April 28, 1828), p. 14.

slavery allegedly freed southern whites for the leisurely pursuit of culture, so did the free Negro worker enable northern whites to engage in more vital activities. In the event Negroes were colonized, a New England journal warned, "white men must hew our wood, draw our water, and perform our menial offices. They supply the place of so many whites, who may be spared for higher purposes." [10] Finally, Negroes performed a psychological service in that their work allowed the whites to assume aristocratic airs on occasion. In New York, for example, an English traveler observed that whites preferred Negro hackney coachmen "because they had no fear that they would assume any thing like equality, — because they could order them about in the tone of masters, — and still more, because it might be thought they were riding in their own carriages — like our cockneys, who put a livery-servant at the back of a glass-coach, and then pass it off as their own." In this way, the Englishman concluded, Negroes were able to improve their economic position "by the means employed to degrade it." [11]

Prevailing racial stereotypes, white vanity, and the widely held conviction that God had made the black man to perform disagreeable tasks combined to fix the Negro's economic status and bar him from most "respectable" jobs. White workers refused to accept the Negro as an apprentice; businessmen rejected his application for credit; and educational restrictions severely hampered his training for the professions. When Frederick Douglass, a skilled caulker, escaped to the North and sought work in the New Bedford shipyards, he was told that his employment would drive every white man away. For the next three years, Douglass worked as a common laborer, a coachman, and a waiter, earning an average of a dollar a day. In 1853, he remarked that it would be easier to find em-

[10] *New England Magazine*, II (1832), 17.
[11] Abdy, *Journal of a Residence and Tour*, III, 185.

ployment for his son in a lawyer's office than in a blacksmith's shop.[12] But even those few Negroes who managed to train themselves for professional careers found obstacles in their way. In Pennsylvania, for example, a committee of the bar refused to examine a qualified Negro applicant, and the district court upheld the decision on grounds that the state did not recognize Negro citizenship.[13] Moreover, trained Negro teachers labored in inferior school buildings at substandard wages.

White labor feared not only the competition of Negroes in the skilled trades but also the loss of social status which resulted from associating with them. White mechanics thus refused to work with Negroes in the same shops, and white servants considered it degrading to eat with them. One English traveler concluded that most white men "would rather starve than accept a menial office under a black."[14] Where the two races worked together, such as in the service occupations, whites insisted on different titles in order to preserve the sanctity of their color. Such distinctions confounded many a foreign observer. "As is well known," one Englishman commented, "a domestic servant of American birth, and without negro blood in his or her veins, who condescends to help the mistress or master of a household in making the beds, milking the cows, cooking the dinner, grooming the horse, or driving the carriage, is not a servant, but a 'help.' 'Help wanted,' is the common heading of advertisements in the North, where servants are required. . . . Let negroes be servants, and if

[12] Douglass, *Life and Times*, pp. 259–63; Foner (ed.), *Life and Writings of Frederick Douglass*, I, 24, II, 234.
[13] *North Star*, January 21, 28, 1848.
[14] John Fowler, *Journal of a Tour in the State of New York* (London, 1831), p. 218; Kenneth and Anna M. Roberts (eds.), *Moreau de St. Mery's American Journey* (New York, 1947), pp. 302–3; James Stirling, *Letters from the Slave States* (London, 1857), p. 55; *Minutes and Proceedings of the Fourth Annual Convention for the Improvement of the Free People of Colour*, p. 27; *North Star*, April 10, 1851; *Frederick Douglass' Paper*, May 18, 1855; Arfwedson, *United States and Canada*, I, 239.

not negroes, let Irishmen fill their place; but for an American, an Englishman, or a Scotsman to be a servant or a waiter is derogatory." This same traveler noted that even the recently arrived Irishman soon began to assert the supremacy of his white blood "and to come out of what he considers the degrading ranks of 'service.'" [15]

Where Negroes competed with whites for the same jobs or threatened to do so, violence often resulted. Such clashes were bound to be more severe during times of economic depression. Unemployed white workers swelled the Philadelphia mobs of 1842 in protest against the hiring of Negroes. In nearby Columbia, "a town meeting of the working men" warned the populace that Negroes were taking jobs formerly reserved for whites and that this might soon lead them into every branch of skilled trade, where "their known disposition to work for almost any price may well excite our fears." [16] The prejudices of white labor and the fear of violence caused New York City authorities to refuse licenses to Negro carmen and porters. If such licenses were granted, authorities warned, "it would bring them [Negro carmen and porters] into collision with white men of the same calling, and they would get their horses and carts 'dumped' into the dock, and themselves abused and beaten." While New York maintained its restriction, Negroes in Philadelphia endured some initial hostility long enough to obtain positions as carmen. [17]

Organized labor reinforced working-class antipathy toward Negro labor competition. Although trade-unions exerted a minor influence on ante bellum workers, they occasionally voiced labor's principal demands, aspirations, and prejudices. Such was the case when they rejected racial unity as a way

[15] Mackay, *Life and Liberty in America*, II, 45–46.
[16] Samuel D. Hastings to Lewis Tappan, August 19, 1842, Tappan Papers, Library of Congress; *The Liberator*, September 20, 1834.
[17] *Colored American*, September 16, 1837; Abdy, *Journal of a Residence and Tour*, III, 318 n.

of achieving higher economic standards, insisted on all-white unions, and vigorously opposed abolitionism. Indeed, anti-slavery advocates, who were themselves often oblivious to the plight of northern industrial labor, found few friends in trade-union ranks. After all, emancipation posed the serious threat of thousands of former slaves pouring into the North to undermine wages and worsen working conditions. Rather than prepare for such an eventuality by organizing Negro workers, trade-unions decided on exclusion. The Industrial Congress — a short-lived national organization of reformers and workingmen — admitted Negro delegates to an 1851 convention, but this had no apparent effect on other labor societies.[18] When New York Negro and white barbers agreed to organize to secure higher prices for their labor, the whites insisted on separate organizations. Carrying these sentiments to an extreme, a Cincinnati "mechanical association" publicly tried its president for teaching a trade to a Negro youth.[19]

Against this background of exclusion and hostility, Negro workers could hardly be expected to rally to the side of organized labor when it sought to press its demands through strike action. Instead, in several cases the Negro laborer willingly acted as a strikebreaker. When New York longshoremen struck in 1855 against wage cuts and an employer attack on their union, Negroes took their jobs on the water front and precipitated some violent clashes. Commenting on the strike, *Frederick Douglass' Paper* expressed little sympathy with the demands of the white longshoremen and pointed out that thousands of idle whites and Negroes would gladly work at half the price. "Of course," the newspaper continued, "colored men can feel under no obligation to hold out in a 'strike' with the whites, as the latter have never recognized them." Despite

[18] *Frederick Douglass' Paper*, June 26, 1851; *The* [12th] *Annual Report of the American and Foreign Anti-Slavery Society* (New York, 1852), p. 21; Wesley, *Negro Labor in the United States*, pp. 57, 73–74.

[19] Ernst, "The Economic Status of New York City Negroes," p. 132; Ohio Anti-Slavery Society, *Condition of the People of Color*, p. 8.

the violent opposition of the strikers, "the sympathies of the employers, the public, and the law, are on the side of the blacks; consequently, the white laborers have been restrained from any overt acts, though, at times, very threatening." [20] Such was the price paid by organized labor in both the ante bellum and post–Civil War years for the maintenance of white supremacy and exclusionism.

In addition to creating anxiety among white workers, the Negro labor force, increasingly augmented by emancipated and fugitive slaves, also aroused the concern of white citizens' groups and several northern legislatures and constitutional conventions. "The white man cannot labor upon equal terms with the negro," a group of Connecticut petitioners declared in 1834. "Those who have just emerged from a state of barbarism or slavery have few artificial wants. Regardless of the decencies of life, and improvident of the future, the black can afford his services at a lower price than the white man." Unless the legislature adopted appropriate entry restrictions, the petitioners warned, the sons of Connecticut would soon be driven from the state by the great influx of "black porters, black truckmen, black sawyers, black mechanics, and black laborers of every description." Agreeing that exclusion constituted the only remedy, delegates to California's constitutional convention warned that local capitalists planned to import Negroes to work in the mines and predicted the outbreak of "fearful collisions." In virtually every ante bellum northern legislature and constitutional convention, similar fears were expressed concerning the entrance of Negroes into occupations which had been dominated by native whites. [21]

[20] *Frederick Douglass' Paper*, February 2, 16, 1855; Wesley, *Negro Labor in the United States*, pp. 79–80; Albon P. Man, Jr., "Labor Competition and the New York Draft Riots of 1863," *Journal of Negro History*, XXXVI (1951), 393–94. See also Abdy, *Journal of a Residence and Tour*, I, 116.

[21] Abdy, *Journal of a Residence and Tour*, III, 246–47; *The Liberator*, February 15, 1834; *California Constitutional Debates of 1849*, pp. 49, 138, 144, 148, 333.

By the 1830's, the rapid increase of the nation's population, urbanization, and competition among whites threatened the Negro's hold on even the lowly employments. The Pennsylvania Abolition Society protested that "prejudice and pride" excluded blacks from turnpikes, canals, coal mines, brickmaking, street-paving, and street-cleaning, and a Philadelphia Negro complained of extensive discrimination among local common laborers. While thousands of persons worked to clean gutters and level drifts during a snowstorm, he found no Negroes so employed, but "hundreds of them . . . going about the streets with shovels in their hands, looking for work and finding none." [22] Although Negroes continued to work in menial jobs, one observer concluded in 1837 that "the time may come when they will not be able to make a living by such means; and then they will be obliged to resort to something still more humble. In this manner the whites will chase and harass them from post to post, until misery will complete their destruction." [23] In addition to the impact of the Panic of 1837 and the ensuing depression, Negro workers faced a new and serious challenge to their already weakened economic position — the Irish immigrant.

Between 1830 and 1860, nearly five million immigrants entered the United States, the bulk of them Irish, Germans, and Scandinavians. While a large number of the Germans and Scandinavians settled on middle western farmlands, the penniless and poverty-stricken Irish usually remained in the cities, crowded into "shanty towns," and sought any kind of employment, regardless of wages or conditions. Such a cheap labor force posed serious dangers to the Negro's economic position.

[22] *Minutes of the Eighteenth Session of the American Convention for Promoting the Abolition of Slavery, and Improving the Condition of the African Race* (Philadelphia, 1824), p. 13; Woodson (ed), *Mind of the Negro*, p. 225.

[23] Francis J. Grund, *The Americans in Their Moral, Social, and Political Relations* (2 vols.; London, 1837), II, 314, 321–22.

"These impoverished and destitute beings,—transported from the trans-atlantic shores," one Negro wrote, "are crowding themselves into every place of business and of labor, and driving the poor colored American citizen out. Along the wharves, where the colored man once done the whole business of shipping and unshipping—in stores where his services were once rendered, and in families where the chief places were filled by him, in all these situations there are substituted foreigners or white Americans." [24]

The Irish immigrant did not immediately displace the Negro laborer. Apparently preferring Negro "humility" to Irish "turbulence," some employers specified in "want ads" that Irishmen need not apply but that Negroes would be acceptable. "WANTED," a New York *Herald* advertisement read, "A Cook, Washer, and Ironer; who perfectly understands her business; any color or country except Irish." [25] Actually, as one English traveler noted, Americans considered both the Irish and the Negroes as outcasts. "To be called an 'Irishman' is almost as great an insult as to be stigmatized as a 'nigger feller,' and in a street-row, both appellations are flung off among the combatants with great zest and vigour." [26] Confronted with these prejudices, the Irish soon channeled their frustrations and anger into hatred of the Negro and began to find what comfort they could in the doctrine of white supremacy. Observers remarked that the Irish detested the Negro more than they did the Englishmen or the native whites, that they considered them "a soulless race," and that they "would shoot a black man with as little regard to moral consequences as they would a wild hog." On election day in New York, the Irish flocked to the polls, shouting, "Down with the Nagurs! Let them go back to Africa, where they belong," and consistently voted against any

[24] *Colored American*, July 28, 1838.

[25] Ernst, "The Economic Status of New York City Negroes," p. 140.

[26] Matilda C. J. F. Houstoun, *Hesperos; or, Travels in the West* (2 vols.; London, 1850), I, 179.

proposal to extend them equal political rights. Fearing that
emancipation in the South would send hordes of free Negroes
into northern cities, the Irish also turned their invectives on
the abolitionists, joined antislavery mobs, and warned that

> . . . when the negroes shall be free
> To cut the throats of all they see
> Then this dear land will come to be
> The den of foul rascality.[27]

Was it not ironical, an English visitor asked, that a respectable Negro often found himself placed in an inferior position
to "a raw Irishman" who might well be more deficient in the
essentials of civilization?[28] Many Negroes agreed that it was
both ironical and deplorable that they should be forced aside
to make room for the Irish. Accordingly, they frequently challenged the superior airs of the new arrivals, referred to them
contemptuously as "white niggers" or "white Buckra," and
considered their presence in Negro neighborhoods undesir-
able.[29] Moreover, they compared the rebellious and lawless
Irishman with the orderly and law-abiding Negro. "Who
makes your mobs on your canal lines, and in the construction
of your railroads?" a Negro leader asked. "Who swell your
mobs in your beer gardens, and in your Sunday excursions?
Who make your Native and Anti-Native American mobs?
Your Forrest and Macready mobs, which the military have to

---

[27] David W. Mitchell, *Ten Years Residence in the United States* (London,
1862), p. 159; Abdy, *Journal of a Residence and Tour*, I, 159; James D. Burn,
Three Years among the Working-Classes in the United States during the War
(London, 1865), p. xiv; Mackay, *Life and Liberty in America*, II, 46–47; Alexander Marjoribanks, *Travels in South and North America* (5th ed.; London and
New York, 1854), p. 435; Hamilton, *Men and Manners in America*, I, 92; New
York *Daily Tribune*, May 11, 1850; Oscar Handlin, *Boston's Immigrants, 1790–
1865* (Cambridge, 1941), p. 137; Godley, *Letters from America*, II, 70.
[28] Charles Daubeny, *Journal of a Tour through the United States and in Canada . . . 1837–38* (Oxford, 1843), p. 79.
[29] Mackay, *Life and Liberty in America*, II, 46–47; Handlin, *Boston's
Immigrants*, p. 213.
[30] *The Liberator*, May 18, 1860.

be called out to put down? I am sure, not the colored people." [30] Frederick Douglass, however, expressed his willingness to excuse the "demoralization" and debasement of the "poor Irish," for these were simply the inevitable products of intemperance, priestcraft, and oppression. But he could not extend this sympathy to the Irish Roman Catholics, for they represented "the enemies of Human Freedom, so far, at least, as *our* humanity is concerned." Finally, Douglass appealed to the Irish to be more consistent in their professions of liberty. How could they condemn English tyranny overseas as long as they sanctioned racial oppression in their new homeland? [31]

Against a background of increasing antipathy and economic competition, violence often erupted between Negro and Irish workers. In 1842, Irish coal miners in Pennsylvania battled with Negro competitors; in 1853, armed Negroes replaced striking Irishmen on the Erie Railroad; and two years later, the Irish and the Negroes battled on New York's docks. [32] The Civil War intensified the conflict, which culminated in the New York Draft Riots of 1863. In at least one instance, however, Negro and Irish workers co-operated to advance their economic position. Underpaid Irish hotel waiters in New York City, advised by their Negro counterparts to demand higher wages, agreed to admit a colored delegate to their meeting. But this experiment in Irish-Negro unity failed miserably as the employers broke the strike, replaced some of the fired workers with Negroes, and finally agreed to retain the best white waiters at higher wages. [33]

In the two decades preceding the Civil War, unskilled Irish labor continued to pour into the menial employments, depress wages, and drive out Negro competitors. Irish workers soon

[31] *Douglass' Monthly*, August, 1859; *Frederick Douglass' Paper*, December 15, 1854.
[32] Carl Wittke, *The Irish in America* (Baton Rouge, La., 1956), p. 126; Wesley, *Negro Labor in the United States*, pp. 79–80; Robert Ernst, *Immigrant Life in New York City, 1825–1863* (New York, 1949), p. 105.
[33] Ernst, "The Economic Status of New York City Negroes," p. 142.

dominated canal and railroad construction and broke the Negro's monopoly on the service occupations. "Within a few years," a Philadelphia newspaper remarked, "they [the Negroes] have ceased to be hackney coachmen and draymen, and they are now almost displaced as stevedores. They are rapidly losing their places as barbers and servants. Ten families employ white servants now, where one did twenty years ago." In 1830, Negroes comprised the majority of New York City's servants; twenty years later, Irish servants outnumbered the entire Negro population by ten to one.[34] The Negro's economic position had been seriously undermined. "Every hour sees us elbowed out of some employment," Frederick Douglass complained in 1855, "to make room perhaps for some newly arrived immigrants, whose hunger and color are thought to give them a title to especial favor. White men are becoming houseservants, cooks and stewards, common laborers and flunkeys to our gentry, and . . . they adjust themselves to their stations with a becoming obsequiousness." Although the Negro now suffered the consequences of economic displacement, Douglass warned, the Irishman would soon find "that in assuming our avocation he also has assumed our degradation."[35]

Economically more secure than the Irish, other immigrant groups had little fear of Negro competition and generally adopted a more tolerant racial outlook. Many German arrivals expressed their sympathy with the Negro's plight and condemned slavery, thus encouraging Frederick Douglass to hail them as "our active allies in the struggle against oppression

[34] *Colored American*, July 28, 1838; Edward Needles, *Ten Years' Progress; or, A Comparison of the State and Condition of the Colored People in the City and County of Philadelphia from 1837 to 1847* (Philadelphia, 1849), p. 5; American Union for the Relief and Improvement of the Colored Race, *Report of the Executive Committee* (Boston, 1836), p. 14; Warner, *New Haven Negroes*, pp. 21–22, 76; Wesley, *Negro Labor in the United States*, pp. 32, 76; *Frederick Douglass' Paper*, March 4, 1853; John A. Finch, *Travels in the United States of America and Canada* (London, 1833), p. 35; Ernst, "The Economic Status of New York City Negroes," p. 140.
[35] Foner (ed.), *Life and Writings of Frederick Douglass*, II, 249–50.

and prejudice." [36] Although many of them remained strongly antislavery, public sentiment gradually permeated the ranks of the new immigrants and modified their racial tolerance. In 1851, a New York German-language newspaper called racial equality "unnatural" and charged that Negroes were the "apes of the white race" and belonged in Africa. German farmers and mechanics gathered in Bucks County, Pennsylvania, in 1837 to condemn Negro suffrage, abolitionism, and English influences. Demanding more extreme action, German residents in Mercer County, Ohio, resolved to resist the further entrance of Negroes "to the full extent of our means, the bayonet not excepted," to remove Negro residents by a specified date, and until that time to refuse them employment, trade, and use of the grinding mills. [37] Although such incidents as these were sporadic and scattered, they nevertheless indicated that the Americanization of the immigrant was not always in the best interest of the Negro.

In California, Negro laborers competed with Chinese immigrants, and both groups faced powerful white prejudices and legislative and judicial discrimination. Although California Negroes expressed sympathy for the plight of the Chinese, they also appeared to share the white man's revulsion at the appearance of this alien population. "The poor Chinese are, indeed, a wretched looking set," the San Francisco correspondent of *Frederick Douglass' Paper* reported. "They are filthy, immoral and licentious — according to our notions of such things. . . . The Chinaman, under the most favorable aspects, is calculated to excite a smile. His vacant Know Nothing face is expressive of nothing but stupidity." Nevertheless, the correspondent added, such grotesqueness did not justify white oppression. When the state legislature threatened to prevent Chinese and others ineligible for citizenship from

[36] *Douglass' Monthly*, August, 1859.
[37] Ernst, "The Economic Status of New York City Negroes," p. 131; *The Liberator*, November 10, 1837; Woodson, *Century of Negro Migration*, p. 56.

168

THE ECONOMICS OF REPRESSION

holding mining claims, this same correspondent protested that
the bill would greatly imperil the economic position of the Negro. How, he asked, could California's legislators justifiably
place the Negro under the same restrictions as the Chinese?
Unlike the Negroes, the Chinese could never really amalgamate with the Americans; since it cost them so little to live, they
were content to work as "coolies" at a third of what would
be necessary to support an average American. Despite such
pleas, California whites applied legal disabilities against both
groups as public opinion sanctioned and enforced social
proscription.[38]

Economic exploitation and segregation produced the Negro
ghetto. In Boston, Negroes congregated on "Nigger Hill" and
along the wharves in "New Guinea"; in Cincinnati, they
crowded into wooden shacks and shanties in "Little Africa";
in New York, they concentrated in a few wards and mixed
with poor whites in the notorious "Five Points," described by
one visitor as "but a step into Hades" and "the worst hell of
America"; and in Philadelphia, they settled in gloomy cellars
and squalid houses located along narrow courts and alleys.[39]
Although some observers also pointed to the remarkable number of fine houses owned by Negroes in attractive neighborhoods, few could turn their eyes from the squalor of the Negro
slums or deny their existence. To southern visitors in the
North, such conditions demonstrated the folly of emancipation. "Thar they was," one southerner wrote, "covered with
rags and dirt, livin in houses and cellars, without hardly any

[38] *Frederick Douglass' Paper*, September 22, 1854, April 6, 13, 1855.
[39] Handlin, *Boston's Immigrants*, p. 100; Crawford, *Romantic Days in Old
Boston*, pp. 93–94; John Daniels, *In Freedom's Birthplace: A Study of the
Boston Negroes* (Boston and New York, 1914), p. 17; Wade, "The Negro in
Cincinnati," p. 44; Ernst, *Immigrant Life in New York City*, pp. 40–41; Robert
H. Collyer, *Lights and Shadows of American Life* (Boston, 1836), pp. 6–7;
*Statistical Inquiry into the Condition of the People of Colour, of the City and
Districts of Philadelphia*, pp. 31–41.

furniture; and sum of 'em without dores or winders. . . .
This, thinks I, is nigger freedom; this is the condition to which
the filanthropists of the North wants to bring the happy black
people of the South!"[40]

Such surroundings obviously had their impact on the general health of the Negro residents. In New York City, tuberculosis proved fatal to twice as many blacks as whites, a
reflection of adverse living conditions.[41] Philadelphia's coro-
ner attributed the high mortality rate in Negro districts to
intemperance, exposure, and malnutrition. After conducting
an inspection in 1848, he reported that many Negroes had
been "found dead in cold and exposed rooms and garrets,
board shanties five and six feet high, and as many feet square,
erected and rented for lodging purposes, mostly without any
comforts, save the bare floor, with the cold penetrating between
the boards, and through the holes and crevices on all sides."
Some bodies had been recovered "in cold, wet, and damp
cellars," while still others had been found lying in back yards
and alleys. Most of these Negroes had sold rags and bones for
a living. Not too far away, however, middle- and upper-class
Negroes maintained some respectable living quarters.[42]

The vigorous exclusion of Negroes from white residential
neighborhoods made escape from the ghetto virtually impossible. The fear of depreciated property values overrode virtually every other consideration. As early as 1793, the attempt
to locate "a Negro hut" in Salem, Massachusetts, prompted
a white minister to protest that such buildings depreciated
property, drove out decent residents, and generally injured
the welfare of the neighborhood. Some years later, New Haven
petitioners complained that the movement of Negroes into

[40] Thompson, *Major Jones's Sketches of Travel*, pp. 103–4. See also Bobo,
Glimpses of New-York City, pp. 94–97, 126–30.

[41] Ernst, *Immigrant Life in New York City*, p. 238.

[42] *Statistical Inquiry into the Condition of the People of Colour, of the City
and Districts of Philadelphia*, pp. 34–36.

previously white neighborhoods deteriorated real estate values from 20 to 50 per cent; an Indianan asserted that the proposed establishment of a Negro tract would reduce the value of nearby white-owned lots by at least 50 per cent.[43] Obviously, then, the Negro had to be contained in his own area. Thus when a Boston Negro schoolmistress considered moving to a better neighborhood, the inhabitants of the block where she proposed to settle resolved either to eject her or to destroy the house. By 1847, the residents of South Boston could boast that "not a single colored family" lived among them — only immigrants "of the better class who will not live in cellars." [44]

Although whites frequently deprecated the Negro slums, some profited from them. In Cincinnati's Little Africa, for example, whites owned most of the wooden shacks and shanties and protested the attempt of municipal authorities to bar further construction of wooden buildings in the center of town. "Heaven preserve the shanties," a Cincinnati editor sarcastically remarked, "and supply the proprietors with tenants from whom the rent can be screwed, without respect to color or character." [45] While white critics continued to deplore Negro housing conditions, white landlords made few, if any, improvements. Both conveniently concluded that Negroes naturally lived that way.

In view of the frequent charge that northern Negroes constituted "a standing monument to the folly of Abolitionism," antislavery societies could not ignore the economic plight of the Negro. In periodic appeals and editorials directed at the Negro community, abolitionists placed particular stress on the need for economic improvement. To destroy prejudice,

[43] Bentley, *Diary*, II, 34; *The Liberator*, February 15, 1834; *Indiana Constitutional Debates of 1850*, I, 446.
[44] Abdy, *Journal of a Residence and Tour*, I, 169; Handlin, *Boston's Immigrants*, p. 102.
[45] Wade, "Negro in Cincinnati," p. 45.

Negroes first had to secure the white man's respect, and this could be most effectively won through a rise in economic status. Accumulate money, William Lloyd Garrison told a Negro audience, for "money begets influence, and influence respectability." This was standard abolitionist advice: wealth alone could truly overwhelm and conquer racial proscription. "A colored man who makes a thousand dollars," a Unitarian clergyman and abolitionist asserted, "does more to put down prejudice, than if he made a thousand moderately good speeches against prejudice, or wrote a thousand pretty fair articles against it. No race in this country will be despised which makes money." Choosing a rather curious analogy, he concluded that if Boston or New York had "ten orangoutangs worth a million dollars each, they would visit in the best society, we should leave our cards at their doors, and give them snug little dinner-parties." [46]

Antislavery organizations made sporadic attempts to implement their appeals to the Negro community. As early as 1796, the American Convention of Abolition Societies urged Negro parents to teach their children useful trades "favorable to health and virtue." Taking more concrete action, the Pennsylvania Society appointed committees to find employment for Negro adults and to place Negro children with persons willing to train them in some skill. "Could they be generally prevailed on to attend to agriculture," the Society hopefully remarked, "were those who remain in the city to become persons of property, and their children brought up to useful trades, we believe many of the evils complained of would gradually disappear." But by 1827, the American Convention could only deplore the Negro's continued exclusion from skilled employments and urge his instruction in handicraft trades. [47] The

---

[46] William Lloyd Garrison, *An Address Delivered before the Free People of Color, in Philadelphia, New York, and Other Cities* (Boston, 1831), p. 10; Clarke, "Condition of the Free Colored People of the United States," pp. 263–64.

[47] *Minutes of the Proceedings of the Third Convention of Delegates from the*

American Anti-Slavery Society, organized by Garrison and his followers in 1833, also encouraged a program of economic uplift; it cheered Negro efforts to shift from menial to agricultural and mechanical employments, called upon sympathetic merchants and master-mechanics to hire Negro apprentices, established a register of Negro mechanics available for work, and moved to found a manual-labor college to train Negro youths.[48]

Abolitionist efforts, however, consisted largely of verbal advice and encouragement and failed to achieve any measurable success. The economic orthodoxy of most abolitionists seriously limited their understanding of the Negro's plight. These were, after all, middle-class reformers, not laboring men or economic radicals. They made no apparent effort to encourage Negro workers to combine among themselves or with white workers for economic gains. Inasmuch as Garrison and many of his followers had expressed no sympathy with the attempts of white workers to form trade unions and strike for better conditions, this attitude is not surprising.[49] The employer's sense of profit, not trade unionism, would override racial prejudice. "Place two mechanics by the side of each other," Garrison declared, "one colored, and the other white," and "he who works the cheapest and best, will get the most custom. In making a bargain, the color of a man will never

Abolition Societies, p. 13; Minutes of the Committee for Improving the Condition of Free Blacks, Pennsylvania Abolition Society, 1790–1803, Historical Society of Pennsylvania, pp. 1–2, 220; *Minutes of the Twentieth Session of the American Convention for Promoting the Abolition of Slavery, and Improving the Condition of the African Race* (Baltimore, 1827), pp. 21–22.

[48] *Fifth Annual Report of the Executive Committee of the American Anti-Slavery Society* (New York, 1838), p. 127; American Anti-Slavery Society, *Address to the People of Color, in the City of New York* (New York, 1834), p. 5; Barnes and Dumond (eds.), *Weld-Grimke Correspondence,* I, 264–65; Minutes of the Committee for Improvement of the Colored People, Pennsylvania Abolition Society, 1837–1853, Historical Society of Pennsylvania, pp. 24–25; *The Liberator,* September 29, 1832.

[49] For Garrison's views on organized labor, see *The Liberator,* January 1, 29, 1831.

be consulted." Rather than combine with white workers, abolitionists advised Negroes, underbid them. "After all," the *New England Magazine* remarked, "the voice of interest is louder, and speaks more to the purpose, than reason or philanthropy. When a black merchant shall sell his goods cheaper than his white neighbor, he will have the most customers. . . . When a black mechanic shall work cheaper and better than a white one, he will be more frequently employed." [50]

At the request of an Ohio Negro convention, three prominent antislavery sympathizers — Cassius M. Clay, Horace Mann, and Benjamin Wade — submitted their recommendations concerning the economic future of the Negro. Clay advised the delegates to forego social equality, which could never be attained in the free or slave states, and immediate political rights in order to concentrate on the accumulation of wealth. Form separate communities apart from the whites, Mann suggested, and thereby advance from menial employments to the professions and skilled trades. Separation would afford all Negroes an equal opportunity to compete for the highest political offices and the best jobs. Arriving at an almost identical conclusion, Wade advised Negroes to withdraw from menial occupations, form separate communities, cultivate the soil, become mechanics, and thus gradually attain economic independence. As long as Negroes remained in white communities, this goal could not be realized. Independence, however, would compel whites to grant them respect and recognition, thus forever destroying the doctrine of racial superiority. "The color of skin is nothing," Wade asserted. "When was it ever known that virtue, industry and intelligence were not respected?" [51]

[50] Garrison, *Address Delivered before the Free People of Color*, p. 10; *New England Magazine*, II (1832), 16–17.

[51] *Proceedings of the Convention of the Colored Freemen of Ohio* (Cincinnati, 1852), pp. 15–25. For some Negro reactions to these suggestions, see *Frederick Douglass' Paper*, October 22, 1852, and *The Liberator*, November 26, 1852.

Such sentiments reflected the limitations of the abolitionist approach. Although these grandiose schemes held forth the promise of economic security at some future date, most Negroes were concerned with more immediate problems and more practical remedies. Not until the late 1850's, when political proscription and economic discrimination showed no sign of diminishing, did a growing number of them agree that separation from the whites might be the only solution. In the meantime, most Negroes would have preferred a job in an abolitionist's shop or office to eloquent messages on the virtues of economic independence.

"To be dependent, is to be degraded," a Negro convention declared in 1848. "Men may indeed pity us, but they cannot respect us" — at least, not until the Negro won economic independence for himself and ceased to rely on the white man for the necessities of life. "The houses we live in are built by white men — the clothes we wear are made by white tailors — the hats on our heads are made by white hatters, and the shoes are made by white shoe-makers, and the food that we eat, is raised and cultivated by white men." Moreover, a Negro leader added, "our fathers are their coachmen, our brothers their cookmen, and ourselves their waiting-men. Our mothers their nurse-women, and our wives their washer women." As long as economic necessity compelled Negro women to perform "the drudgery and menial offices of other men's wives and daughters," it was nonsensical for Negroes to prate about political and social equality.[52]

Since at least 1828, Negro leaders, newspapers, and conventions had been voicing similar sentiments. David Walker, for example, had berated Negroes in his *Walker's Appeal* for relying solely on bootblacking, waiting, and barbering for a livelihood. Although he had no objections to such pursuits as

[52] *North Star*, September 22, 1848; Delany, *Condition, Elevation, Emigration, and Destiny of the Colored People*, pp. 41–45.

a necessary means of subsistence, he warned his people not to be satisfied with inferior employment. At the same time, the first Negro newspaper — *Freedom's Journal* — had recommended to its readers the virtues of economy and industry, as well as the proper training of Negro youths for useful and respectable trades. After 1831, Negro state and national conventions repeatedly called upon their people to shift from menial jobs to mechanical and agricultural pursuits, to form joint-stock companies, mutual-savings banks, and county associations in order to pool capital for the purchase of real estate, and to patronize Negro-owned businesses. The competition of immigrant labor added to the urgency of these appeals. "Learn trades or starve!" Frederick Douglass warned in 1853. Since Negroes could no longer monopolize the menial occupations, they had to find new opportunities; they had to master the mechanical arts, advance into the skilled trades, educate their children along these lines, "and learn not only to black boots but to make them as well." Otherwise, Douglass concluded, the Negro faced economic deterioration and disaster.[53]

Excluded from the workshops, crowded into filthy slums, and confined to the lowest of employments, some Negroes became convinced that economic improvement could best be achieved by abandoning the cities for the simple and virtuous attractions of agrarian life. This was among "the most happy and honorable of pursuits," Negro leaders pointed out, for it elevated its workers through "wealth, virtue, and honor" and made them economically independent and respectable. The city, on the other hand, shortened lives, seduced its inhabitants through gambling and general licentiousness, and excluded blacks from remunerative employment and enterprise. More-

[53] Walker, *Walker's Appeal*, p. 34; *Freedom's Journal*, March 16, 1827; *Frederick Douglass' Paper*, March 4, 1853; Foner (ed.), *Life and Writings of Frederick Douglass*, II, 234.

176   THE ECONOMICS OF REPRESSION

over, an "enormous combination of capital" was "slowly in-
vading every calling in the city, from washing and ironing
to palace steamers." In time, this process would make the
urban poor nothing but the slaves of increasingly low wages
and high rents. Through rigid economy and hard work, however, Negroes could move into the country and become successful farmers. Here was "a positive road to wealth, influence,
and usefulness." [54] Virtually every ante bellum Negro convention — state and national — reiterated these sentiments.

In an effort to encourage such a move, Gerrit Smith, an
antislavery leader and philanthropist, offered to distribute
approximately 140,000 acres of his land in upstate New York
to 3,000 Negroes. Such grants of 40 to 60 acres, Smith hoped,
would establish a large population of independent Negro
farmers and qualify them to vote under New York laws. Soon
after the offer had been made, Negro leaders appealed to
their people to take advantage of this "unexampled benevolence" and assert their economic independence. Once in possession of land, "we will be our own masters, free to think,
free to act; and if we toil hard, that toil will be sweetened
by the reflection, that it is all, by God's will and help, for ourselves, our wives and our children. Thus placed in an independent condition, we will not only be independent, in
ourselves, but will overcome that prejudice against condition,
which has so long been as a mill stone about our necks."
Despite such enthusiasm, the project failed miserably. Much
of the land was poor and unfit for cultivation, and the cost of
moving, settling, seeding, and waiting for the first crops compelled many Negroes to abandon their grants. In 1848, two

[54] *Minutes of the National Convention of Colored Citizens: held at Buffalo
. . . August, 1843, for the Purpose of Considering their Moral and Political
Condition as American Citizens* (New York, 1843), pp. 31–36; *Proceedings of
the Connecticut State Convention of Colored Men* (New Haven, 1849), pp. 16–17;
*Proceedings of the First Convention of the Colored Citizens of the State of
Illinois* (Chicago, 1853), pp. 14, 30–31; *Ohio Colored Convention of 1852*, p. 10;
North Star, April 10, 1851.

years after Smith's offer, less than 30 Negro families had settled on the new lands.[55]

By the 1850's, it became clear that the virtues of agrarian life had made little impression on urban Negroes. "From some cause or other," Douglass lamented in 1853, "colored people will congregate in the large towns and cities; and they will endure any amount of hardship and privation, rather than separate, and go into the country." They are obviously "wanting in self-reliance — too fond of society — too eager for immediate results — and too little skilled in mechanics or husbandry to attempt to overcome the wilderness." As an alternative, Douglass proposed that an industrial college be established for the training of Negroes. Although heartily indorsed by the 1853 national Negro convention, plans for such a school met with as little success in the 1850's as they had in the 1830's. White abolitionist apathy and Negro factional disputes helped to doom them. Finally, in 1855, various Negro leaders publicly denounced the proposed industrial college as "a complexional institution" designed to separate Negro youth from the rest of the population, and they suggested instead the establishment of a central bureau to collect funds and encourage mechanics among Negroes. Delegates to the 1855 national convention agreed to form "Industrial Associations" to encourage Negro artisans, but the plan came to nothing.[56]

White hostility prevented Negroes from playing any significant role in the ante bellum labor movement. In 1850, New York Negroes did form a short-lived organization — the American League of Colored Labourers — which sought to

[55] Harlow, *Gerrit Smith*, pp. 244–52; *An Address to the Three Thousand Colored Citizens of New-York, who are the owners of one hundred and twenty thousand acres of land, in the State of New York, given to them by Gerrit Smith, Esq. of Peterboro* (New York, 1846); *North Star*, January 7, February 18, 1848, January 5, March 2, June 1, 1849.

[56] Foner (ed.), *Life and Writings of Frederick Douglass*, II, 35–37, 231–35; *Frederick Douglass' Paper*, January 20, 1854, May 18, 25, 1855; *National Colored Convention of . . . 1855*, p. 26.

promote a union of skilled workers, the commercial, mechanical, and agricultural education of Negro youths, an industrial fair, and a fund to assist Negro mechanics in establishing independent businesses. But the organization apparently expired before any of its plans could be executed. Meanwhile, *Frederick Douglass' Paper* reported "some talk . . . of organizing a society of the laboring classes" to secure more constant and profitable employment — "a thing that should have been done long since" — but again, talk failed to materialize into action. Convention recommendations that Negroes organize "Trade Unions on a small scale" or "Co-partnerships" of businessmen met a similar fate.[57]

By 1860, a growing number of Negroes had obtained the necessary education and capital to enter the professions, small businesses, and the skilled trades, but the great mass of them still labored as unorganized and unskilled workers competing with newly arrived immigrants for the menial jobs. Both Negro and white labor failed to realize the consequences of this division, especially under the conditions imposed by postwar industrial capitalism, and firmly held to the vision of an eventual rise into the hierarchy of propertied entrepreneurs. White hostility, exclusion, and economic privation continued to confront Negro workers, and depressions fell upon them with particular force. "Whenever the interests of the white man and the black come into collison in the United States," an English visitor remarked in 1851, "the black man goes to the wall. . . . It is certain that, wherever labour is scarce, there he is readily employed; when it becomes plentiful, he is the first to be discharged."[58]

In their efforts to maintain racial supremacy and purity,

[57] Wesley, *Negro Labor in the United States*, pp. 55–56; Ernst, "The Economic Status of New York City Negroes," p. 141; *Frederick Douglass' Paper*, February 23, 1855; *National Colored Convention of . . . 1855*, p. 19.
[58] James F. W. Johnston, *Notes on North America* (2 vols.; Edinburgh and London, 1851), II, 315.

the whites did not differentiate among the various classes of Negro society. By virtue of the color of his skin alone — and regardless of economic status — a Negro had to endure the disabilities imposed by white citizens and legislators. Whites might distinguish "good niggers" from "uppity niggers" or express a preference for hiring mulattoes over blacks, but that was all. Otherwise, Negroes were all alike — a homogeneous and degraded mass which had to be carefully regulated. Nevertheless, although it was seemingly irreconcilable with the Negro's low economic status, social stratification did exist, especially in the larger cities of the North. Among Philadelphia Negroes, for example, one observer — Joseph W. Wilson — found broad social distinctions equaling those of any other community: an upper class, residing "in ease, comfort and the enjoyments of all the social blessings of this life"; a middle class, "sober, honest, industrious, and respectable"; and a lower class, "found in the lowest depths of human degradation, misery and want." [59]

Wealth, occupation, family, nativity, color, and education largely determined a Negro's position in the social order. By 1860, inroads into business and the professions provided the basis for an increasing accumulation of propertied and liquid wealth.[60] Social segregation afforded a growing number of opportunities and insured an important position in the Negro class structure for doctors, lawyers, shopkeepers, ministers, and undertakers. Within the narrowly circumscribed economic world of the Negro, the upper and middle classes included professionals, successful businessmen, large-scale farmers, carpenters, skilled mechanics, barbers, and high-placed

[59] [Joseph W. Wilson], *Sketches of the Higher Classes of Colored Society in Philadelphia* (Philadelphia, 1841), p. 14.

[60] Delany, *Condition, Elevation, Emigration, and Destiny of the Colored People*, pp. 92–137; Abram L. Harris, *The Negro as Capitalist* (Philadelphia, 1936), pp. 5–23; Nell, *Colored Patriots*, pp. 327–28; Ernst, "The Economic Status of New York City Negroes," p. 142; *The Liberator*, January 27, 1854, July 2, 1858; Furness, "Walt Whitman Looks at Boston," p. 356.

waiters, servants, and coachmen, while the lower class consisted of common laborers and comprised the bulk of the population. Rather than admit a permanent working-class status, however, many lower-class Negroes attempted to improve their position by obtaining regular employment and an education, virtual prerequisites for any successful escape from slum neighborhoods and for admission into the middle class. But the segregated Negro community provided a limited number of opportunities for a Negro bourgeoisie and sharply curtailed the amount of social mobility.

Successful Negro entrepeneurs often extended their services beyond their own communities. In several cities, for example, Negro restaurateurs, caterers, bootmakers, tailors, and barbers acquired a fashionable white clientele. Of course the maintenance of a good reputation among whites required Negro businessmen to show proper respect and not to tamper with deep rooted prejudices. In the restaurant and barbering businesses, for example, Negroes frequently, if not generally, had to bar members of their own race. A New York restaurateur called a friend from the dining-room and offered to serve him behind a screen or in the kitchen, explaining that "his customers *now* were not as those in William Street, where he formerly kept." [61] After witnessing the ouster of a prospective Negro customer from a New York barber-shop, an astonished English visitor requested an explanation from the Negro barber. "Ay, I guessed you were not raised here," the barber replied. "Now I reckon you do not know that my boss [also a Negro] would not have a single . . . gentleman come to his store, if he cut coloured men; now my boss, I guess, ordered me to turn out every coloured man from the store right away, and if I did not, he would send me off slick." That evening, the English visitor related the incident to three American "gentlemen . . . of education and of liberal

[61] *Colored American*, June 5, 26, July 10, 1841.

opinions." "Ay right, perfectly right," one exclaimed, "I would never go to a barber's where a coloured man was cut!" [62] Such practices finally prompted an Ohio Negro convention to condemn any "colored man who refuses to shave a colored man because he is colored" as "much worse than a white man who refuses to eat, drink, ride, walk, or be educated with a colored man . . . for the former is a party *de facto* to riveting chains around his own neck and the necks of his much injured race." Inasmuch as the same convention called upon Negroes to equal the "Saxon" in wealth and enterprise, this must have presented somewhat of a dilemma to many successful Negro entrepreneurs. [63]

Nativity proved less important to status than occupation in the Negro class structure. A recently arrived southern-born immigrant who obtained a good economic position would find little to bar him from acceptance in the Negro upper or middle classes, but the fact that so many of the newcomers had neither education nor skill and comprised "the most numerous in those crowded streets and alleys where the destruction and wretchedness is most intense and infectious" resulted in some hostility between the northern-born free Negro and the escaped or emancipated southern slave. [64] Upper- and middle-class northern Negroes often held aloof from the new immigrants and complained that they threatened to besmirch the reputation of the community. In Philadelphia, for example, Joseph W. Wilson attributed much of the disaffection within the Negro upper class to "real or pretended sectional preferences," such as those between "the natives and the southern families." Although he concluded that the natives generally respected their southern brethren, he also found that some of them "can't bear

[62] Fearon, *Sketches of America*, pp. 58–60. See also Candler, *Summary View of America*, p. 284.

[63] *Ohio Colored Convention of 1852*, p. 6.

[64] *Statistical Inquiry into the Condition of the People of Colour, of the City and Districts of Philadelphia*, p. 31.

the southerners!" [65] Among the lower classes, there existed more substantial grounds for antagonism because native Negro workers resented additional competition. When an English traveler arrived in Philadelphia in 1846, two Negro porters greeted him and offered to carry his baggage. While one claimed he was "in de cheap line," the other retorted: "Cheap! — neber mind him, Sa; he's only a nigga from Baltimore, just come to Philadelphy. I'se born her, Sa, and know de town like a book. Dat ere negga not seen good society yet — knows nuffin — habn't got de polish on." [66]

Equally significant in determining a Negro's place in the social order was the relative darkness of his skin. By 1850, mulattoes comprised some 25 per cent of the northern Negroes. [67] Although a light color did not automatically secure a Negro's place in the hierarchy, it often afforded him greater economic opportunities, which, in turn, assured him of a high rank in Negro society. In many cases, whites simply preferred to hire mulattoes, feeling that their closer proximity to Caucasian features also made them more intelligent and physically attractive. Such preference invariably had its effect on some mulattoes and made them feel socially superior to the blacks. Nevertheless, a mulatto was still not welcome in white society and had to share the legal disabilities of the blacks. In most cases, then, he took his place in the Negro community and, in fact, produced much of its militant leadership, including such men as Frederick Douglass, James Forten, Robert Purvis, Charles L. Remond, James McCune Smith, William Still, John Mercer Langston, William Wells Brown, and David Walker.

Although whites understandably associated a lighter skin with a superior type of Negro, the surprising fact is that so

[65] Wilson, *Sketches of the Higher Classes,* pp. 47–48.

[66] Alexander Mackay, *The Western World; or, Travels in the United States in 1846–47* (3 vols.; London, 1850), I, 132–33.

[67] John Cummings, *Negro Population in the United States, 1790—1915* (Washington, D.C., 1918), p. 210.

many Negroes consciously or unconsciously accepted this color valuation. The mulatto's high social position thus resulted in large measure from the strong tendency among Negroes, particularly those in the upper and middle classes, to envy a light complexion, accept white standards of beauty, and do everything possible to alter their own appearances accordingly. In too many cases, one Negro protested, parents taught their children "that he or she is pretty, just in proportion as the features approximate to the Anglo-Saxon standard." To conform to these standards, "flat noses must be pinched up. Kinky hair must be subjected to a straightening process — oiled, and pulled, twisted up, tied down, sleeked over and pressed under, or cut off so short that it can't curl, sometimes the natural hair is shaved off, and its place supplied by a straight wig, thus presenting the ludicrous anomaly of Indian hair over negro features. Thick lips are puckered up. . . . Beautiful black and brown faces by the application of rouge and lily white are made to assume unnatural tints, like the livid hue of painted corpses." Such attempts to alter nature, he concluded, illustrated the power of public sentiment and required that parents cultivate in their children a respect for their race and color and refrain from characterizing straight hair as "good hair" or Anglo-Saxon features as "good features." [68] Ironically, the persistence of such practices, as well as the force of social segregation, formed the basis for some important Negro economic enterprises.

As more schools for Negro youths opened, education became increasingly important and necessary for social status, especially if it led to professional employment. It also tended to solidify class lines. Economic comfort and security enabled upper- and middle-class parents to insure the regular attendance of their children at public or private schools, while lower

[68] M. H. Freeman, "The Educational Wants of the Free Colored People," *Anglo-African Magazine*, I (April, 1859), 116–19.

class children frequently had to start work at an early age. Among the upper classes, education served important social and economic functions. In Philadelphia, for example, Joseph W. Wilson found that upper-class Negroes often pursued an education "more for its own sake — the adornment which it gives them — than from any relative or collateral advantages," and they did not necessarily utilize it to learn a specific trade. Actually, the relative merits of a classical or vocational education would long be a subject of dispute among Negroes. Moreover, Wilson found that the educated Negro was by no means "the happiest man." Qualified for a useful and honorable place in life, he still found it difficult to secure a good position and thus felt more acutely than others the effects of racial prejudice.[69] Partly for this reason, professional and educated men furnished the most numerous and aggressive portion of Negro leadership.

In social intercourse, upper- and middle-class Negroes sought to achieve much of the decorum and display of white society. Observing Philadelphia's Negro society, Wilson found social exchanges conducted on a very respectable and dignified level, a remarkable degree of refinement and cultivation, ease and grace of manner, and "a strict observance of all the nicer etiquettes, proprieties and observances that are characteristic of the well bred."[70] Although both races indulged in ostentatious displays of their real or pretended wealth, foreign travelers particularly noted such excesses among Negroes. "Many of the blacks carry walking-canes," an Englishman wrote, "and parade the streets arm in arm, bowing most affectedly to the negresses, who are often dressed in a style so costly, that it is difficult to conceive how they can procure such finery." In Philadelphia, another visitor noted that the "most extravagant funeral" he had seen "was that of a black; the coaches were

[69] Wilson, *Sketches of the Higher Classes*, pp. 95–97.
[70] *Ibid.*, pp. 54, 56, 60.

very numerous, as well as the pedestrians, who were all well dressed, and behaving with the utmost decorum." [71] Such ostentation, contrasting sharply with the general enonomic status of the Negro, disgusted many white and Negro abolitionists. The Pennsylvania Abolition Society, for example, accused Negroes of aping "those silly white people who pride themselves in their outward adorning to the neglect of their minds," and a Negro leader berated his brethren for spending thousands of dollars each year "for an hour's display of utter emptiness." [72] But protests such as these largely ignored the fact that middle- and upper-class Negroes, having been segregated from white society and in most public places, had few other opportunities to demonstrate their social success and position.

Class distinctions sometimes manifested themselves in dissension and conflict. In the upper and middle classes, for example, one observer noted envy of advancement and success, antagonism toward newcomers, and constant competition for place and self-exaltation in political meetings. Travelers remarked that Negroes often reproached one another as "dirty black naygurs," an insult usually reserved for especially dark Negroes, lower-class blacks, or newly arrived southern immigrants. "So much does the oppressed or lower class always strive to imitate the superior," Francis Lieber observed, "that even the name which is bestowed by the latter upon the former,

[71] John Howison, *Sketches of Upper Canada . . . and Some Recollections of the United States of America* (Edinburgh, 1821), pp. 312–13; Arfwedson, *United States and Canada*, I, 27; Francis Lieber, *Letters to a Gentleman in Germany* (Philadelphia, 1834), p. 68; Duncan, *Travels through Part of the United States and Canada*, I, 60; Edward D. Seeber (ed.), *Edouard de Montule Travels in America, 1816–1817* (Bloomington, Ind., 1951), p. 181; Marryat, *Diary in America*, I, 294.

[72] Pennsylvania Anti-Slavery Society, *Address to the Coloured People of the State of Pennsylvania* (Philadelphia, 1837), p. 6; Henry Highland Garnet, *The Past and the Present Condition, and the Destiny, of the Colored Race* (Troy, N. Y. 1848), p. 19.

by way of contempt, is adopted and used by them." [73] Such language, carrying with it derogatory implications, not only set Negroes to fighting each other but, when used by whites, could precipitate a major riot.

By the 1830's, abolitionists — white and black — frequently expressed dismay and disappointment over the growing clannishness of Negro society. How could prejudice be conquered when mulattoes and Negroes found it difficult to live together, or when Negroes insulted each other as "niggers," or when they excluded members of their own race from their business establishments? "I mourn over the aristocracy that prevails among our colored brethren," Sarah Grimke wrote to Theodore Weld. "I cherished the hope that suffering had humbled them and prepared them to perform a glorious part in the reformation of our country, but the more I mingle with them the fainter are my hopes. They have as much caste among themselves as we have and despise the poor as much I fear as their pale brethren." [74] Nevertheless, class distinctions persisted. The Negro bourgeoisie, however, although often contemptuous of the less successful, could not dissociate itself from the lower classes. In the segregated community, it depended on Negro patronage. Moreover, racial pride and the fact that legislation applied to all colored classes insured the existence of a Negro community with common grievances, interests, and goals.

[73] Lieber, *Letters to a Gentleman*, p. 90. See also Isaac Holmes, *An Account of the United States of America, Derived from Actual Observation, during a Residence of Four Years in that Republic* (London, 1823), p. 331.

[74] Pennsylvania Anti-Slavery Society, *Address to the Coloured People*, p. 6; Barnes and Dumond (eds.), *Weld-Grimke Correspondence*, I, 498.

VI

The Church and
The Negro

Seeking an escape from the drudgery and disabilities of everyday existence, many Negroes found spiritual comfort and opportunities for social expression in the church. Indeed, the
minister was unquestionably the most important and influential
figure in the ante bellum Negro community. While exercising
a powerful political, social, and moral influence, he contributed some of the most militant leadership to the Negro's
struggle for equal rights, a fact well demonstrated by such
men as Theodore S. Wright, Henry Highland Garnet, Samuel
R. Ward, Charles B. Ray, J. W. C. Pennington, Amos G.
Beman, and Daniel A. Payne. Both a politician and a spiritual
leader, the Negro minister frequently used his position and
prestige to arouse his congregations on issues affecting their
civil rights as well as their morals; he not only condemned
colonization, segregation, and disfranchisement, but persistently attacked "licentious literature," the immoral and cor-
rupting influence of the theater, infidelity, and atheism.[1]

[1] See, for example, *Colored American*, edited by the Reverend Samuel Cornish,
January 28, February 4, 11, 1837.

Encompassing virtually every aspect of Negro life, the church provided innumerable services. In addition to being a center of religious devotion and ceremony, it was a school, a political meeting hall, a community recreation and social center, and, not too infrequently, a haven for fugitive slaves. Amos G. Beman, pastor of New Haven's African Congregational Church, effectively illustrated the pivotal importance of the ante bellum Negro religious leader and the church as a center of community life. Under his direction, New Haven Negroes organized a benevolent association, a library club, "Circles of Improvement," and forums; at the same time, they helped to organize a four-state temperance society which not only condemned alcoholic beverages but also discussed slavery, education, national organization, employment offices, and the merits of mechanical arts and agriculture. In addition to using the church for these various activities, Negro children displayed their school work in the basement and received regular Sunday School instruction. As an antislavery leader, Beman welcomed fugitive slaves, convened abolitionist meetings in his church, helped to organize state and national Negro conventions, campaigned for Negro suffrage, published a newspaper, and contributed to the various abolitionist journals. In short, Beman effectively combined the roles of Sunday orator, politician, and social leader.[2]

In his sermons, the Negro minister exerted considerable authority, for this was an age in which churchmen could still mold public opinion and set social standards. Segregated, politically proscribed, and economically oppressed, many Negroes could find at least some solace and encouragement in the plight of the Israelites under the yoke of Egypt or of the early Christians in the catacombs of Rome. Such analogies made sense to ante bellum Negro congregations and helped to drama-

[2] Warner, *New Haven Negroes*, pp. 92–94; Robert A. Warner, "Amos Gerry Beman — 1812–1874: A Memoir on a Forgotten Leader," *Journal of Negro History*, XXII (1937), 200–221.

tize their own everyday struggles. The minister also sought to encourage racial pride among his parishioners, telling them, for example, that "the pages of history furnish us with abundant proofs, from the achievements of our ancestors, that heaven has designed us to be an equal race." Regardless of their present situation, he told them, the Negro people should not lose hope, for they would eventually conquer the oppressor — if not in this world, then certainly in the next. "If 'he that oppresseth the poor reproacheth his maker,' " a Negro bishop declared, "how great must be the reproach cast upon the Infinite when one man oppresses another on account of the color which distinguishes him from his fellow mortals!" The Kingdom of God, in other words, had no place for racial bigots.[3]

Recognizing that moral encouragement and guidance freed few of their southern brethren, Negro ministers increasingly turned their attention to the plight of the slave and reflected the growing militancy of Negro abolitionism. Early Negro churchmen, such as Richard Allen, had urged caution, moderation, and patience. God would eventually free the bondsmen and eradicate prejudice, but, in the meantime, slaves had to be obedient and affectionate and place their trust in the Almighty; free Negroes had to show gratitude toward their former masters and not allow any past mistreatment to manifest itself in "rancour or ill-will." By 1827, however, several Negro ministers had prophesied the doom of slavery — "a hateful monster, the very demon of avarice and oppression . . . the scourge of heaven, and the curse of the earth." Twenty-one years later, the Reverend Henry H. Garnet, pastor of the Liberty Street (New York) Negro Presbyterian Church, appealed to his enslaved brethren to strike for freedom or perish. "If a band of heathen men should attempt to enslave a race of Christians, and to place their children under the influence of some false

[3] Benjamin E. Mays, *The Negro's God as Reflected in His Literature* (Boston, 1938), pp. 45, 53.

religion," he declared, "surely Heaven would frown upon the men who would not resist such aggression, even to death." [4]

Although frequently expressing an aggressive abolitionist spirit, the Negro church also exerted a conservative influence on the community. Churchmen failed to agree on the proper political and social role of their institutions; indeed, some ignored the important issues of the day and endeavored instead to inure their congregations to the bitterness of life by turning their attention to the hope of a better existence in the next world. Between 1834 and 1853, for example, many of the sermons preached in the African Protestant Episcopal Church of Philadelphia had no relation to the vital questions of that period. In fact, one minister admonished Negroes who centered their hopes "in this lower world" to place their faith in God and rejoice that the time neared "when angels at the gate of Paradise, shall hail you as an immortal born." Rather than agitate for equal rights, then, Negroes should patiently allow God to improve conditions in His way; in the meantime, they should prepare for that next world, where blacks would no longer confront the trials of an oppressed race. [5]

Many Negro ministers and laymen had little use for such admonitions, and some asked if the all-consuming fervor of religious instruction had not obscured certain basic realities. After all, God would not do for the Negro what he had to do himself. The idea that man must pray for what he received, one Negro leader contended, had long been disproved. Had not experience demonstrated that man could live on earth without any semblance of religion as long as he conformed to the physical laws? "It is only necessary," he concluded, "in order to convince our people of their error and palpable mistake in this matter, to call their attention to the fact, that there are no people more religious in this Country, than the colored people,

---

[4] *Ibid.*, pp. 34–35, 42; Carter G. Woodson (ed.), *Negro Orators and Their Orations* (Washington, D.C., 1925), pp. 64–77, 150–57.

[5] Mays, *The Negro's God*, pp. 54–56.

and none so poor and miserable as they." [6] Despite such skepticism, most Negroes appeared to maintain religious affiliations, at least for social, if not for spiritual, reasons.

In November, 1787, an incident in Philadelphia helped to launch the independent Negro church movement in the North. Two prominent Negro leaders — Richard Allen and Absalom Jones — and several of their friends entered the St. George Methodist Episcopal Church for a regular Sunday service. Large numbers of Negroes had been drawn to this church and had been permitted to occupy comfortable seats on the main floor, but the increasing popularity of St. George's finally prompted church officials to announce that henceforth Negroes would be expected to sit in the gallery. Aware of this new seating arrangement, Allen, Jones, and other Negroes took seats in the front of the gallery, overlooking the places which they had previously occupied. But the church authorities had actually reserved an even less conspicuous place for their Negro worshipers in the rear of the gallery, and they soon made this quite apparent. "We had not been long upon our knees," Allen later recalled, "before I heard considerable scuffling and low talking. I raised my head up and saw one of the trustees . . . having hold of the Reverend Absalom Jones, pulling him up off of his knees, and saying, 'You must get up — you must not kneel here.' " Jones thereupon requested that the officials wait until the prayers had been completed. When the trustees persisted, however, and threatened forcible removal, "we all went out of the Church in a body, and they were no more plagued with us." In fact, "we were filled with fresh vigor to get a house erected to worship God in." [7]

[6] Delany, *Condition, Elevation, Emigration, and Destiny of the Colored People*, pp. 37–39.

[7] Richard Allen, *Life, Experience, and Gospel Labors* (Philadelphia, 1887), pp. 14–15; William Douglass, *Annals of the First African Church in the USA, now styled the African Episcopal Church of St. Thomas, Philadelphia* (Phila-

Several other factors, including personal ambitions and growing race consciousness, contributed to the final separation, but the Philadelphia incident dramatically illustrated the plight of the Negro in the white man's church. Actually, Allen had previously favored separate facilities to accommodate the large number of Negro worshipers; however, opposition from both races had compelled him to abandon the idea. Even after the secession from St. George's, religious differences prevented any immediate organization of a new church. Instead, a group of Philadelphia Negroes, led by Allen and Jones and representing "the scattered appendages of most of the churches in the city," met on April 12, 1787, and organized the Free African Society, a mutual-aid association "without regard to religious tenets, provided the persons lived an orderly and sober life." Strict, Quaker-like practices and discipline governed the conduct of the members, and the society provided benefits for the sick and for widows and orphans, communicated with free Negroes in other cities, applied for a plot in Philadelphia's potter's field as a burial place for its members, and offered its assistance to the Pennsylvania Abolition Society for a proposed study of the free Negro population.[8]

As the movement for an independent Negro church gained momentum, the Free African Society organized a campaign to raise funds for the purchase of a church site and enlisted the assistance of several prominent whites, including Benjamin Rush, Benjamin Franklin, George Washington, and Thomas Jefferson. Local white churches, particularly the Episcopalian and Quaker, expressed grave doubts over the wisdom of the Negro move. The Episcopal bishop of Pennsylvania frankly asserted that the project "originated in pride," although, in

delphia, 1862), p. 11; Charles H. Wesley, *Richard Allen* (Washington, D.C., 1935), pp. 52–53.

[8] Wesley, *Richard Allen*, pp. 59–68; W. E. Du Bois, *The Philadelphia Negro* (Philadelphia, 1899), pp. 19–20; L. H. Butterfield (ed.), *Letters of Benjamin Rush* (2 vols.; Princeton, 1951), I, 608.

fact, white pride bore the greater responsibility for the break. Nevertheless, such opposition undoubtedly made it more diffi- cult to secure white support and funds. Most of the contri- butions, Benjamin Rush remarked, would probably have to come from Deists, "swearing captains of vessels," and Phila- delphia brokers. "The old and established societies look shy at them [the Negroes], each having lost some of its members by the new associations. To feel or to exercise the true Spirit of the Gospel nowadays seems to require a total separation from all sects, for they seem more devoted to their forms or opinions than to the doctrines and precepts of Jesus Christ." Two years after they had launched their fund-raising campaign, Phila- delphia Negroes held a dinner to celebrate the raising of the church roof. "About 100 white persons, chiefly carpenters, dined at one table," Rush recorded, "who were waited upon by Africans. Afterward about 50 black people sat down at the same table, who were waited upon by white people. Never did I see people more happy." Contributing a toast to the occasion, Rush proposed: "May African Churches everywhere soon suc- ceed African bondage." The assembled throng cheered him enthusiastically.[9]

Although Philadelphia Negroes united to erect a church building, they could not agree on the issue of religious affili- ation. Recalling the treatment accorded them by St. George Methodist Episcopal Church, most of the members of the Free African Society voted to affiliate with the Episcopalians. In accordance with this decision, Absalom Jones parted company with Richard Allen to head the first independent northern Negro church — the St. Thomas Protestant Episcopal Church of Philadelphia. Refusing to abandon his old sect, Allen then took steps to form a Methodist church, contending that its

[9] Butterfield (ed.), *Letters of Benjamin Rush*, I, 600, 602, 608, 620–21, 624, II, 636, 639; George W. Corner (ed.), *The Autobiography of Benjamin Rush* (Princeton, 1948), pp. 202–3, 228–29; Wesley, *Richard Allen*, pp. 69–71.

"plain and simple gospel" best answered the spiritual needs of
the Negro people. "All other denominations," Allen asserted,
"preached so high flown that we were not able to comprehend
their doctrine. Sure I am that reading sermons will never prove
as beneficial to the colored people as spiritual or extempore
preaching." Before the end of 1794, Bishop Frances Asbury
had dedicated the Bethel African Methodist Episcopal Church.
Justifying their separation from the whites, the Bethelites recalled that racial mixing in public assemblies, particularly
churches, had caused considerable grief. An independent
church, however, made such mixing unnecessary, provided a
convenient assembling place for Negroes, and might protect
"our weak-minded brethren . . . from the crafty wiles of the
enemy." Although admitting only descendants of the African
race to membership, the new church denied any schismatic intentions and welcomed reciprocal meetings with whites, such
as "bands, classes, and love feasts." In 1799, Bishop Asbury
ordained Allen a deacon, and the following year, the General
Conference of the Methodist Episcopal church officially indorsed the separation and agreed to the ordination of Negro
ministers.[10]

Although they were still affiliated with their white counterparts, several Negro churches moved quickly to affirm their
virtual independence in local matters. Bishop Asbury of Philadelphia noted, for example, that local Negro worshipers desired full control of temporal matters and had asked for even
greater rights and privileges than any white trustees had ever
demanded. By 1816, the Bethelites won most of their demands
for local autonomy and established a pattern followed by other
Negro denominations. In that year, Negro Methodists from
various cities gathered in Philadelphia, established the national African Methodist Episcopal church, and elected Rich-

[10] Wesley, *Richard Allen*, pp. 71–73, 90–91; Du Bois, *The Philadelphia Negro*,
pp. 21–22; *Colored American*, October 14, 1837.

ard Allen as its first bishop. Eight years later, their membership reached 9,888, including 14 elders, 26 deacons, and 101 itinerant and local licentiates, and the rapid organization of Methodists in Ohio necessitated the formation of a western conference.[11]

While Negro Methodists and Episcopalians laid the foundation for an independent northern Negro church, the Baptists took steps to effect a similar separation. On May 14, 1809, thirteen Philadelphians formed the first African Baptist church, and in that same year, the Reverend Thomas Paul organized independent Baptist churches in Boston and New York. Already active in the South, the independent Negro Baptist church attracted a large northern following and soon vied with the Methodists as the most important and powerful Negro denomination. The formation of separate groups within the other religious affiliations was much less extensive.[12]

By 1830, the Negro church movement reflected much of the chaos and multiplicity of sects that prevailed among the whites. Although the Methodists and Baptists exerted the greatest influence, Negroes could be found in almost all of the organized religions. In New York, many Negroes attended the newly established and fashionable St. Philip's Episcopal Church or the African Methodist Episcopal Zion Church, while in New Haven, middle- and upper-class Negroes crowded into Beman's prosperous and active Temple Street Congregational Church. Within those denominations which had already broken away from the whites, further splits occurred and new Negro sects emerged. Having hoped that Negroes might forego religious differences, many "friends of the colored people" soon lamented the fact that "the same causes which produced sects and dissonant creeds throughout Christendom, operated to di-

[11] Wesley, *Richard Allen*, pp. 86–91, 134–41, 150–57; Carter G. Woodson, *The History of the Negro Church* (2d ed.; Washington, D.C., 1945), pp. 65–66, 87.
[12] Woodson, *History of the Negro Church*, pp. 73–78, 81–84.

vide and subdivide the colored people." [13] Nevertheless, the
Negro church had become a reality in the North. Although it
further separated the two races, it proved to be the most dy-
namic social institution in the Negro community, affording its
members an all too rare opportunity to assemble freely, vote
for officers, and express themselves spiritually, socially, and
politically.

Apparently unmoved, if not relieved, at the loss of much of
their Negro membership, white churches continued to reflect
the popularly held prejudices of ante bellum Americans. In
white society, the church possessed great social as well as
spiritual importance. To preserve proper decorum, church
officials assigned an inconspicuous position to their colored
parishioners. When attending services, Negroes found themselves segregated, either in an "African corner," a "Nigger
Pew," seats marked "B.M." (Black Members), or aloft in
"Nigger Heaven." The Sabbath schools also provided separate
quarters for Negro and white children. Religious bodies which
offered the Lord's Supper generally compelled Negroes to wait
until the whites had partaken of the bread and wine. "Who
would have believed it?" a French traveler asked. "Ranks and
privilege in Christian churches!" [14]

The "Nigger Pew" most dramatically symbolized the Negro's inferior status in the church. Property-minded whites
generally deeded their pews on condition that no Negro be permitted to purchase them, for this would depreciate the pecuniary value of nearby pews. A Boston Negro once acquired a
white man's pew in payment of a debt, tried unsuccessfully to

[13] William R. Staples, *Annals of the Town of Providence* (Providence, 1843),
p. 490.
[14] Chambers, *American Slavery and Colour*, pp. 129–31; Duncan, *Travels
through part of the United States and Canada*, I, 332; Houstoun, *Hesperos*, I,
195; Charles Lyell, *Travels in North America, Canada, and Nova Scotia* (2d ed.;
2 vols.; London, 1855), I, 211–12; Roberts (ed.), *Moreau de St. Mery's American
Journey*, p. 302; Beaumont, *Marie*, p. 76.

sell it, and then decided to occupy it with his family. But a church committee immediately notified him that any attempt to occupy his pew might lead to disastrous consequences and that he would be well advised to confine himself to those seats reserved for Negroes in the upper gallery. Ignoring this warning, the Negro entered the church on the following Sunday, found a constable barring his way into the pew, and finally agreed not to press his property rights against such formidable opposition. In nearby Randolph, Massachusetts, a Negro won a legal suit against persons who had ejected him from his pew in the local Baptist church, but constant harassment, including the removal of his chair and a pitch-and-tar covering of his pew area, forced him to seek spiritual guidance elsewhere. Some churches protected themselves against such incidents simply by inserting into all pew deeds a restriction which confined any transfer to "respectable white persons." [15]

In their assault on northern prejudice, abolitionists singled out for particular scorn the practices of white churches. Pointing to the "obscure, remote and inconvenient boxes" reserved for colored parishioners, *The Liberator* charged that any Negro who entered such "a human menagerie" dishonored his race. Some abolitionists deliberately sat in the sections reserved for Negroes; indeed, a women's antislavery convention urged its members to sit with Negroes in segregated churches as long as such distinctions remained. When Lewis Tappan adopted this policy and also influenced a minister to distribute the sacramental bread and wine to his colored members first, he set off considerable excitement in a New York community. Public reaction finally compelled the bold minister to acknowledge before his congregation that this departure from previous custom had been "ill-timed" and should have been presented

[15] *National Anti-Slavery Standard*, December 3, 1840; *The Liberator*, November 5, 1836; Abdy, *Journal of a Residence and Tour*, I, 133–36; Charles K. Whipple, *Relations of Anti-Slavery to Religion* (Anti-Slavery Tracts No. 19, New York, n.d.), pp. 7–8; Chambers, *American Slavery and Colour*, pp. 130–31.

before the entire church for approval.[16] Elsewhere, white congregations registered similar protests against any racial mixing. In Newark, New Jersey, the introduction of a Negro into a white Presbyterian pulpit resulted in the virtual destruction of the church building; in New Rochelle, New York, a Negro minister had scarcely begun an address before a largely white audience when an unruly crowd rushed through the door, crying "Bring him out!" and forced him to flee.[17]

In the face of increasing abolitionist criticism, southern apologists had stressed the general contentment of the slave population; similarly, white church officials told their critics that segregation worked successfully and caused no great anguish among most Negro members. Irresponsible agitators had provoked much fuss and furor over an otherwise peaceful and orderly arrangement. Segregation not only preserved peace within the church but, wherever practiced, it also safeguarded the caste structure. When William Lloyd Garrison reproached a Hartford church for separating its congregation, for example, a religious journal replied that Negroes sat in "two pews in the gallery, pleasantly situated," and that any attempt to alter this arrangement obviously proposed to level all distinctions in society. Although each individual admittedly had a right to consort socially with Negroes, the journal ventured to predict that "a distinction in society, as regards the colored population of this country, will not cease during this, or the succeeding century." In the meantime, it implied, the

[16] *The Liberator*, May 21, 28, 1831; *Proceedings of the Anti-Slavery Convention of American Women* (New York, 1837), p. 17; Diary of Lewis Tappan, February 23, 1836 to August 29, 1838, Tappan Papers, Library of Congress, pp. 123–28. See also James G. Birney, *The American Churches, the Bulwarks of American Slavery* (Newburyport, Mass., 1842) ; [Harvey Newcomb], "*The Negro Pew*" (Boston, 1837) ; Davies, *American Scenes and Christian Slavery*, pp. 218–21; Chambers, *American Slavery and Colour*, pp. 129–30; Aptheker (ed.), *Documentary History*, pp. 189–91.

[17] Thomas Brothers, *The United States of North America as They Are* (London, 1840), p. 379; *The Friend of Man*, October 11, 1837.

church should carefully scrutinize public opinion before conceding any equality to its Negro worshipers.[18]

Since several denominations included Negro and white churches, both adhering to the same tenets and discipline, there soon arose disputes over what rights and privileges were to be accorded the new member bodies. The Episcopal church, where Negroes and white sympathizers fought steadily to grant affiliated Negro churches the right to send delegates to the diocesan conventions and to secure the admission of qualified Negroes into the theological seminaries, afforded a good illustration of this struggle within the national religious groups. As early as 1819, church authorities had reason to believe that the matter had been settled peacefully and permanently. The New York Diocese, apparently hoping to set a precedent for future policy, voted to admit a Negro applicant to candidacy in the Holy Orders, provided that neither he nor any congregation he might head be entitled to a seat in the diocesan convention. Episcopal Bishop John H. Hobart and the Negro applicant both accepted these conditions.[19]

Twenty-seven years later, the issue of representation again confronted the New York Diocese. In reaffirming the previous decision that no Negro congregation be granted representation, the majority report of the convention committee demonstrated the extent to which ante bellum religious leaders mirrored prevailing racial attitudes. Church administration, the committee first explained, resulted from experience, adaptation to circumstances, and expediency; these factors, in turn, determined the persons with whom white worshipers wished to associate and permit to participate in the government of the church. The plight of American Negroes, the report admitted,

[18] *The Liberator*, August 13, 1831.
[19] *Journal of the Proceedings of the Sixty-second Convention of the Protestant Episcopal Church in the Diocese of New York* (New York, 1846), pp. 75–77.

deserved sympathy, and even compassion, but this could not obscure the fact that "they *are* socially degraded, and are not regarded as proper associates for the class of persons who attend our Convention." Expediency alone made it unwise to force whites to associate on equal terms in the affairs of the diocese "with those whom they would not admit to their tables, or into their family circles — nay, whom they would not admit to their pews, during public worship." Had not the Negro himself recognized these basic differences and founded separate churches to avoid humiliation and inferiority in white congregations? "It is impossible, in the nature of things," the report stated, "that such opposites should commingle with any pleasure or satisfaction to either." The efforts of "zealous philanthropists" to defy custom and force an unnatural racial equality in the public schools had already caused dissension, conflict, and injury to those institutions; they would produce, the committee warned, similar turmoil in the church.

Although they submitted a separate report in favor of the admission of Negro delegates, even the minority members found little fault in the fundamental arguments of the majority and deprecated "most earnestly any prolonged or excited discussion of this subject." Exclusion might have been "wise and salutary" at one time, they asserted, but subsequent events cast serious doubts upon the propriety and expediency of continuing restrictions. Should the present policy be maintained, the minority members warned, Negroes might establish their own apostolic succession, form a new Episcopal church, and provoke a serious schism in the old one. Distinctions might be just and proper in ordinary society, but in the church, they should be made subservient to "self-denial, holiness, and virtue." [20]

Evading both reports, the convention tabled the matter and avoided any policy changes until the 1850's. By that time, John

[20] *Ibid.*, pp. 72–74, 76, 78–79.

Jay, grandson of the first Chief Justice and a frequent delegate to the diocesan convention, had launched a persistent campaign to revoke the ban on Negro representation, calling it a violation of constitutional rights, catholic unity, apostolic precedent, and Christian brotherhood. In 1853, after a seven-year battle, Jay scored a significant triumph as the Episcopal Convention voted to admit representatives from St. Philip's Episcopal Church, a Negro congregation in New York. "Another Revolution," one prominent New Yorker recorded with dismay, "John Jay's annual motion carried at last, and the nigger delegation admitted into the Diocesan Convention." [21]

In Philadelphia, the St. Thomas African Episcopal Church met with similar difficulties in its efforts to secure representation in the Pennsylvania Diocese. The Convention had voted in 1795 that the newly established Negro church could not send a clergyman or deputies to the annual meetings or interfere in any way with church government. When the question again arose in 1842, the Convention sustained its previous ruling and extended it to other Negro churches in the diocese. Fear of racial mixing even prompted Pennsylvania Episcopalians to refuse representation to Philadelphia's Church of the Crucifixion, which was composed of a Negro congregation and a white vestry and pastor, on grounds that it might conceivably decide to elect Negro delegates to the diocesan meetings. [22]

The Episcopal church, unlike certain other denominations, extended its proscriptive practices to the theological seminaries. In 1836, for example, Isiah D. DeGrasse applied for

[21] *The Thirteenth Annual Report of the American and Foreign Anti-Slavery Society* (New York, 1853), pp. 90–93; Allan Nevins and Milton H. Thomas (eds.), *The Diary of George Templeton Strong* (4 vols.; New York, 1952), II, 131.

[22] Jay, *Miscellaneous Writings on Slavery*, pp. 445–47; Pennsylvania Anti-Slavery Society, *Thirteenth Annual Report* (Philadelphia, 1850), pp. 29–30, and *Fifteenth Annual Report* (Philadelphia, 1852), pp. 32–34; American and Foreign Anti-Slavery Society, *Eleventh Annual Report* (New York, 1851), p. 90, and *Thirteenth Annual Report*, p. 153.

admission into the General Theological Seminary of the Protestant Episcopal Church of New York, selected a room in the dormitory, and prepared to take the entrance examinations. Bishop Benjamin T. Onderdonk of the New York Diocese thereupon informed the Negro applicant that his attempt to enter and live in the school had provoked a great deal of opposition. "There were fears," DeGrasse wrote, "that my presence there as a regular inmate, and especially my eating in common with the *pious* students, would give rise to much dissatisfaction and bad feeling among them." Since the seminary depended on southern students for much of its support, the admission of Negroes "might deprive them of their present pecuniary benefits and prevent Southern gentlemen from connecting themselves with this School of Divinity." Moreover, in the present state of tension, many feared that the mixing of Negroes and whites actually jeopardized the school buildings and the personal safety of their occupants.

In a "compromise" move, Bishop Onderdonk indicated his willingness to permit DeGrasse to continue to attend classes, provided he vacate his room and neither apply for formal admission nor consider himself a regular member of the school. "Never, never will I do so!" DeGrasse wrote in his diary that night. Declining the Bishop's offer, he called it "utterly repugnant" to his feelings as a man and too great a sacrifice of principle. Once DeGrasse had made his decision to leave, the Bishop made no move to dissuade him; instead, he welcomed it as serving the best interests of the seminary and the ultimate good of both races. "This day," the rejected applicant concluded, "I am driven in the presence of the students of the Seminary, and the sight of high Heaven, from the School of the Prophets." [23] Other Negro seminary candidates faced similar obstacles, despite the vigorous protests of John Jay that this

[23] [John Jay], *Caste and Slavery in the American Church* (New York, 1843), pp. 14–17; Barnes and Dumond (eds.), *Weld-Grimke Correspondence*, I, 445–46.

constituted "a new principle, a new doctrine, a new order in the Church." [24]

In a move to preserve religious unity and eradicate any disruptive influences, New York Episcopal authorities attempted to silence antislavery agitation by Negro ministers. On July 12, 1834, Bishop Onderdonk strongly urged the Reverend Peter Williams of St. Philip's Episcopal Church in New York City publicly to resign from the American Anti-Slavery Society. The Church had to avoid such controversial issues, the Bishop wrote, and maintain itself "on the Christian side of meekness, order, and self-sacrifice to common good, and the peace of the community." In an open letter to the citizens of New York, Williams reviewed his contributions to the struggle for Negro rights, admitted past association with abolitionists in educational endeavors, but maintained that he had declined serving on their executive committee or attending their conventions. After confessing the extent of his political sins, Mr. Williams announced his resignation from the American Anti-Slavery Society. Nevertheless, he concluded, the abolitionists were still "good men, and good Christians, and true lovers of their country, and of all mankind," although, unfortunately, they attempted to advance Negroes "faster than they were prepared to be advanced" or further than public opinion would countenance. [25]

The Episcopal church actually attracted relatively few Negroes, but its discriminatory racial policy demonstrated the extent to which prejudice could invade the citadels of organized religion. Such attitudes, however, were not universal; indeed, they often differed with each congregation, diocese, and denomination. Although refused admission to the General Theological Seminary, for example, one Negro applicant—

[24] Jay, *Caste and Slavery in the American Church*, pp. 6–9, 12, and *Miscellaneous Writings on Slavery*, pp. 442–46.
[25] Woodson (ed.), *Mind of the Negro*, pp. 629–34.

Alexander Crummell — secured ordination in the Massachusetts Diocese. The Presbyterians, in the meantime, admitted
Negro churches to their presbyteries and synods and apparently practiced no racial discrimination at Union Theological Seminary. When public indignation forced two Negro
delegates to the Pennsylvania Presbyterian Synod to leave
town, that body immediately protested the incident and affirmed the right of Negroes to sit in their conventions on an
equal basis with whites.[26] The Catholic church impressed several observers, since it extended equal privileges to Negroes
and permitted no segregated seating arrangements.[27] Consistency was difficult to find, however, even among such staunch
advocates of Negro rights as the Quakers.

Among the various organized religions, none had been more
vigorous in its antislavery efforts than the Society of Friends.
By 1800, the Quakers had abolished slaveholding among their
members and had taken steps to improve the economic and
educational level of free Negroes. Co-operating with the early
antislavery societies, the Quakers adopted a moderate approach, appealed to the moral judgment of slaveholders, and
urged Negroes to be patient and industrious. With the advent
of a more aggressive abolitionism in the 1830's, however,
Quakers were advised to dissociate themselves from the anti-
slavery societies and adopt more gradual and less conspicuous
methods.[28] Garrisonian abolitionism alarmed many of the
more moderate Friends and helped to explain their disincli-
nation to co-operate with the new movement, but the force of
public opinion also had its effect. "Friends have been exposed

---

[26] Jay, *Miscellaneous Writings on Slavery*, p. 450.

[27] *Frederick Douglass' Paper*, February 5, 1852; Woodson (ed.), *Mind of the Negro*, p. 278; Thomas L. Nichols, *Forty Years of American Life* (London, 1874), p. 369; Beaumont, *Marie*, pp. 76–77. An early French traveler noted, however, that Philadelphia's Irish Catholic Church refused to bury Negroes in its cemetery. Roberts (ed.), *Moreau de St. Mery's American Journey*, p. 302.

[28] Drake, *Quakers and Slavery*, pp. 114–200.

to the influences of a corrupt public sentiment," an English
Quaker reported after a trip to the United States in 1841.
"They have, to a considerable extent, imbibed the prejudice
against colour, while some of them have been caught by the
gilded bait of southern commerce." [29]

As early as the 1780's, the question of Negro membership
provoked much discussion and excitement among the Quakers.
In the absence of any clearly formulated policy, the Philadelphia Yearly Meeting agreed in 1783 that the application of a
woman of white, Indian, and Negro origin might be "safely"
considered on an equal basis with other membership applications. The Society subsequently admitted the candidate. Twelve
years later, a Philadelphia Friend expressed great concern
over those of his brethren who argued that popularly held prejudices made it inexpedient to admit Negroes under any circumstances. But such concern appeared to be premature. Making
even more explicit its previous position, the Philadelphia
Yearly Meeting resolved in 1796 that prospective members
should be admitted on the basis of "their views and practices"
and "without respect of persons or colour." [30]

Although this decision became a part of the Friends' Book
of Discipline, it failed to settle the question permanently. After
the 1830's, for example, several abolitionists publicly charged
that Friends deliberately excluded Negroes from membership.
"I do not think the present generation have or would receive
a coloured member," Sarah Grimke wrote in 1840. "I have
heard it assigned as a reason that of course no white member
would marry them and then if they infringed the Discipline
they must be disowned." Arnold Buffum, a Garrisonian abo-

[29] Sturge, *A Visit to the United States in 1841*, p. 128. See also Elizabeth B.
Chace and Lucy B. Lovell, *Two Quaker Sisters* (New York, 1937), pp. 115–16.
[30] Henry J. Cadbury, "Negro Membership in the Society of Friends," *Journal
of Negro History*, XXI (1936), 170–74; Thomas E. Drake, "Joseph Drinker's
Plea for the Admission of Colored People to the Society of Friends, 1795," *ibid.*,
XXXII (1947), 110–12.

litionist and Rhode Island Quaker, claimed that Negroes had made a number of membership applications but that none had been accepted.[31] On the other hand, Quaker officials denied these charges and pointed to meetings where Negroes had been admitted. After an intensive study of this question, a contemporary Quaker historian has concluded that the Society probably excluded few, if any, Negroes on specifically racial grounds but instead discouraged colored applicants, postponed consideration, or cited other reasons for rejection.[32]

Although scholarly disagreement concerning the question of Negro membership still prevails, overwhelming evidence points to the segregation of Negroes and whites in many Quaker meeting halls. As early as 1756, plans to extend Philadelphia's "Great Meeting House" provided "suitable places" for Negroes. Several foreign visitors later expressed their astonishment at finding separate seats for Negroes in a religious body that had been noted for its antislavery efforts and educational facilities for free blacks. The rules of discipline ostensibly forbade "such unchristian distinctions," Edward Abdy remarked; nevertheless, Negroes "are reminded, even in the Quaker meeting-houses, of the mark which has been set upon them, as if they were the children of Cain." Reporting on a visit to the United States in 1841, Joseph Sturge, an English Quaker, told of visiting a New Bedford meeting and finding both races "sitting promiscuously." But this, he added, had been the only racial mixing he had seen, for, ordinarily, Negroes rarely attended Quaker meetings.[33]

Concerned over the conduct of her American brethren, Eliz-

[31] Barnes and Dumond (eds.), *Weld-Grimke Correspondence*, II, 829; Cadbury, "Negro Membership in the Society of Friends," pp. 178–81.
[32] Cadbury, "Negro Membership in the Society of Friends," p. 183.
[33] *Ibid.*, p. 168; Abdy, *Journal of a Residence and Tour*, III, 189; Edward S. Abdy to Maria (Weston) Chapman, May 24, 1844, Weston Papers; Sturge, *A Visit to the United States in 1841*, p. 100. See also James Flint, *Letters from America* (Edinburgh, 1822), p. 37, and Roberts (ed.), *Moreau de St. Mery's American Journey*, p. 302.

abeth Pease, an English Friend and a frequent correspondent of American abolitionists, resolved to collect and publish pertinent material on the Quakers and the Negro. Complying with a request for such information, Sarah M. Douglass, a Philadelphia Negro schoolteacher and an inactive Friend, asserted that years of experience had convinced her of the existence of separate Negro benches in the Arch Street meeting hall. Not only had she been consigned to such a bench with her mother, but a Friend had sat at each end of the bench to prevent whites from mistakenly taking seats there. As a child, Miss Douglass recalled "hearing five or six times during the course of one meeting this language of remonstrance addressed to those who were willing to sit by us, 'This bench is for the black people,' 'This bench is for the people of color.' And oftentimes I wept, at other times I felt indignant and queried in my own mind are these people Christians." Although Miss Douglass no longer attended meetings, her mother still went, and often "has a *whole long bench* to herself." After citing other examples of such segregation, the Negro schoolmistress concluded that little evidence pointed to any diminution of racial prejudice among the Friends. "I have heard it frequently remarked and have observed it myself, that in proportion as we become intellectual and respectable, so in proportion does their disgust and prejudice increase." Additional testimony from other sources told much the same story — separate benches, separate schools, and membership restrictions. Upon compiling and publishing these observations, Miss Pease expressed her grief that American Friends were "falling from the noble position wh[ich] they once held and deviating from the principles and spirit — they profess." [34]

[34] Sarah M. Douglass to William Bassett, December, 1839, in Sarah M. Grimke to Elizabeth Pease, April 16, 1840, and Bassett to Pease, August 3, 1839, Garrison Papers. (These letters comprised the major portion of [Elizabeth Pease], *Society of Friends in the United States: Their Views of the Anti-Slavery Question and Treatment of the People of Colour* [Darlington, 1840].) See also Barnes and

Foreign criticism, much of it abolitionist inspired, caused few immediate changes in Quaker policy. Like other denominations, the Society of Friends simply found it difficult to inure itself against the force of public sentiment, and this proved much stronger than the sting of an occasional English critic. Some Friends, perhaps in desperation, turned to the American Colonization Society for a permanent solution to the problem of race relations. Others maintained their efforts to improve Negro educational and moral standards, refrained from any undue defiance of the social code, and perhaps comforted themselves with the more favorable judgments of some of their English co-religionists. On the eve of the Civil War, one such sympathetic observer, William Tallack, warned his English brethren not to be too harsh with the conduct of American Friends and not to judge American Negroes by the few respectable ones sent to Great Britain as lecturers. Indeed, American Quakers should be commended for their efforts to improve the general condition of a depraved race, but such assistance, Tallack maintained, should not require the Friends "to depart from the ordinary customs of white society in respect to non-intimacy with the colored race." Until the now unpleasant habits of that race improved considerably, the relative social condition of blacks and whites would remain unaltered. Englishmen, Tallack concluded, should think twice before prating about the shameful conduct of Americans, "for it is pretty certain that if we were in their place our policy would not be very different." [35]

While maintaining separate and independent churches, Negro leaders persistently assailed the proslavery and caste nature of white religious bodies. Churches which sanctioned

Dumond (eds.), *Weld-Grimke Correspondence*, II, 744, 756, 829, 855; Pease to Jane Smeal, March 3, 1840, Pease to Maria (Weston) Chapman, April 23–25, 1840, Garrison and Weston Papers.

[35] William Tallack, *Friendly Sketches in America* (London, 1861), pp. 231–32.

209

racial distinctions, they charged, violated the true spirit of Christianity. How could such institutions propagate the teachings of Jesus Christ and ignore, or even countenance, the ruthless suppression of a human race? How could they send missionaries to convert heathens in other parts of the globe when "there are not a more wretched, ignorant, miserable, and abject set of beings in all the world, than the blacks in the Southern and Western sections of this country"? Those religious sects which tolerated such degradation, a Negro convention concluded, were "nothing more than synagogues of Satan."[36]

Until the white churches should purge themselves of these sins, Negro leaders urged their people to boycott such institutions. Some adopted this advice without any prompting. Attending a Methodist service in New Bedford, Frederick Douglass found himself placed in a separate seat and saw his brethren stand meekly aside as the whites attended the Lord's Supper. The pastor then called upon his "colored friends" to come forward, declaring, "You, too, have an interest in the blood of Christ. God is no respecter of persons." By this time, Douglass had had enough. "The colored members — poor, slavish souls — went forward as invited. I went out, and have never been in that church since." Apparently, few Negroes reacted so dramatically. "It is with pain and anguish of soul," the Colored American complained, "that we have seen the southern tier of pews, in Broadway Tabernacle, crowded with our colored brethren. We should rather worship God at our own churches or in our own houses, than to occupy proscribed seats in any other churches." How, the newspaper asked, could Negroes regard as a brother any man who oppressed them in the very house of God? Moreover, why should Negroes sanction their own degradation? If Negroes had to go to white churches,

[36] Woodson (ed.), *Mind of the Negro*, pp. 490–94; Walker, *Walker's Appeal*, pp. 45–46; *National Colored Convention, Troy, 1847*, p. 16.

they should at least scatter into several churches throughout
the city and dramatize their protest by avoiding the segregated
pews. "Stand in the aisles, and rather worship God upon your
feet, than become a party to your own degradation. You must
shame your oppressors, and wear out prejudice by this holy
policy." [37]

Devoting considerable attention to the practices of white
Christians, the Negro convention movement registered some
violent protests against segregated seating and proslavery ministers. Samuel Davis of Buffalo set the tenor of such protests
in his welcoming address to the 1843 convention: "Behold her
gigantic form, with hands upraised to heaven! See her increased and made rich by the toil, and sweat, and blood of
slaves! View her arrayed in her pontifical robes, screening
the horrid monster, slavery, with her very bosom — within her
most sacred enclosures; that the world may not gaze on its
distorted visage, or view its hellish form!" After this keynote
speech, the convention delegates agreed that any "true Church
of Christ" opposed the sin of slavery, that most American
sects practiced prejudice and ignored human bondage, and that
the ministers of such sects constituted "the greatest enemies to
Christ and to civil and religious liberty." In an appeal to American Negroes, the convention urged a mass exodus from any
church — white or black — which refused to pray for the oppressed slaves, denied its facilities for antislavery meetings, or
maintained any racial distinctions. Several delegates objected
to withdrawal from discriminatory churches, maintaining that
antislavery sentiment had increased in recent years and that
such a move would alienate sympathetic whites and curtail
growing demands for reform. But the advocates of a more
aggressive policy replied that the leading ecclesiastical establishments had so wedded themselves to public opinion and

[37] Frederick Douglass, *My Bondage and My Freedom* (New York, 1855), pp.
350–53; *Colored American*, August 19, 1837.

popularity-seeking that no Negro could in good conscience retain his membership in them. Most of the delegates indorsed this position and concluded that divine worship in one's own house was preferable to continued fellowship with hypocritical Christians.[38]

While concentrating their attack on the white churches, Negro leaders also recognized some serious deficiencies within their own religious community. Several colored churches had maintained a policy of discreet silence or apathy on the issues of slavery agitation and equal rights. What was perhaps even more reprehensible, some had adopted an obsequious attitude in order to win public approval and acceptance. In Cincinnati, for example, members of the Negro Methodist Episcopal church refused in 1829 to join in an appeal to the legislature for abrogation of the Black Laws but asked instead for "a continuation of the smiles of the white people as we have hitherto enjoyed them."[39] To Negro abolitionists, this must have been true heresy. When the Negro Methodist Conference failed to act against slavery, an Ohio convention charged that the church deliberately sanctioned the institution so that it might extend its influence into the South and reap religious tithes from the unfortunate bondsmen. If such criticism were unwarranted, the convention ventured, then Negro Methodists should clarify their position on slavery and explain why their newspaper refused to publish any discussion of the subject. Subsequently, another Ohio meeting resolved that any Negro church which refused to agitate against slavery deserved "the disfellowship of all good men."[40]

Reflecting this impatience with certain Negro churches, as well as the growing attack on segregated schools, several Negro leaders began to regret the establishment of separate

[38] *National Colored Convention, Buffalo, 1843*, pp. 6, 11, 14–15.
[39] Sheeler, "The Struggle of the Negro in Ohio for Freedom," p. 212.
[40] *Minutes of the State Convention of the Colored Citizens of Ohio* (Columbus, 1850), p. 19; *Ohio Colored Convention of 1852*, p. 11.

religious bodies. Such institutions, they contended, helped to maintain prejudice and Christian caste and served as a constant reminder of the Negro's inferiority. "We regret that there ever was a separate church or any kind of separate institution built for colored people," the *Colored American* asserted in 1837, for they "have contributed more largely to the persecution, and neglect of our colored population, than all the politics of the land." Indorsing this sentiment, the Moral Reform Society — an otherwise frequent critic of the *Colored American* — resolved that separate churches fostered prejudice and insulted the true spirit of reform. Since both races acknowledged the same God and expected to find the same hereafter, why should they not associate in Christian fellowship? [41]

Joining the opposition to separate churches, Frederick Douglass' *North Star* castigated them as *"negro pews, on a higher and larger scale,"* differing only in location and dimension but equally obnoxious. After all, it asked, had not the Negro pew been designed on the grounds that colored people were offensive to whites and should therefore be separated from them? Did not Negro churches merely extend that separation and thus justify those grounds? Enemies of the Negro, Douglass charged, had long sought to separate the two races, either through African colonization or by means of separate schools, churches, temperance societies, and social clubs. Although enormous grievances and insults had at first justified ecclesiastical independence, separate churches now served to impede the progress of the Negro people and to countenance their segregation in other fields. "If there be any good reason for a colored church," Douglass asserted, "the same will hold good in regard to a colored school, and indeed to every other institution founded on complexion. Negro pews in the church; negro boxes in the theatre; negro cars on the railroad; negro berths in the steamboat. . . ."

[41] *Colored Americans*, April 22, 29, 1837; Nell, *Colored Patriots*, p. 355.

Douglass also contended that separate churches resulted in inferior religious instruction, for many Negro ministers lacked those mental qualifications necessary for the proper training of their congregations. The existence of so many of these "would be ministers," some of them unable to write their own names, accounted in large measure for "the ignorance and mental inactivity, and general want of enterprise among us as a class." Now was the time, Douglass concluded, for Negroes to demand equal rights in all institutions. Why not follow the example of those New England Negroes who refused to sit in Jim Crow railroad cars, even if it meant being dragged from the train? Such resistance had contributed mightily to the abolition of discriminatory cars in New England; it could also end racial distinctions in the church. On the next Sabbath, every Negro should abandon his colored church, enter the white institutions, and demand his equal rights. "Colored members should go in and take seats, without regard to their complexion, and allow themselves to be dragged out by the ministers, elders, and deacons. Such a course would very soon settle the question, and in the right way."[42]

Such militancy apparently did not go beyond the confines of Frederick Douglass' newspaper. Some Negroes, such as Henry Bibb, quickly commended Douglass for questioning the validity of separate churches. "I see no more use in having a colored church exclusively," Bibb wrote, "than having a colored heaven and a colored God."[43] Nevertheless, this criticism had few visible effects on the general development of the Negro church. On the eve of the Civil War, its growing numerical and financial strength easily made it the very bulwark and center of the Negro community.

[42] *North Star*, February 25, March 3, 10, 1848.
[43] *Ibid.*, April 7, 1848.

VII

Abolitionism:
White and
Black

On January 6, 1832, twelve white men gathered in a school-room under Boston's African Baptist Church and dedicated a new organization — the New-England Anti-Slavery Society — to the cause of immediate abolition and the improvement of the political and economic position of northern Negroes. One member of this group, William Lloyd Garrison, had already gained considerable notice through his editorship of *The Liberator*; now he moved to organize the antislavery sentiment aroused by his scathing denunciations of the sins of southern bondage and northern prejudice. "We have met tonight in this obscure school-house," he remarked. "Our numbers are few and our influence limited; but, mark my prediction, Faneuil Hall shall ere long echo with the principles we have set forth. We shall shake the nation by their mighty power."[1]

[1] Francis and Wendell P. Garrison, *William Lloyd Garrison*, I, 279–80; *The Liberator*, February 18, 1832.

Although the antislavery movement eventually divided into
several factions, abolitionists generally agreed that slaves and
free Negroes shared a similar plight. Consistency demanded
that they move against both northern and southern abuses of
the Negro population. Had not slaveholders and their spokesmen continually defended the "peculiar institution" on the
grounds that Negroes were unfit to enjoy the rights and privileges exercised by whites? Had they not pointed to northern
treatment of the Negro as substantial proof of the benevolence
of slavery and the hypocrisy of antislavery arguments? The
debasement of northern Negroes, abolitionist Gerrit Smith
charged, "gives the greatest efficiency to the main argument for
justifying slavery." As long as northern laws, institutions, and
customs rendered "the freedom of the colored people but an
empty name — but the debasing mockery of true freedom,"
how could the antislavery movement condemn racial oppression in the South?[2] Abolitionists, in short, had to strike at the
roots of slavery, show the Negro's capacity for self-improve-
ment, and demonstrate the sincerity of their own professed
sympathy for the Negro's plight. In no other way, agreed James
Russell Lowell, could abolitionists more effectively serve
"their holy cause."[3]

Improving the condition of northern Negroes thus formed
an integral part of the antislavery movement. In the first issue
of *The Liberator*, William Lloyd Garrison advised his "free
colored brethren" that the struggle for equal rights in the
North constituted "a leading object" of abolitionism.[4] By

[2] Gerrit Smith, *Letter . . . to Hon. Julian C. Verplanck* (Whitesboro, New
York, n.d.), p. 5. See also *Human Rights*, February, 1837; *Second Annual Report
of the American Anti-Slavery Society* (New York, 1835), pp. 6, 68–69; *Proceedings
of the First Annual Meeting of the New York State Anti-Slavery Society* (Utica,
1836), p. 57; Sophia Davenport to Anne Warren Weston, June 30, 1838, Weston
Papers.
[3] James Russell Lowell, *The Anti-Slavery Papers of James Russell Lowell* (2
vols.; Boston and New York, 1902), I, 22.
[4] *The Liberator*, January 1, 1831.

1860, antislavery societies could point to some notable victories. What made them especially remarkable was the fact that abolitionists scored these successes in the face of powerful public hostility and in spite of dissension and racial prejudice within the antislavery movement itself.

Although they deplored racial prejudice and indorsed the Negro's claim to full citizenship, white abolitionists were divided over the question of social intercourse with their Negro brethren. Since racial mixing flouted the prevailing social code and might easily precipitate mob action, antislavery advocates faced a real dilemma. If an abolitionist fought for equal rights, some argued, it did not necessarily follow that he also had to consort with Negroes socially. Indeed, such an act might endanger the effectiveness and success of the antislavery cause. "May we not find it more efficient to go for their improvement in . . . civil privileges," James Birney asked, "leaving their introduction to *social* privileges out of the public discussion? Would it not be better to leave this matter rather more at rest for the present time than to press it upon the whole community? May not urging it *now* be throwing too much in our way the prejudice against it, and defeat the elevation of the Col'd people to civil privileges?"[5]

Although several Negroes actively participated in the organization and activities of the antislavery societies, white abolitionists continued to disagree on the expediency of Negro membership and social relations. In 1835, for example, William Lloyd Garrison found it necessary to criticize William Ellery Channing, an antislavery sympathizer, for expressing the belief that "we ought never to have permitted our colored brethren to unite with us in our associations."[6] The following

[5] Barnes and Dumond (eds.), *Weld-Grimke Correspondence*, I, 163.
[6] William Lloyd Garrison to Lewis Tappan, December 16, 1835, quoted in Charles H. Wesley, "The Negro's Struggle for Freedom in its Birthplace," *Journal of Negro History*, XXX (1945), 74.

year, Charles Follen admitted before the Massachusetts Anti-Slavery Society that abolitionists had been advised "not unnecessarily to shock the feelings, though they were but prejudices, of the white people, by admitting colored persons to our Anti-Slavery meetings and societies. We have been told that many who would otherwise act in union with us, were kept away by our disregard of the feelings of the community in this respect." Such advice, Follen added, posed serious dangers for the antislavery forces. Excluding Negroes would not only deprive the movement of some effective workers, but it would also comply with "inhuman prejudice," sanction the principle of slavery, and "give the lie to our own most solemn professions." Although abolitionists ought to select their social friends according to their own principles, "how can we have the effrontery to expect the white slaveholders of the South to live on terms of civil equality with his colored slave, if we, the white abolitionists of the North, will not admit colored freemen as members of our Anti-Slavery Societies?" [7]

Such liberal sentiments did not always prevail. When abolitionist leaders met in New York on March 9, 1836, to arrange a program for the anniversary meeting of the American Anti-Slavery Society, Lewis Tappan proposed that a Negro minister be invited to deliver one of the addresses. Considerable opposition thwarted such a bold plan. "This is a ticklish point," Tappan wrote that night. "I insisted upon it as we must act out our principles, but it was said the time has not come to mix with people of color in public. So to prevent disunion I submitted." One month later, an even more heated discussion occurred at a meeting of the executive committee of the American Anti-Slavery Society, and one member threatened to resign if "true abolitionism" required social intercourse between Negroes and whites. "I have observed," Tappan wrote after the meeting,

[7] *Fourth Annual Report of the Board of Managers of the Massachusetts Anti-Slavery Society*, p. 50.

"that when the subject of acting out our profound principles in treating men irrespective of color is discussed heat is always produced. I anticipate that the battle is to be fought here, and if ever there is a split in our ranks it will arise from collision on this point." [8]

The meetings of a Philadelphia antislavery society vividly demonstrated abolitionist concern with the questions of Negro membership and social intercourse. Organized in 1836, this society dedicated itself to arrest the progress of slavery and to strive for eventual abolition. One year after its formation, however, the organization found itself spending five sessions to discuss the question "Is it expedient for colored persons to join our Anti-Slavery Societies?" After hearing speakers on both sides, the members finally decided in the affirmative by a margin of two votes. Subsequent meetings discussed such questions as "Ought Abolitionists to encourage colored persons in joining Anti-Slavery Societies?" and "Is it expedient for Abolitionists to encourage social intercourse between white and colored families?" While resolving at its 1837 quarterly meeting to remove public prejudice and encourage the intellectual, moral, and religious improvement of Negroes, the society's members debated — and eventually tabled — a resolution which declared that social intercourse with Negroes would strengthen the bitterness of public prejudice, retard the acquisition of civil and religious privileges, and fasten the chains of bondage even tighter. Instead, the convention resolved that it was neither "our object, or duty, to encourage social intercourse between colored and white families" but agreed, by a narrow margin, that it would be expedient to accept Negroes as members of antislavery societies.[9]

[8] Diary of Lewis Tappan, February 23, 1836 to August 29, 1838, Tappan Papers, Library of Congress; Barnes and Dumond (eds.), *Weld-Grimke Correspondence*, I, 276–77.
[9] Minutes of the Junior Anti-Slavery Society of Philadelphia, 1836–1846, Historical Society of Pennsylvania.

Such problems apparently troubled foreign as well as American antislavery societies. Edward Abdy, a staunch English abolitionist who visited the United States in the years 1833–34, later wrote to an American friend: "We cannot, I am ashamed to say, claim exemption from the prejudice of color. . . . De Beaumont, when asked why Bisette was not a member of the Committee of the French abolition society replied — Why! he is a colored man! Here we have a religious man and a liberal expressing sentiments opposed to every rational idea of what we owe to God and humanity. Thus it is that Benevolence is employed to foster Pride — we humiliate while we relieve. . . . It really seems as if many considered an African . . . as entitled to the same sort of sympathy and subscribed to the anti-slavery society as they subscribe to the society for the prevention of cruelty to animals." [10]

While abolitionists searched their consciences for a way out of these perplexing problems, Lewis Tappan engaged in a bitter controversy with revivalist leader and antislavery sympathizer Charles G. Finney over the wisdom of mixing Negroes and whites in public functions. When, for example, Negro and white choirs shared the same platform at the first-anniversary meeting of the American Anti-Slavery Society in May, 1835, certain abolitionist sympathizers, including Finney, intimated that such intercourse had helped to provoke the July anti-Negro riots in New York City. But "the choirs sat separately in the orchestra," Tappan explained, "the whites on one side and the colored on the other!" Having "been cruelly *slandered* about attempts to mix black and white people," Tappan asserted that the seating of the two choirs was "the only attempt I ever made to mix up the two colors in any public assembly or elsewhere," and "this I did by order of a committee of which I was chairman." Tappan admitted, however, that he had once dined with

[10] Edward S. Abdy to Maria (Weston) Chapman, May 24, 1844, Weston Papers.

two Negro members of the executive committee of the American Anti-Slavery Society and occasionally with "a few colored 'gentlemen,'" but this constituted "the [head] and front of my offending. . . . And yet many abolitionists have talked about efforts at amalgamation, etc." [11]

Acting as an intermediary in the Tappan-Finney dispute, Theodore Weld, the leading western abolitionist, expressed his own views on the delicate subject of social intercourse. "Take *more pains* to treat with attention, courtesy, and cordiality a colored person than a white," Weld advised Tappan, "from the *fact* that he *is* colored." But in mixing the two races on a social basis, abolitionists should first ask whether its effect on the general public would be "a *blessing* or a *curse* to the Colored people." Weld felt that his own feelings toward Negroes had been sufficiently demonstrated by his actions while attending Lane Seminary in Cincinnati. "If I attended parties," he declared, "it was *theirs—weddings—theirs—Funerals—theirs — Religious meetings — theirs —* Sabbath schools — Bible classes — theirs." But this did not oblige him, Weld quickly added, to walk arm in arm with a Negro woman at midday down the main street of Cincinnati. Such an act "would bring down a storm of vengeance upon the defenceless people of Color, throw them out of employ, drive them out homeless, and surrender them up victims of popular fury"; indeed, such "an ostentatious display of superiority to prejudice and a *blistering bravado defiance*" would misconstrue the true motives and objectives of abolitionists and turn public attention from their major goal — the destruction of slavery — to a "collateral" point. Although it would be sinful to manifest any unkindness toward Negroes, abolitionists had to realize, Weld concluded, that "there are times when we *may refrain* from making *public visible demonstrations* of feelings about differences of color in

[11] Barnes and Dumond (eds.), *Weld-Grimke Correspondence*, I, 275–76.

practical exhibitions, when such demonstrations would bring down persecutions on them." [12]

Charges of racial mixing also deeply annoyed Arthur Tappan. Defending his conduct as late as 1863, the New York abolitionist leader and philanthropist wrote to an English friend regarding his past views and actions. Although Christian conduct had bound him to treat Negroes without respect to color, Tappan explained that he had always felt that public sentiment on the subject required "great prudence" on the part of abolitionists. He had consistently shown his willingness "*publicly*" to associate with "a well educated and refined colored person," but he considered it best to refrain from social intercourse until "the public mind and conscience were more enlightened on the subject." It was thus a "malignant falsehood" to accuse him of "any gross assault on the fastidiousness of the age." With regard to the charges that he or any member of his family "have ever put arms into hands of colored men or women in New York or anywhere else, it is without the slightest foundation." [13]

The problems of Negro membership and social intercourse aroused considerable discussion among women's antislavery organizations. When two Quaker women formed the Female Anti-Slavery Society in Fall River, Massachusetts, and invited several interested Negroes to join, it "raised such a storm among some of the leading members that for a time, it threatened the dissolution of the Society." Although the opposition denied any objections to Negroes' attending their meetings, they considered it improper to invite them to become members of the Society, "thus putting them on an equality with ourselves." [14] The Fall River group finally decided in favor of admission, but "wicked prejudices about colour" barred Negroes from membership in the New York women's anti-slavery

[12] *Ibid.*, I, 270, 272–74.
[13] Lewis Tappan, *The Life of Arthur Tappan* (New York, 1870), pp. 201–2.
[14] Chace and Lovell, *Two Quaker Sisters*, pp. 119–20.

society. [15] Delegates to the national convention of antislavery women approved, although not unanimously, a resolution by Sarah M. Grimke calling upon abolitionists to associate with their oppressed brethren, to sit with them in churches, to appear with them on the streets, to grant them equal rights in steamboats and stagecoaches, and to visit them in their homes and receive them "as we do our white fellow citizens." Less than a month after the convention, two Philadelphia abolitionists wrote that the recently passed resolution "greatly alarmed" some of "our timid friends" who unsuccessfully attempted to expunge it from the published convention report. Not content with this setback, these "pseudo-abolitionists" endeavored to induce leading Philadelphia Negroes to deny publicly any desire to mix socially with whites; only such a disavowal, they warned, would avert "destruction and bloodshed." [16] In Cincinnati, several of the women teachers at the Negro school complained to Theodore Weld that some "half-hearted" abolitionist co-workers expressed alarm "if perchance we lay our hands on a curly head, or kiss a coloured face." Since such actions seemed to "offend their nice taste," it became increasingly difficult to work with these prejudiced women in the company of Negroes. "Dear Br[other]," they pleaded, "do pray the Lord to send us co-workers instead of anti-workers." [17]

Regardless of public opposition and personal doubts, some abolitionists considered social intercourse with Negroes a demonstration of true devotion to the cause of their oppressed brethren. Although conceding that one could advocate "the

[15] Anne Warren Weston to Deborah Weston, October 22, 1836, Weston Papers. "Every body has their own troubles and the New York brethren have theirs. Mrs. Cox is the life and soul of the New York Society and she is in a very sinful state of wicked prejudices about colour; they do not allow any coloured woman to join their society. . . . The Tappans have none of this prejudice therefore they and Mrs. Cox are hardly on speaking terms."

[16] *Proceedings of the Anti-Slavery Convention of American Women* (Philadelphia, 1838), p. 8; James and Lucretia Mott to Anne Warren Weston, June 7, 1838, Weston Papers.

[17] Barnes and Dumond (eds.), *Weld-Grimke Correspondence*, I, 217.

civil emancipation of those whom he would still be unwilling to associate with," the American Anti-Slavery Society reprimanded its members for yielding too readily to prejudice. If color or public opinion alone explained an abolitionist's reluctance to associate with Negroes, then "he wrongs the cause in which he is engaged." [18] When abolitionists did mix with Negroes, it became almost fashionable to tell others about this novel experience, treating it as a personal triumph over the amassed forces of prejudice and evil. Weld, for example, related at great length his daily intercourse with Negroes in Cincinnati. When Negro ministers and friends mixed with whites at the Weld–Angelina Grimke wedding, the new bride explained, "They were our invited guests and we thus had an opportunity to bear our testimony against the horrible prejudice which prevails against colored persons." Both Negroes and whites attended the funeral of James Forten, a prominent Philadelphia Negro leader, and one white participant proudly described it as "a real amalgamation funeral." [19]

Such intercourse was, after all, novel and often dangerous in the ante bellum United States. In facing this annoying problem, many abolitionists did indeed appear hesitant, careful, apprehensive — but always curious. "I hear that Mrs. [Lydia] Child has had a party lately, and invited colored persons," a Massachusetts woman abolitionist wrote. "Do write me about it." [20]

The aversion to intimate social relations with Negroes arose from the fact that most whites, whether abolitionists or not, acknowledged the existence of vast differences — physical and mental — between the two races. Some abolitionists, for example, failed to question the validity of commonly accepted

---

[18] *Fourth Annual Report of the American Anti-Slavery Society*, p. 107.
[19] Barnes and Dumond (eds.), *Weld-Grimke Correspondence*, II, 679; Anna Davis Hallowell, *James and Lucretia Mott* (Boston, 1884), p. 232.
[20] Sophia Davenport to Caroline Weston, June 5, 1836, Weston Papers.

stereotypes of the Negro character; they contended instead
that these peculiar racial qualities constituted no just grounds
for denying Negroes freedom or equal political rights. On the
other hand, such abolitionists as William Lloyd Garrison
argued that, unfortunately, the Negro could do nothing about
the color of his skin and this alone perpetuated prejudice. "The
black color of the body, the wooly hair, the thick lips, and
other peculiarities of the African," Garrison's *Liberator* remarked, "forms so striking a contrast to the Caucasian race,
that they may be distinguished at a glance. . . . They are
branded by the hand of nature with a perpetual mark of disgrace." [21]

Nevertheless, abolitionist literature contributed its share to
the popular conception of the Negro, frequently referring to
his meek, servile, comical, minstrel-like qualities. William
Ellery Channing, writing in an antislavery tract, described the
Negro as "among the mildest, gentlest of men"; his nature was
"affectionate, easily touched" and was therefore more open to
religious impression than the white man's; the European races
manifested "more courage, enterprise, invention," but the
Negro "carries within him, much more than we, the germs of
a meek, long-suffering, loving virtue"; if civilized, the African
would undoubtedly show less energy, courage, and intellectual
originality than the Caucasian but would surpass him in ami-
ableness, tranquility, gentleness, and content"; he might never
equal the white man "in outward condition," but he would
probably be "a much happier race." [22] The Ohio Anti-Slavery
Society found that Negroes "endure with more patience the
scorn and wrong under which they are pressed down — are
more grateful for the favors which they receive — more tract-

[21] *The Liberator*, January 22, 1831.
[22] William Ellery Channing, "The African Character," in John A. Collins (ed.),
*The Anti-Slavery Picknick: A Collection of Speeches, Poems, Dialogues and
Songs; intended for use in Schools and Anti-Slavery Meetings* (Boston, 1842),
pp. 56–58. See also Abdy's interview with Channing in *Journal of a Residence
and Tour*, III, 217–37.

able than persons of like information and intelligence among the whites." [23] Abolitionist author Charles Stuart reported that Negroes were guilty of fewer "atrocious crimes" because they were "less ferocious, less proud, and passionate and revengeful, than others." [24] Accepting this composite picture of the Negro character, abolitionists might well argue that social intercourse with the blacks not only seemed impolitic but unnatural.

Negro efforts to break away from this stereotype did not always win approval within the abolitionist movement. Frederick Douglass, for example, proved to be a formidable antislavery orator, but several abolitionists became concerned over Douglass' rapid intellectual development; perhaps people would no longer believe that he had ever been a slave. "The public have itching ears to hear a colored man speak," antislavery agent John A. Collins pointed out to William Lloyd Garrison, "and particularly *a slave*. Multitudes will flock to hear one of this class speak. . . . It would be a good policy to employ a number of colored agents, if suitable ones can be found." By 1841, however, Douglass' suitability seemed to be in question. "People won't believe that you were ever a slave, Frederick, if you keep on in this way," one abolitionist told Douglass. Collins added: "Better have a little of the plantation speech than not; it is not best that you seem too learned." [25]

In seeking to eradicate prejudice while at the same time accepting certain popular notions about the Negro, abolitionists frequently exhibited a curious racial attitude. They might, for example, refer to their African brethren — innocently or otherwise — as "niggers" or emphasize some alleged physical or mental characteristic. At times they seemed to sense this dual attitude. When a prominent Massachusetts woman aboli-

[23] Ohio Anti-Slavery Society, *Condition of the People of Color*, p. 4.
[24] Charles Stuart, "On the Colored People of the United States," *Quarterly Anti-Slavery Magazine*, II (October, 1836), 16.
[25] Douglass, *Life and Times*, pp. 269–70.

tionist described an antislavery fund-raising fair in New Bedford, she wrote to her sister: "All the fashionables of the town were there and all the 'niggers' (don't let this letter get into the Mass. Abolitionist)."²⁶ Usually, however, abolitionists appeared unaware that they might be using offensive language in describing Negroes. Arnold Buffum, a New England antislavery leader, thus informed Garrison about his activities in behalf of a school "where honors may be dispensed to wooly heads."²⁷ Abolitionist James W. Alvord, after visiting a school in Clifton, Connecticut, wrote to Theodore Weld that one Negro girl sat with the white students. "Can't tell how it will go," he remarked. "Should not be surprised if some of the white parents should smell her very bad, tho I could not perceive the girls on either side were at all aware of her niggerly odour." At the same time, however, Alvord asked Weld what more he could do for "the salvation" of the Negro. "To this object," he declared, "I *would dedicate my life*."²⁸

Negroes frequently demonstrated their appreciation of the efforts and accomplishments of the antislavery societies, but they did not hesitate to condemn prejudice within the abolitionist movement. "Even our professed friends have not yet rid themselves of it," a Negro teacher lamented. "To some of them it clings like a dark mantle obscuring their many virtues and choking up the avenues to higher and nobler sentiments." As an example, she cited the comment of "one of the best and least prejudiced men" in the antislavery cause: "'Ah,' said he, 'I can recall the time when in walking with a colored brother, the darker the night, the better Abolitionist was I.'" Although this person no longer expressed such feelings, she feared that

²⁶ Deborah Weston to Mary Weston, January 5, 1840, Weston Papers. The "Mass. Abolitionist" refers to a weekly newspaper edited by Elizur Wright, Jr., which generally disagreed with the Garrisonian position, particularly on political action.
²⁷ Francis and Wendell P. Garrison, *William Lloyd Garrison*, I, 327.
²⁸ Barnes and Dumond (eds.), *Weld-Grimke Correspondence*, II, 697.

similar sentiments "oftentimes" manifested themselves among the white friends of the Negro. Of course, she added, "when we recollect what great sacrifices to public sentiment they are called upon to make, we cannot wholly blame them. Many, very many anxious to take up the cross, but how few are strong enough to bear it." [29]

Several Negro leaders complained that white abolitionists devoted so much time to fiery condemnations of southern slavery that they tended to overlook the plight of northern Negroes. One Negro newspaper charged in 1839 that making "abolition in the North" an objective of secondary importance clearly constituted "a primordial defect" in the antislavery movement: "At this moment more is known among abolitionists of slavery in the Carolinas, than of the deep and damning thralldom which grinds to the dust, the colored inhabitants of New York. And more efforts are made by them to rend the physical chains of Southern slaves, than to burst the soul-crushing bondage of the Northern states." [30] Even when white abolitionists turned their attention to the condition of northern Negroes, it appeared to some that they stressed only political rights and industrial education. Was it not "strange," a Negro leader asked, that the constitution of the American Anti-Slavery Society failed to mention social equality as an objective? [31]

Although some Negro leaders criticized abolitionist apathy, others contended that Negroes had placed too much reliance on the efforts of white agitators, thus impairing their own independent development and hampering the struggle for equal rights. The antislavery societies, Martin R. Delany charged, have always "presumed to *think* for, dictate to, and *know* better what suited colored people, than they know for themselves."

[29] *Ibid.*, I, 380.
[30] *Colored American*, May 18, 1839.
[31] James McCune Smith to Gerrit Smith, March 1, 1855, quoted in Howard Holman Bell, *A Survey of the Negro Convention Movement, 1830–1861* (Ph.D. diss., Northwestern University, 1953), p. 41.

He applauded the constructive work of these societies, but he
felt that Negroes placed too much faith in the "miracle" of
abolition and demonstrated too little confidence in their own
efforts. After some white abolitionists appeared at the 1831
national Negro convention to propose a manual-labor college,
Negroes suddenly ceased their independent activities, Delany
lamented, "and with their hands thrust deep in their breeches-
pockets, and their mouths gaping open, stood gazing with astonishment, wonder, and surprise, at the stupendous moral co-
lossal statues of our Anti-Slavery friends and brethren, who in
the heat and zeal of honest hearts . . . promised a great deal
more than they have ever been able half to fulfill, in thrice the
period in which they expected it." Since that time, Negroes had
waited patiently, and largely in vain, for a practical application of abolitionist dogma. Consequently, Delany concluded,
"we find ourselves occupying the very same position in relation
to our Anti-Slavery friends, as we do in relation to the proslavery part of the community — a mere secondary, underling
position, in all our relations to them, and any thing more than
this, is not a matter of course . . . but . . . by mere sufferance." [32]

In assessing the weaknesses of the antislavery movement,
Negro critics particularly referred to the economic depression
of their people and the failure of abolitionists to offer Negroes
decent job opportunities in their business establishments or
even in the antislavery offices. After all, abolitionist speeches
and editorials could not correct the prevailing prejudices of
white society — this required a demonstration of Negro economic improvement. "Our white friends are deceived," a
Negro newspaper charged, "when they imagine they are free
from prejudice against color, and yet are content with a lower
standard of attainments for colored youth, and inferior ex-

[32] Delany, *Condition, Elevation, Emigration, and Destiny of the Colored
People*, pp. 10, 24–25, 27.

hibitions of talent on the part of colored men." [33] Abolitionists possessed the means to assist Negro laborers, these critics maintained, and yet few of them showed any willingness to train or hire Negroes. "They might employ a colored boy as a porter or packer," a Negro leader remarked, "but would as soon put a hod-carrier to the clerk's desk as a colored boy, ever so well educated though he be." [34] The question arose at a convention of the American and Foreign Anti-Slavery Society when a Negro delegate deprecated the failure of leading members to employ Negroes in their commercial houses or in the antislavery offices. Moreover, another Negro delegate added, fellow-abolitionist Arthur Tappan, owner of a large New York City department store, used Negroes only in menial employments. Replying to this charge, Tappan claimed that he had recently hired a Negro porter but that this person had left his job before being qualified for advancement to a clerical position. In any case, Tappan asserted, he would not ask "an Irishman sawing wood in the street, and covered with sweat" to dine with his family; neither would he ask a Negro in a similar condition. He required only that his associates be gentlemen, irrespective of color. Whatever the relevance of this remark, Tappan concluded that abolitionists had to guard against unwarranted racial prejudices and "act out, at all times, the principles they professed." [35]

It is difficult to measure the extent of racial prejudice within the abolitionist movement or to chart its course during the ante bellum period. More significant, perhaps, is the fact that abolitionists could hold differing views on the propriety of social relations with Negroes and still combine to assist northern Negroes to secure equal political rights and economic improve-

[33] *Colored American*, November 4, 1837, July 28, 1838. See also Delany, *Condition, Elevation, Emigration, and Destiny of the Colored People*, pp. 26–28.

[34] *Frederick Douglass' Paper*, May 18, 1855.

[35] *Twelfth Annual Report of the American and Foreign Anti-Slavery Society*, pp. 29–30.

ment. The Garrisonians, for example, worked successfully
with Massachusetts Negroes to secure the repeal of the ban on
interracial marriages, the abandonment of Jim Crow seating
in railroad cars, and the integration of Boston's public schools.
Elsewhere, abolitionists maintained active campaigns to repeal
statutory and extralegal racial distinctions and rendered both
moral and material assistance to Negro schools.

In evaluating the work of the white abolitionists, one should
not overlook these important contributions to the cause of human freedom in the North or the consistency with which abolitionists struck at both northern and southern racial oppression.
The antislavery movement did indeed suffer from factionalism,
extreme partisanship, narrow class attitudes, prejudice, and
even hypocrisy, but it shared these weaknesses with nearly
every organized social movement and political party in ante
bellum America. The fact that abolitionists did not allow these
weaknesses to interfere materially with their struggle for civil
rights is at least a tribute to their sincerity. Forced at times to
endure mob violence, severe public censure, frustration, and
defeat, these dedicated agitators displayed an ability to apply
theoretical arguments about equal rights to concrete situations.
Although frequently hesitant and uncertain in their own social
relations with Negroes, abolitionists nevertheless attempted to
demonstrate to a hostile public that environmental factors,
rather than any peculiar racial traits, largely accounted for
the degradation of the northern Negro.

The widely publicized activities of white antislavery
workers and the commanding figures of William Lloyd Garrison, Wendell Phillips, and Theodore Weld have tended to obscure the important and active role of the Negro abolitionist.
The antislavery movement was not solely a white man's movement. Through their own newspapers, conventions, tracts, orations, and legislative petitions, Negroes agitated for an end to

southern bondage and northern repression. The white abolitionist encountered strong and often violent public opposition,
but the Negro abolitionist risked even greater hostility, for his
very presence on the antislavery platform challenged those
popular notions which had stereotyped his people as passive,
meek, and docile. As a common laborer, the Negro might be
tolerated, even valued, for his services; as an antislavery agi-
tator, he was frequently mobbed.

Negro abolitionism preceded by several years the appearance of Garrison and *The Liberator.* Encouraged by the post-
Revolutionary emancipation movement, Negroes worked with
sympathetic whites to remove the last traces of slavery in the
North and to call for its abolition in the South. As early as
1797, four illegally manumitted North Carolina Negroes, who
had fled to the North to escape re-enslavement, petitioned Congress to consider "our relief as a people." Three years later, a
group of Philadelphia free Negroes appealed directly to Congress to revise the federal laws concerning the African trade
and fugitive slaves and to adopt "such measures as shall in due
course emancipate the whole of their brethren from their present situation." [36] In addition to legislative petitions, meetings
commemorating the abolition of the African slave trade or the
end of slavery in a particular state afforded opportunities for
such prominent Negro leaders as Peter Williams, Nathaniel
Paul, William Hamilton, and Joseph Sidney to voice their sentiments on public issues. [37] The organization of independent
churches, Free African societies, Masonic lodges, and anti-

[36] Aptheker (ed.), *Documentary History,* pp. 39–44.

[37] For a convenient guide to the published addresses of these early Negro
leaders, see Dorothy P. Porter, "Early American Negro Writings: A Bibliographical Study," *Papers of the Bibliographical Society of America,* XXXIX
(1945), 192–268. Especially valuable for an early Negro's views on national affairs
is Joseph Sidney, *An Oration, Commemorative of the Abolition of the Slave Trade
in the United States; Delivered before the Wilberforce Philanthropic Association,
in the City of New York, on the second of January, 1809* (New York, 1809).
Copy in Schomburg Collection, New York Public Library.

colonization meetings further intensified a growing race consciousness and helped to arouse the Negro community in
several areas to a more vigorous defense of its civil rights.

Four years before the publication of the first issue of *The
Liberator*, two Negro leaders, John Russwurm and Samuel E.
Cornish, launched the first Negro newspaper — *Freedom's
Journal* — in an effort to disseminate useful ideas and information and to attract public attention to the plight of those still
in bondage. In the first issue, the editors announced that Negroes had to plead their own cause: "Too long have others
spoken for us. Too long has the publick been deceived by misrepresentations." [38] During its two years of publication, *Freedom's Journal* featured articles on the evils of slavery and
intemperance, the importance of education and the progress of
Negro schools, literary and historical selections, moral lessons,
information on the various Afro-American benevolent societies, and a discussion of colonization. Cornish subsequently
withdrew from the partnership and established a short-lived
newspaper, *The Rights of All*, and Russwurm abandoned his
editorial duties to join the colonizationists. [39]

Negro antislavery agitation took on a more aggressive tone
in 1829 as David Walker, a Boston clothing dealer and local
agent for *Freedom's Journal*, contributed a powerful tract to
abolitionist literature — *Walker's Appeal, in Four Articles*.
Addressing his sentiments to the "coloured citizens" of the
world, but particularly to those of the United States, Walker
described American Negroes as "the most degraded, wretched,
and abject set of beings that ever lived since the world began."
Indeed, he asked, "Can our condition be any worse? — Can it
be more mean and abject? If there are any changes, will they
not be for the better, though they may appear for the worst at
first? Can they get us any lower? Where can they get us? They

---

[38] *Freedom's Journal*, March 16, 1827.
[39] For some bitter criticism of Russwurm after his conversion to colonization,
see Woodson (ed.), *Mind of the Negro*, pp. 160–63.

are afraid to treat us worse, for they know well, the day they do it they are gone."

In Walker's estimation, four major factors accounted for this wretched state of affairs: slavery, ignorance, "the preachers of Jesus Christ," and the African colonization movement. Consequently, Negroes had to strive for economic and educational improvement and resist the encroachments of the colonizationists. ("America is as much our country, as it is yours.") The southern Negro, on the other hand, faced an even greater challenge, for he had to strike directly and perhaps violently for his freedom as a natural right. Once that thrust for liberty had been made, Walker advised, "make sure work — do not trifle, for they will not trifle with you — they want us for their slaves, and think nothing of murdering us in order to subject us to that wretched condition — therefore, if there is an *attempt* made by us, kill or be killed." To prevent the outbreak of racial war, Walker warned the white man, recognize the legal rights of Negroes. There can be no mistaking the alternative. "Remember, Americans, that we must and shall be free and enlightened as you are, will you wait until we shall, under God, obtain our liberty by the crushing arm of power? Will it not be dreadful for you? I speak Americans for your good. We must and shall be free I say, in spite of you. . . . And wo, wo, will be to you if we have to obtain our freedom by fighting."[40]

Within a year after its publication, the apparent popularity — or notoriety — of Walker's pamphlet warranted a third edition. The often violent reaction to its contents and the mysterious death of the author in 1830 undoubtedly assisted its circulation.[41] Indeed, it had already caused some consternation

[40] David Walker, *Walker's Appeal, in Four Articles; together with a Preamble, to the Coloured Citizens of the World, but in particular, and very expressly to those of the United States of America, written in Boston, State of Massachusetts, September 28, 1829* (3d ed.; Boston, 1830).

[41] See Vernon Loggins, *The Negro Author* (New York, 1931), p. 86; Woodson (ed.), *Mind of the Negro*, p. 222.

in the North, and it understandably created outright alarm in
portions of the South. Already beset by a growing fear of slave
uprisings, the South could not afford to tolerate the potentially
explosive appeal of a Boston clothing dealer. The governor of
North Carolina denounced it as "an open appeal to their [the
slaves'] natural love of liberty . . . and throughout expressing sentiments totally subversive of all subordination in
our slaves"; the mayor of Savannah wrote to the mayor of
Boston requesting that Walker be arrested and punished, and
Richmond's mayor reported that several copies of *Walker's
Appeal* had been found in the possession of local free Negroes;
the governors of Georgia and North Carolina submitted the
pamphlet to their state legislatures for appropriate action; and
the Virginia legislature held secret sessions to consider proper
measures to prevent the pamphlet's circulation. Finally, four
southern states — Georgia, North Carolina, Mississippi, and
Louisiana — seized upon the pamphlet to enact severe restrictions to cope with such "seditious" propaganda.[42]

The South was not alone in its critical reaction. Walker's
medicine for the ills of American Negroes was too strong for
many white abolitionists. "A more bold, daring, inflammatory
publication, perhaps, never issued from the press of any country," antislavery publisher Benjamin Lundy declared. "I can
do no less than set the broadest seal of condemnation on it."[43]
Lundy's disciple, William Lloyd Garrison, had just launched
his own career as an aggressive antislavery publicist and was
more equivocal in his reaction. The editor of *The Liberator*
found it difficult to reconcile his belief in nonresistance with
his unconcealed admiration of Walker's courage and forth-
rightness. While deploring the circulation of this "most injudi-
cious publication" and "its general spirit," Garrison admitted

[42] Clement Eaton, "A Dangerous Pamphlet in the Old South," *Journal of
Southern History*, II (1936), 323–34.
[43] *Genius of Universal Emancipation*, April, 1830; *The Liberator*, January 29,
1831.

235

that it contained "many valuable truths and seasonable warnings." [44]

The appearance of *The Liberator* in 1831 and the formation of the American Anti-Slavery Society two years later thus found northern Negroes already engaged in a variety of abolitionist activities. In addition to publishing a newspaper and several antislavery tracts, Negroes had taken steps to co-ordinate their actions through annual national conventions. On September 15, 1830, delegates gathered in Philadelphia's Bethel Church to launch the first in a series of such conventions. Against a background of increasing repressive legislation in the North, the delegates adopted an address to the free Negro population, pointing out that their present "forlorn and deplorable situation" demanded immediate action. Where Negroes were subjected to constant harassment and denied even the right of residence, the most recent and blatant case being Ohio, such action would have to take the form of emigration to Canada. There, the convention advised, Negroes could establish themselves "in a land where the laws and prejudices of society will have no effect in retarding their advancement to the summit of civil and religious improvement." Meanwhile, those Negroes who chose to remain in the United States would have to utilize every legal means to improve their political and economic position. Before adjourning, the delegates called upon Negroes to establish auxiliary societies and send delegates to the next annual convention. [45]

Convening annually up to 1835 and periodically thereafter, the national Negro conventions regularly condemned the American Colonization Society, deprecated segregation and "oppressive, unjust and unconstitutional" legislation, stressed the importance of organization, education, temperance, and economy, and set aside the Fourth of July as a day of "humilia-

[44] *The Liberator*, January 29, 1831.
[45] "The First Colored Convention," *Anglo-African Magazine*, I (October, 1859), 305–10; Aptheker (ed.), *Documentary History*, pp. 102–7.

tion, fasting and prayer" when Negroes would ask for divine intervention to break "the shackles of slavery." [46] Meanwhile, the formation of auxiliary state organizations, temperance groups, moral-reform societies, and educational associations created an unprecedented amount of unity and activity among northern Negroes, developed new leadership, and contributed mightily to the strength of the newly formed white antislavery societies.

While engaged in these independent activities, Negro abolitionists also hailed the appearance of a new militancy among their white supporters; they not only welcomed the publication of *The Liberator* but actually outnumbered white subscribers in the early years. "It is a remarkable fact," William Lloyd Garrison wrote in 1834, "that, of the whole number of subscribers to the *Liberator*, only about one-fourth are white. The paper, then, belongs emphatically to the people of color — it is their organ." [47] In addition to contributing articles and letters to the antislavery press, Negroes also attended and addressed abolitionist conventions and, notwithstanding some opposition, served as members of the executive committee and board of managers of both the American Anti-Slavery Society and its later rival, the American and Foreign Anti-Slavery Society. [48]

Negro abolitionists did not confine their activities to the United States. In the 1840's and 1850's, several of them toured the British Isles to promote antislavery sentiment and raise money for abolitionist enterprises. Englishmen crowded into meeting halls to see and hear leading American Negroes tell of the plight of their people and their own experiences as slaves or freemen. Frederick Douglass, for example, described his

[46] Selected proceedings of several of the national Negro conventions may be found in Aptheker (ed.), *Documentary History*, pp. 114–19, 133–37, 141–46, 154–57, 159, 226–33, and 341–57.

[47] Francis and Wendell P. Garrison, *William Lloyd Garrison*, I, 432.

[48] Herbert Aptheker, "The Negro in the Abolitionist Movement," *Essays in the History of the American Negro* (New York, 1945), pp. 154–55; Foner (ed.), *Life and Writings of Frederick Douglass*, I, 33, 426.

years of bondage in the South; William G. Allen told of his narrow escape from an enraged northern mob after proposing to marry a white girl; William and Ellen Craft related their flight to freedom and their subsequent exile to avoid prosecution under the Fugitive Slave Act; and Henry Highland Garnet undoubtedly mentioned the mob that ejected him from a Connecticut boys' academy.[49] While arousing their foreign audiences with these tales of slavery and racial violence, Negroes also found much to amaze them. "Here the colored man feels himself among friends, and not among enemies," one Negro "exile" wrote from England, "among a people who, when they treat him well, do it not in the patronizing (and, of course insulting) spirit, even of hundreds of the American abolitionists, but in a spirit rightly appreciative of the doctrine of human equality." [50] For some of these Negro abolitionists, returning home must have been difficult. After extensive travels in England and Europe, for example, William Wells Brown came back to Philadelphia, only to find himself proscribed from the Chestnut Street omnibus on his first day home. "The omnibuses of Paris, Edinburgh, Glasgow, and Liverpool, had stopped to take me up," he recollected, "but what mattered that? My face was not white, my hair was not straight; and, therefore, I must be excluded from a seat in a third-rate American omnibus." [51]

Both Negro and white abolitionists suffered from internal dissension over fundamental questions of policy and ideology. While the white antislavery societies split over the issues of political action, nonresistance, women's rights, disunion, and the nature of the Constitution, Negroes argued the merits of moral suasion and separate conventions. By 1835, the American Moral Reform Society, dominated largely by Philadelphia

[49] Benjamin Quarles, "Ministers Without Portfolio," *Journal of Negro History*, XXXIX (1954), 27–42.

[50] *The Liberator*, July 22, 1853.

[51] William Wells Brown, *The American Fugitive in Europe* (Boston, 1855), pp. 312–14.

Negroes, replaced the regular convention movement. Dedicated to "improving the condition of mankind," the new organization urged Negroes to abandon the use of the terms "colored" and "African," to refrain from holding separate colored conventions, to integrate as fully as possible into white society, to support the equality of women, and to adopt the principles of peace, temperance, brotherly love, and nonresistance "under all circumstances." In adopting such a program, the moral reformers obviously allied themselves with the Garrisonians in the growing factional struggle within the antislavery movement.[52]

The American Moral Reform Society found little support outside the Garrisonian strongholds of Philadelphia and Boston. Meanwhile, New York Negro leaders launched a new weekly newspaper, the *Colored American,* which expressed dismay over the growing split in abolitionist ranks and the activities of the moral reformers. Editor Samuel Cornish noted that the delegates to a recent moral-reform convention had impressed him as "vague, wild, indefinite and confused in their views." Only drastic reorganization and the adoption of a more vigorous program of action could possibly salvage the society. As for their efforts to substitute the term "oppressed Americans" for "colored people," Cornish called this sheer nonsense. "Oppressed Americans! *who are they?*" he asked. "Nonsense brethren!! You are COLORED AMERICANS. The indians are RED AMERICANS, and the white people are WHITE AMERICANS and *you are good as they, and they are no better than you.*"[53]

[52] *Minutes of the Fifth Annual Convention for the Improvement of the Free People of Colour in the United States* (Philadelphia, 1835), pp. 4–5, 9, 14–15, 31–32; *The Emancipator,* September 22, 1836; *The Minutes and Proceedings of the First Annual Meeting of the American Moral Reform Society* (Philadelphia, 1837); *Minutes of Proceedings at the Council of the Philadelphia Association for the Moral and Mental Improvement of the People of Color* (Philadelphia, 1837); *National Anti-Slavery Standard,* October 1, 1840.
[53] *Colored American,* August 26, September 2, 9, 16, 1837.

While scolding the moral reformers, the *Colored American* also engaged in a controversy with the pro-Garrison *National Anti-Slavery Standard* over the advisability of colored conventions. "We oppose all exclusive action on the part of the colored people," the *Standard* announced in June, 1840, "except where the clearest necessity demands it." As long as Negroes contented themselves with separate churches, schools, and conventions, public sentiment would remain unaltered. Instead, Negroes should join with their white friends to demand equal rights as men, not as colored persons, and thus confirm the abolitionists' contention that racial distinctions had no place in American society. The moral reformers enthusiastically indorsed the position of the *Standard*. Other Negro leaders, however, immediately condemned it and upheld the need for independent action. The abolitionists had done much for the Negro, Samuel R. Ward wrote to the editor of the *Standard*, but too many of them "best love the colored man at a distance" and refuse to admit or eradicate their own prejudices. In the meantime, Negroes had to meet and act for themselves.[54]

Although the American Moral Reform Society had a short life, the split in white abolitionist ranks continued to undermine Negro unity. By 1840, Garrisonians shared the field of agitation with the American and Foreign Anti-Slavery Society and the Liberty party. New England and Philadelphia Negroes generally supported the American Anti-Slavery Society and condemned the critics of Garrison as unworthy of confidence or support. New York Negroes, on the other hand, not only dissociated themselves from the moral reformers but generally indorsed direct political action and contributed to the leadership and campaigns of the Liberty party. At one point, the *Colored American* attempted to restore some semblance of sanity and unity to abolitionists by urging them to avoid pe-

[54] *National Anti-Slavery Standard*, June 18, July 2, August 20, September 10, October 1, 1840.

ripheral issues and petty bickering and get back to opposing
slavery. "Why . . . make governments or anti-governments
— resistance or non-resistance — women's rights or men's
rights — Sabbaths or anti-Sabbaths, a bone of contention?" the
Negro newspaper asked. "None of these should have any thing
to do with our Anti-Slavery efforts. *They are neither parts nor
parcels of that great and holy cause*, nor should they be in-
truded into its measures." Rather than promote abolitionist
harmony, however, such sentiments, coupled with the editors'
indorsement of political action and their refusal to censure
Garrison's critics, induced some severe attacks and threats to
cut off financial support from the paper. Defending their right
to differ with Garrison on any issue and to adopt an independent editorial policy, the editors of the *Colored American*
warned Negroes that as long as they permitted white abolitionists to act and think for them, "so long they will outwardly
treat us as men, while in their hearts they still hold us as
slaves." [55]

In a desperate effort to retain their hold on the antislavery
movement, Garrison and his associates made every effort to
secure Negro support. In Boston and New Bedford, Negro
meetings acclaimed Garrison as a "friend and benefactor" and
indorsed his antislavery position.[56] Already abandoned by
many of his white followers, Garrison expressed gratification
over such reactions. The opposition knew, he wrote, "that, so
long as I retain the confidence of my colored friends, all of
their machinations against me will prove abortive." [57] Had
Garrison known that his most important Negro ally, Frederick

[55] *Colored American*, October 7, 14, 1837, May 11, August 17, October 5, 19,
November 2, 1839.

[56] *The Liberator*, June 7, 21, 1839. See also *Eighth Annual Report of the Board
of Managers of the Massachusetts Anti-Slavery Society* (Boston, 1840), pp. 36–
37; *The Liberator*, October 6, 1837, April 3, 1840; Dwight L. Dumond (ed.),
Letters of James Gillepsie Birney, 1831–1857 (2 vols.; New York, 1938), I,
575–79.

[57] William Lloyd Garrison to Elizabeth Pease, September 1, 1840, Garrison
Papers.

Douglass, was about to desert him, he would have had much less cause for optimism.

As late as September 4, 1849, Douglass had insisted that he was a loyal Garrisonian abolitionist, and there was little reason to doubt him. According to the tenets of that faith, he had excoriated the Constitution as "a most foul and bloody conspiracy" against the rights of three million slaves, had supported disunion as the most effective means to remove federal protection from the "peculiar institution," had belittled political action as futile and necessarily compromising, and had advocated moral persuasion rather than violence in attacking slavery.[58] Nevertheless, signs of revolt became increasingly apparent. After founding the *North Star* in 1847 against the advice of his Boston friends and moving from New England to Rochester, Douglass carefully re-evaluated his position and listened to the arguments of various New York abolitionists who had already broken with Garrison. Before long, the Negro leader reached the conclusion that disunion would only place the slaves at the complete mercy of the South, that political action constituted "a legitimate and powerful means for abolishing slavery," that southern bondage would probably have to expire in violence, and that the Constitution made no guarantees to slavery but in fact implied its eventual extinction.[59] In May, 1851, Douglass utilized the annual convention of the American Anti-Slavery Society to proclaim his heresy publicly. "There is roguery somewhere," Garrison reputedly declared as he moved to strike the *North Star* from the list of approved abolitionist publications.[60] Douglass had gone over to the enemy.

Although he voiced his new position on the lecture platform and in the *North Star*, Douglass hoped to avert a complete

[58] Foner (ed.), *Life and Writings of Frederick Douglass*, II, 49–52.
[59] Douglass, *Life and Times*, pp. 322–24; Foner (ed.), *Life and Writings of Frederick Douglass*, II, 52–53, 149–50, 152–53, 155–57.
[60] Foner (ed.), *Life and Writings of Frederick Douglass*, II, 53–54, 155–56.

break with Garrison. "I stand in relation to him something like that of a child to a parent," he wrote to Charles Sumner.[61] Nevertheless, Garrisonian anxiety and alarm soon changed to vigorous denunciation and even personal defamation. *The Liberator* now placed Douglass' editorials in the section usually reserved for proslavery sentiments, and it charged that the Negro leader had betrayed his former friends for the sake of financial gain, that he possessed ambitions to become the spokesman of the colored race, and that he had lost much of his moral fervor and influence.[62] When Douglass reduced the size of his newspaper, one Garrisonian gleefully wrote to an English friend that the Negro editor "has the confidence of very few, the respect . . . of none. Do what he may, we shall take no notice of him, and I think his career — on professedly anti-slavery grounds — will soon come to an end." Although Garrison generally allowed his followers to deal editorially with the Negro upstart, he confided to friends that he regarded Douglass as a malignant enemy, "thoroughly base and selfish," "destitute of every principle of honor, ungrateful to the last degree, and malevolent in spirit," and unworthy of "respect, confidence, or countenance." Such was the thoroughness of the Garrison indictment.[63]

Replying to his critics with equal bitterness, Douglass called them "vigilant enemies" and labeled their Negro followers as "practical enemies of the colored people" and contemptible tools. The Garrisonians had first attempted to silence his newspaper, he charged, and now they sought to expel him from the antislavery fold as a dangerous heretic. "They talk down there [Boston] just as if the Anti-Slavery Cause belonged to them — and as if all Anti-Slavery ideas originated with them and that

[61] *Ibid.*, II, 210–11.
[62] *The Liberator*, September 16, 23, 30, December 16, 30, 1853.
[63] Samuel May, Jr., to Richard Davis Webb, February 8, 1857, May Papers; William Lloyd Garrison to Samuel J. May, September 5, 1857, September 28, 1860, Garrison Papers.

no man has a right to 'peep or mutter' on the subject, who does not hold letters patent from them." [64] Douglass also sought to clarify his differences with Garrison, but these appeared to be lost in the bitter editorial war. Before long, Negroes in various parts of the country were meeting to discuss the conflict and to choose sides. Chicago Negroes condemned Garrison's "vile crusade" against "the voice of the colored people"; a Rhode Island convention hailed Douglass as "our acknowledged leader"; and an Ohio gathering decisively defeated a proposal calling on Negroes to abstain from voting in those areas where they enjoyed the franchise. Meanwhile, Garrisonian Negro leaders reiterated the charges of *The Liberator* and claimed to speak for "all the true colored men in the country." [65]

Efforts to reconcile the two antislavery leaders met with no success — only time could heal the deep wounds left by this useless and wasteful struggle. To many Negro and white abolitionists, the entire affair presented a rather sordid and dreary spectacle. "Where is this work of excommunication to end?" Harriet Beecher Stowe wrote Garrison. "Is there but one true anti-slavery church and all others infidels? — Who shall declare which it is." [66] While the dispute helped to reduce the effectiveness of the antislavery movement, it also clearly demonstrated some of the weaknesses in Garrison's ideological and tactical position. Nonresistance, the rejection of political action, disunion, and a proslavery interpretation of the Constitution did not strike many abolitionists in the 1840's and 1850's as being either suitable or realistic weapons with which to abolish southern bondage or northern proscription. Indeed, the final triumph of Garrisonian objectives resulted almost

[64] *Frederick Douglass' Paper*, December 9, 1853; Foner (ed.), *Life and Writings of Frederick Douglass*, II, 270.
[65] Foner (ed.), *Life and Writings of Frederick Douglass*, II, 61–62; *Minutes of the State Convention of the Colored Citizens of Ohio* (Columbus, 1851), pp. 11–12.
[66] Foner (ed.), *Life and Writings of Frederick Douglass*, II, 64.

entirely from the employment of strictly non-Garrisonian methods — political agitation and armed force.

Internal dissension hampered but did not stifle the independent activities of Negro abolitionists. Despite the Garrisonian antipathy to "complexional conventions," local and state organizations continued to meet in the 1840's, and several national conventions revived interstate co-operation. On August 15, 1843, Negroes from various states met in Buffalo to consider "their moral and political condition as American citizens." After several heated debates — which partly reflected the growing split in abolitionist ranks — the convention adopted a series of resolutions which denounced the American Colonization Society and the proslavery churches, indorsed the Liberty party, stressed the value of temperance, education, the mechanical arts, and agriculture, and attributed the plight of free Negroes — North and South — to the evils of slavery.[67]

Henry Highland Garnet, a New York Negro leader, hoped to secure from the Buffalo delegates a more aggressive stand against slavery. Indicting the cruelties of southern bondage and praising as martyrs those Negroes who had led revolts for freedom, Garnet delivered a powerful plea to the slave population in tones reminiscent of David Walker's *Appeal*. "Brethren arise, arise!" he declared. "Strike for your lives and liberties. Now is the day and the hour. Let every slave throughout the land do this, and the days of slavery are numbered. You cannot be more oppressed than you have been — you cannot suffer greater cruelties than you have already. *Rather die freemen than live to be slaves*. Remember that you are FOUR MILLIONS! . . . Let your motto be resistance! resistance! RESISTANCE!" Although the Garrisonians had suffered a defeat on the issue of political action, they managed to steer the convention away from such a commitment to physical violence in overthrowing slavery. By a vote of nineteen to eighteen,

[67] *National Colored Convention, Buffalo, 1843*, pp. 11, 14–16, 19–22, 25, 27, 31–36.

the delegates refused to indorse Garnet's address. Instead, the convention affirmed its faith in the ultimate righteousness of human government and the abolition of slavery through its instrumentality.[68] Relieved at this outcome, one Garrisonian intimated that Garnet, who had also been one of the first Negroes to indorse the Liberty party, had fallen under the influence of bad advisers. "If it has come to this," Garnet replied, "that I must think as you do, because you are an abolitionist, or be exterminated by your thunder, then I do not hesitate to say that your abolitionism is abject slavery."[69]

Although the Buffalo delegates refused to indorse Garnet's address, its contents and the closeness of the convention vote indicated the emergence of a new militancy among Negro abolitionists. Six years later, Garnet's address and Walker's appeal appeared together in a published pamphlet — reportedly at the expense of an obscure New York farmer, John Brown.[70] An Ohio Negro convention immediately ordered five hundred copies to be "gratuitously" circulated.[71] That same year, a New York Negro editor reminded the governor and legislature of Louisiana that their recent expressions of sympathy for Hungarian rebels might be equally applicable to their own bondsmen. "Strike for your freedom now, at the suggestion of your enslavers," the editor wrote. "Make up your minds to die, rather than bequeath a state of slavery to your posterity."[72]

By the end of the 1840's, the appeals of Garnet and Walker — once deemed too radical — received growing support in Negro conventions, newspapers, and antislavery tracts. Even Frederick Douglass, who had bitterly opposed Garnet's ad-

[68] Woodson (ed.), *Negro Orators and Their Orations*, pp. 150–57; Brewer, "Henry Highland Garnet," p. 46; *National Colored Convention, Buffalo, 1843*, p. 16.
[69] *The Liberator*, December 3, 1843.
[70] Loggins, *The Negro Author*, p. 192; Woodson (ed.), *Negro Orators and Their Orations*, p. 150.
[71] *Ohio Colored Convention of 1849*, p. 18.
[72] Aptheker (ed.), *Documentary History*, pp. 290–91.

dress, abandoned his previous conviction that moral persuasion and nonresistance alone could abolish slavery. While still a loyal Garrisonian, he created a "marked sensation" in 1849 when he told a Faneuil Hall audience that he would "welcome the intelligence to-morrow, should it come, that the slaves had risen in the South, and that the sable arms which had been engaged in beautifying and adorning the South were engaged in spreading death and devastation there." Three years later, Douglass told the national Free Soil party convention that the slaveholders had forfeited their right to live. The potential horrors of a slave insurrection should no longer be allowed to obstruct the path to freedom. "The slaveholder has been tried and sentenced," he declared in 1857. "He is training his own executioners." The following year, John Brown visited the Douglass home and remained there for several weeks, devoting most of his time to writing financial appeals for a yet un-revealed plan.[73]

[73] *North Star*, June 15, 1849; *Frederick Douglass' Paper*, August 20, 1852; Chambers, *American Slavery and Colour*, p. 174 n.; Foner (ed.), *Life and Writings of Frederick Douglass*, II, 88.

The Crisis of
The 1850's

In the decade preceding the Civil War, new challenges tested the physical and moral stamina of the North's two hundred thousand Negroes. During the previous fifty years, the nation's political and material advances had been largely confined to whites. Disfranchised and segregated in most states, legally barred from settling in some, confined to a diminishing number of inferior jobs, American Negroes found little cause for optimism in the era that witnessed the election of Abraham Lincoln and the dissolution of the Union. Instead, they looked with dismay at the passage of more repressive state and federal legislation, a Supreme Court decision that stripped them of citizenship, a revived colonization movement, and a new anti-slavery political party which demonstrated little regard for the plight of northern blacks.

Nevertheless, some encouraging signs did brighten an other-wise dismal outlook. The Negro community, bolstered by vig-orous leadership, had never been stronger, and it had joined

247

with abolitionist sympathizers to effect some notable advances
in civil rights, especially in New England. At the same time,
the threatened expansion of southern slavery had awakened
the dormant consciences of many whites; it had increased
public interest in the Negro's plight, spurred the organization
of a new political movement, forced the old parties to commit
themselves, and produced a new group of national leaders to
challenge the alleged aggressions of the "slavocracy." Anti-
slavery tracts and fugitive-slave memoirs appeared in growing
numbers to arouse white sympathies, and Harriet Beecher
Stowe's description of "Life among the Lowly" in *Uncle Tom's
Cabin* was moving white audiences to tears in the North's
segregated theaters. Beyond this, however, there appeared to
be little hope for any early integration of northern Negroes
into American society.

Submitting to the southern demand for strengthened fugitive-slave legislation, northern political leaders obtained a
momentary sectional truce but simultaneously created an atmosphere of fear in the Negro community. The Fugitive Slave
Act of 1850 sought to insure a speedier return of runaway
bondsmen to the South; any claimant who could establish affidavit proof of ownership before a special federal commissioner could take possession of a Negro. The captive had no
recourse to common legal safeguards, such as a jury trial or
a judicial hearing. In fact, the new law awarded ten dollars to
the commissioner if he directed the captive's return, but only
five dollars if he ordered the runaway's release. The relative
cost of paper-work involved in the two transactions allegedly
justified this differential. Critics, however, called it an open
bribe. The Act further empowered federal officers to call upon
all citizens to help enforce its provisions and imposed fines,
imprisonment, and civil damages for concealing or rescuing a
fugitive. It posed an obvious threat to free northern-born Ne-

groes: any of them might be "mistakenly" identified as fugitives and carried to the South.

Encouraged by the new legislation, slaveholders appeared in northern communities or employed agents to reclaim their lost chattel. Paid informers of both races, some of whom gave false testimony, heightened the tension under which northern Negroes lived.[1] In the first six years of the Act, more than two hundred alleged fugitives were arrested, approximately twelve of whom successfully defended their claim to freedom. Rather than risk consignment to southern bondage, many Negroes, including some of the leading figures of the Negro community who had been active abolitionists and admitted fugitives, fled to Canada or England. "The night is a dark and stormy one," *Frederick Douglass' Paper* lamented in 1851. "We have lost some of our strong men.— Ward has been driven into exile; Loguen has been hunted from our shores; Brown, Garnet and Crummell, men who were our pride and hope, we have heard signified their unwillingness to return again to their National field of labors in this country. Bibb has *chosen* Canada as his field of labor — and the eloquent Remond is comparatively silent."[2] Although an estimated twenty thousand fled to Canada between 1850 and 1860, most Negroes chose to remain in the North and resist this latest threat to their precarious freedom. "The only way to make the Fugitive Slave Law a dead letter," Frederick Douglass told them, "is to make half a dozen or more dead kidnappers."[3]

While the South demanded full compliance with the new act, the North divided in its response. Several northern communities and states decided that enforcement was too great a

[1] For the fate of one such Negro informer, see Woodson (ed.), *Mind of the Negro*, pp. 346–48.
[2] Wilbur H. Siebert, *The Underground Railroad from Slavery to Freedom* (New York, 1898), pp. 240–42, 249–51; Fred Landon, "The Negro Migration to Canada after the Fugitive Slave Act of 1850," *Journal of Negro History*, V (1920), 22–23; *Frederick Douglass' Paper*, November 27, 1851.
[3] *Frederick Douglass' Paper*, August 20, 1852.

price to pay, even for sectional peace. Whites might differ on extending political and social rights to Negroes, but many of them shared a common revulsion at the sight of slave-hunters searching for human prey in northern neighborhoods. The uprooting of respectable Negroes from their jobs and families to be returned to slavery seemed to defy any code of common decency. Consequently, some communities openly defied the law, forcibly ejected claimants, or collected money to buy the victim's freedom. Several states virtually annulled the Fugitive Slave Act through the passage of personal-liberty laws which enabled alleged fugitives to secure legal counsel, guaranteed them a hearing and a jury trial, forbade their confinement in state jails, and enjoined state officers from issuing writs or granting any assistance to claimants. Such legislation made it increasingly difficult to capture alleged runaways and soon prompted the South to charge that northerners had betrayed a solemn promise.[4]

With personal freedom at stake, northern Negroes organized and, when necessary, armed themselves to sabotage the operation of the new law. This gave some substance to the sentiments of a New York City protest rally that the Fugitive Slave Act "must be trampled under foot, resisted, disobeyed, and violated at all hazards."[5] Turning to direct action, Negroes assisted escaped slaves and joined with abolitionists to hamper the efforts of southern slaveholders to recover them. In one dramatic case, the Boston Vigilance Committee kidnaped an accused fugitive from the courtroom during a recess in his trial and sent him to Canada. Although unsuccessful in another such attempt, the Committee prompted Boston authorities to call out three hundred policemen to escort a fugitive from the court-

[4] Siebert, *Underground Railroad*, pp. 245–46.
[5] *The Fugitive Slave Bill: Its History and Unconstitutionality* (New York, 1850), p. 32. See also *North Star*, April 5, October 24, 31, 1850; *The Liberator*, October 4, 11, November 8, 1850; *New York Colored Convention of 1851*, pp. 29–30; *Ohio Colored Convention of 1851*, p. 16.

house to the wharf. In other northern communities, similar rescue attempts, many of them classics in abolitionist history, resulted in freeing fugitives or causing claimants considerable expense.[6]

As bitterness and tension mounted, resistance frequently erupted into violence. In Christiana, Pennsylvania, for example, the efforts of a slaveholder to recover some fugitives cost him his life. The accused Negro assailants, ably defended by Thaddeus Stevens, were subsequently acquitted. An abolitionist attack on the Boston Court House to free a fugitive slave took the life of an acting United States marshal and quickly brought President Franklin Pierce to order federal troops to the scene. Commenting on this incident, Frederick Douglass discussed a question that must have occasioned some interesting debates among abolitionists: "Is it Right and Wise to Kill a Kidnapper?" Although he had once identified himself with the Garrisonian principle of nonviolence, Douglass now urged Negroes to abandon any scruples about force when dealing with a slave-hunter, for such a person had forfeited his right to live. Moreover, Douglass insisted, Negroes had long been stereotyped as patient, passive, and meek. "This reproach must be wiped out," he declared, "and nothing short of resistance on the part of colored men, can wipe it out. Every Slavehunter who meets a bloody death in his infernal business, is an argument in favor of the manhood of our race."[7]

Already shaken by the personal-liberty laws, southern defenders expressed their shock at the sight of organized and armed Negroes openly defying federal authority. Ignoring its own repeated suppression of the rights of antislavery advocates and free Negroes, the South demanded full recognition of the

[6] Wilbur H. Siebert, *The Underground Railroad in Massachusetts* (Worcester, 1936), pp. 45–53, 57–63; Siebert, *Underground Railroad*, pp. 327–33; Allan Nevins, *Ordeal of the Union* (2 vols.; New York, 1947), I, 387–89.

[7] Aptheker (ed.), *Documentary History*, pp. 323–24; *Frederick Douglass' Paper*, June 2, 1854.

rights of slaveowners to repossess their human property and
urged that steps be taken to break northern resistance. When
news of the successful abolitionist rescue of a fugitive slave
reached Washington, D.C., Senator Henry Clay of Kentucky
suggested that the President immediately investigate the
outrage and recommend appropriate congressional action.
Vigorously condemning the Boston rescue, Clay cited with
particular alarm the color of the participants and the obvious
implications. "By whom was this mob impelled onward?" he
asked. "By our own race? No, sir, but by negroes; by African
descendants; by people who possess no part, as I contend, in
our political system; and the question which arises is, whether
we shall have law, and whether the majesty of the Government
shall be maintained or not; whether we shall have a Government of white men or black men in the cities of this country." [8]
Despite Clay's alarm, a frequently sympathetic public opinion
encouraged Negroes and abolitionists to continue their resistance until enforcement of the detested law became impractical,
if not impossible.

Against a background of sectional bitterness and growing
concern over the future of American Negroes, the Colonization
Society found even more compelling reasons to urge support
of its Liberian colony. The Fugitive Slave Act, the Dred Scott
decision, anti-immigration laws, and the overwhelming defeat
of suffrage proposals bolstered previous colonizationist arguments that Negroes could never secure equal rights within the
United States. Adding to this plight, new waves of foreign
immigrants drove many Negroes from the menial employments they had once monopolized and threatened what little
economic security they possessed. What more evidence could
be adduced to demonstrate to hitherto skeptical Negroes the
impossibility of integration into white society and thus the

[8] *Congressional Globe*, 31 Cong., 2 sess., p. 597.

desirability, if not the inevitability, of African colonization? "He cannot stay where he is," a colonization leader declared in 1860. "He is excluded from other parts of the United States; he can find no enduring home in the west; . . . where is he to find a home?" Fortunately, God himself had at one time supplied the answer — the western coast of Africa.[9]

In its appeals for Negro volunteers and white support, the Colonization Society repeated the familiar arguments of the 1820's and indicated how recent events had merely added to the urgency of the problem. Several states, through constitutional conventions or the legislature, renewed their indorsement of colonization, and some hoped to make it virtually obligatory by further proscribing Negro rights. The Indiana constitutional convention agreed to contribute all fines collected from violations of the new anti-immigration law to the cause of colonization. The state legislature subsequently appropriated $5,000 for a special colonization fund. In Ohio, the state house of representatives petitioned Congress to inquire into the expediency of surveying and appropriating a portion of the territory recently acquired from Mexico for the exclusive benefit of Negro settlers; a Connecticut legislative committee indorsed the Liberian project after affirming the hopelessness of Negroes' ever attaining social or political equality in the United States; and Governor Washington Hunt of New York, after discussing in his annual message to the legislature the "anomalous position" of the Negro, pointed to the practicality and desirability of colonization and urged liberal state and federal financial support.[10]

Aside from state indorsements, colonization attracted sup-

[9] *Forty-third Annual Report of the American Colonization Society* (Washington, D.C., 1860), p. 26.

[10] *Indiana Constitutional Debates of 1850*, II, 1586, 1793–96, 2045; Richard W. Leopold, *Robert Dale Owen* (Cambridge, Mass., 1940), p. 285; *House Miscellaneous Document*, 31 Cong., 1 sess., No. 19 (1850) ; Warner, *New Haven Negroes*, p. 107; Lincoln (ed.), *Messages from the Governors*, IV, 619–23.

port in the 1850's from various sources and for different reasons. Some southerners urged the removal of free Negroes as a nuisance and a subversive influence on the slave population. Most colonizationists, however, apparently hoped that colonization would solve an admittedly hopeless problem and benefit both races, but this did not necessarily tie them to the Liberian plan. A Cleveland Free Soil newspaper, for example, suggested in 1851 that some productive section of the United States be set aside for the exclusive residence of free Negroes. On the eve of the Civil War a Springfield, Massachusetts, journal, discussing the question "What Shall Be Done With The Darkies?" berated Negro leaders for dereliction of duty, lack of racial pride and independence, and a tendency to cling to the coattails of white society. Colonization, it maintained, was not a degrading removal but an opportunity to build a new and constructive society. When Negroes demonstrated that they possessed the necessary spirit, enterprise, and intelligence to create and properly govern an independent colony, the editorial concluded, they would have taken a crucial step toward universal emancipation.[11]

Most abolitionists maintained a strong anticolonization stand and continued to view the Colonization Society as a "bitter, malignant and active enemy" of the antislavery cause. In the 1850's, however, a growing uncertainty concerning the wisdom of this long-held opposition manifested itself in abolitionist ranks. Harriet Beecher Stowe's *Uncle Tom's Cabin*, for example, evoked considerable controversy by dealing sympathetically with colonization. In the closing pages of the book, George Harris departs, with his family, for Liberia, where a

[11] Cleveland *Daily True Democrat*, February 27, 1851, in Works Projects Administration (eds.), *Annals of Cleveland, 1818–1935* (59 vols.; Cleveland, 1937–38), XXXIV, 175; *The Liberator*, August 31, 1860. See also Jacob Dewees, *The Great Future of America and Africa* (Philadelphia, 1854), and W. S. Brown, "A Plan of National Colonization," in Josiah Priest, *Bible Defence of Slavery* (Glasgow, Kentucky, 1853), pp. 491–509.

new and promising republic has arisen. Although this land has been used by his oppressors to retard emancipation, Harris maintains that such sinister designs cannot obstruct its value as the nucleus of a new Negro nation. "I want a country, a nation, of my own," he declares. "I think that the African race has peculiarities, yet to be unfolded in the light of civilization and Christianity, which, if not the same with those of the Anglo-Saxon, may prove to be, morally, of even a higher type. . . . As a Christian patriot, as a teacher of Christianity, I go to *my country*, — my chosen, my glorious Africa !" Unmoved by Mrs. Stowe's eloquent plea for the new republic, Negro delegates to the American and Foreign Anti-Slavery convention called this passage an "evil influence," referred to its enthusiastic acceptance by a recent colonization meeting, and hoped that something would be done to counteract its influence. In a note to the convention, Mrs. Stowe reaffirmed her opposition to the American Colonization Society, assured the delegates that she was not a colonizationist, and admitted that if she were to rewrite the book, Harris would not be sent to Liberia. At the same time, however, she called the African colony "a fixed fact" and advised Negroes not to disregard completely this opportunity to construct an independent nation.[12]

While Mrs. Stowe suggested the need for another look at Liberia, several other abolitionists sought to draw a line — though an admittedly precarious one — between the general merits of colonization and the questionable designs of the American Colonization Society. James Birney, who had abandoned colonization for abolitionism in the 1830's, dismally concluded in 1852 that little hope remained for the Negro in the United States. Although he refused to indorse the Society,

[12] *Proceedings of the American Anti-Slavery Society, at its Second Decade* (New York, 1854), p. 15; Harriet Beecher Stowe, *Uncle Tom's Cabin* (2 vols.; Boston, 1852), II, 302–3; American and Foreign Anti-Slavery Society, *Twelfth Annual Report*, p. 28, *Thirteenth Annual Report*, pp. 192–93; *Frederick Douglass' Paper*, May 20, 1852.

Birney called upon each Negro to decide for himself whether or not he could best better his position here or elsewhere. Some abolitionists went even further and maintained that the Colonization Society had had a change of heart, that it had altered its tactics and thus deserved more careful consideration. Moreover, Liberia now stood as an independent Negro state, rather than as an appendage of the Society, so why not urge Negroes to go there and demonstrate to the world their capabilities? But few abolitionists actually joined in these sporadic calls for a re-evaluation of colonization; most of them reaffirmed their previous opposition to the Society, and even those who appeared otherwise sympathetic concluded that the entire scheme was inexpedient and impractical. Apparently, the federal government had reached a similiar conclusion.[13]

Despite state and public appeals, the federal government remained largely indifferent to the colonization scheme. President Millard Fillmore indorsed it but at the same time deleted from his 1852 Message to Congress some intended remarks on the subject. After citing the deplorable condition of the free Negro population, Fillmore had planned to demonstrate the practicality and necessity of African colonization. "There can be no well-grounded hope," he had written, "for the improvement of either their moral or social condition, until they are removed from a humiliating sense of inferiority in the presence of a superior race." Although the proposed remarks were omitted from the delivered address, several newspapers alluded to them.[14] One year later, the Senate also indicated an unwillingness to take any specific action. During the debate on the naval appropriations bill, a New Jersey senator offered an amendment which would have appropriated $125,000 to equip

[13] Betty L. Fladeland, *James Gillespie Birney* (Ithaca, N.Y., 1955), pp. 280–81; *Twelfth Annual Report of the American and Foreign Anti-Slavery Society*, p. 29.

[14] Frank H. Severance (ed.), *Millard Fillmore Papers* (2 vols.; Buffalo, 1907), I, 313 n., 320–24.

and maintain an exploratory expedition to Africa to ascertain its resources and to aid the colonization of free Negroes. Urging approval of the measure, the senator declared that "the negro is a timid creature; he feels in his soul that which the white man boldly avows: that he is an inferior being, and therefore the subject of deception and wrong." Government support, he pointed out, would enhance the prestige of the colonization cause, remove previous suspicions about its motives, and encourage Negro participation. Congress rejected the amendment and continued to maintain a hands-off position.[15]

Although Negro conventions and newspapers reiterated their opposition to African colonization, the hard-pressed Negro community reacted much more favorably in the 1850's to the idea of emigration, particularly to other parts of the Western Hemisphere. After the establishment of the "independent" Liberian Republic, some Negroes even urged a new approach to that area. Henry Highland Garnet, once a vigorous critic of colonization, now praised the beneficial influence of Liberia on the rest of Africa and recommended emigration to those Negroes who despaired of ever improving their position in the United States.[16] Agreeing that colonization should be re-evaluated, a Hartford, Connecticut, Negro businessman charged that colored leadership had betrayed its responsibility by encouraging hopes that could never be realized in this country. After a realistic look at the present plight of free Negroes, how could anyone not conclude "that the friendly and mutual separation of the two races is not only necessary to the peace, happiness and prosperity of both, but indispensable to the preservation of the one and the glory of the other?" [17] Most Negroes undoubtedly denied — or at least wanted to deny —

[15] *Congressional Globe*, 32 Cong., 2 sess., pp. 1064–65; *Appendix to the Congressional Globe*, 32 Cong., 2 sess., pp. 231–34.

[16] *North Star*, January 26, March 2, 1849.

[17] Woodson (ed.), *Mind of the Negro*, pp. 133–44.

such a pessimistic conclusion, but a growing minority nevertheless felt that it warranted further consideration and that some
outlet should be opened, either overseas or on this continent,
for the emigration of the restless, the disgruntled, and the
ambitious.

In the 1850's, Negro emigrationist sentiment looked more
to Central America than to Africa as a place of permanent
refuge. Martin R. Delany, a prominent Negro leader, physician, and journalist, took a leading part in encouraging interest in these areas and in the general value of emigration. The
United States, he wrote in 1852, had violated its professed
principles of republican equality by maintaining the Negro
population in political and economic bondage. The appearance of respectable and competent Negro businessmen, literary figures, and professionals had done little to alter white
hostility. Meanwhile, most Negroes had become so accustomed
to economic inferiority that they now regarded the menial
jobs as "fashionable" and "second nature." Under these circumstances, Delany argued, the Negro was compelled to
choose between two alternatives: continued degradation here
or emigration and the establishment of a useful and free community elsewhere. However, all colonization roads did not
necessarily lead to Liberia or require support of the "anti-
Christian" and "misanthropic" Colonization Society. If anything, the Liberian colony was geographically and climatically
unacceptable, a slaveholder's device to secure his chattel, and
"a burlesque" on government. The destiny of American Negroes, Delany concluded, lay in the Western Hemisphere; not
in Canada, which faced imminent annexation to the United
States, but in Central and South America, which afforded the
Negro a favorable geographic location and climate, untapped
natural resources, unlimited opportunities for individual
enterprise, and a "Promised Land" where he could live with-

out any fear of annexation or political and economic oppression.[18]

To promote and organize emigrationist sentiment, Negro proponents called a national convention for 1854 and invited only those who favored colonization in the Western Hemisphere to participate in the proceedings. The proposed meeting immediately set off a lively debate among northern Negroes. Calling it "unwise, unfortunate, and premature," Frederick Douglass charged that such a project contemplated a separate nationality. "We are Americans," he asserted. "We are not aliens. We are a component part of the nation. Though in only some of the States, are we an acknowledged necessary part of the 'ruling element,' we have no disposition, to renounce our nationality. We do not wish to form a separate nation in these United States." Some day, Douglass optimistically concluded, the whites would grant full citizenship rights to the Negro. Until that time, his people should not allow themselves to be distracted from immediate goals by far-fetched plans based upon "despondency and despair." Indorsing Douglass' position, Negro conventions in Illinois, California, and Massachusetts opposed the pending emigrationist convention as impeding the struggle for equal rights; an Ohio meeting had previously rejected a resolution urging voluntary emigration on the grounds that no Negro should leave the United States while any of his southern brethren remained in bondage.[19]

On August 24, 1854, despite mounting opposition, delegates from eleven states convened in Cleveland for the National Emigration Convention of the Colored People. Drawing

[18] Delany, *Condition, Elevation, Emigration, and Destiny of the Colored People*, pp. 14–15, 30–35, 159–98.
[19] *Frederick Douglass' Paper*, August 26, September 30, October 28, 1853, March 10, July 6, 1854; *Illinois Colored Convention of 1853*, p. 13; *Ohio Colored Convention of 1852*, p. 9. See also Frederick Douglass, William J. Watkins, James M. Whitfield, *Arguments, Pro and Con, on the Call for a National Emigration Convention, to be held in Cleveland, Ohio, August, 1854* (Detroit, 1854).

its support primarily from Pennsylvania and Ohio, the Convention attracted the most outspoken emigrationists of the 1850's — Delany, James T. Holly, James M. Whitfield, and H. Ford Douglass. The Platform and Address to the Negro People neatly summarized their position. Despite years of patient waiting and agitation, the Negro had been doomed to constant "disappointment, discouragement and degradation." Disfranchisement had deprived him of any political power; statutes and extralegal customs had relegated him to an inferior position and had paralyzed his creative energies; the Fugitive Slave Act now threatened him with enslavement. The American Negro had thus carefully to consider emigration or face deterioration.

Emigrationists made it quite clear, however, that the establishment of an independent Negro colony signified more than a simple desire to escape political oppression: it also symbolized a growing feeling of national consciousness and racial pride. Negroes had to be made to realize that they were a different race, that they had little in common with the Anglo-Saxons, and that they possessed certain commendable "inherent traits" and "native characteristics" which required only cultivation before the rest of the world would attempt to emulate them. In the various arts and sciences, ethics, metaphysics, theology, and legal jurisprudence, "there is no doubt but the black race will yet instruct the world."

Some day, the Cleveland delegates agreed, the "question of black and white" will decide the world's destiny. In the past three centuries the territorial aggrandizement of the whites had been based upon the subjugation of the colored peoples of the world; in fact, "the Anglo-American stands pre-eminent for deeds of injustice and acts of oppression, unparalleled perhaps in the annals of world history." But this imbalance could not persist, the convention warned, and every individual would soon have to identify himself with the whites or the blacks. The colored races formed two-thirds of the world's population and were drawing closer together; the white races comprised but one-third. How much longer would "that two-thirds . . . passively submit to the universal domination of this one-third?"

After this prophetic glance at the future, the delegates returned to more immediate matters and noted the important changes that had taken place among American Negroes. While their fathers had submitted to slavery and had contented themselves with small favors from their white masters, the new generation was securing an education and learning the meaning of natural rights. Previously satisfied with white sufferance, Negroes now demanded their rights as "an innate inheritance." Since these could not be acquired within the United States, Negroes would have to go elsewhere — settle in the West Indies or Central or South America — assert their manhood, and develop a new civilization. In these areas the Negro would finally achieve political equality and social and economic betterment, and the natives would most certainly encourage such development as "a check to European presumption, and insufferable Yankee intrusion and impudence." Emigration, then, afforded American Negroes an opportunity to escape a degraded position and commence a new and productive life. Not only did the Cleveland delegates enthusiastically indorse this position, but they also proceeded to form a "National Board of Commissioners," headed by Delany, to begin immediate implementation of it.[20]

The Cleveland convention ably publicized the emigrationist cause, but it did not win the support of the Negro community. Many whites expressed their approval, and this undoubtedly helped to increase Negro suspicions concerning the motives and aims of the emigrationists. "We are surprised to learn,"

[20] *Proceedings of the National Emigration Convention of Colored People; held at Cleveland, Ohio . . . the 24th, 25th and 26th of August, 1854* (Pittsburgh, 1854), pp. 16–18, 23–27, 33–37, 40–41, 43–46, 55–56, 71–77.

a Cleveland newspaper remarked, "that the objects of the convention met with but little favor from our colored citizens." [21] This lack of enthusiasm doomed the project from the beginning. Moreover, the emigrationists themselves divided into various factions. Each proposed area of settlement — Canada, Haiti, Central America, South America, and Africa — had its adherents and colonizing companies. Indeed, in some cases the emigrationist leaders appeared to outnumber their followers.

After the outbreak of the Civil War, emigrationist interest diminished considerably among Negroes but increased among whites, especially when emancipation seemed inevitable. Some Negroes, however, continued to press for emigration as the only alternative to continued oppression in the United States, regardless of the outcome of the civil conflict. In 1862, for example, 242 California Negroes petitioned Congress to colonize them "in some country in which their color will not be a badge of degradation." The true interests of both races, they maintained, required such a separation; any of the proposed sites would be preferable to this country, where the future of the Negro appeared to be dismal, if not hopeless. "It seems to be the settled policy of the nation," the petitioners concluded, "as evinced in the action of both the State and federal governments, to discountenance in every manner the increase of persons of color in their midst, and to use every legal means to induce those now here to emigrate; and there is probably no point on which the public sentiment of every section of the country and of every class of society is so perfectly unanimous as upon this." [22] Most Negroes, however, refused to leave, hoping instead that the impact of the Civil War might create for them a "Promised Land" in the United States.

[21] Cleveland *Leader*, August 25, 1854, in W.P.A. (eds.), *Annals of Cleveland*, XXXVII, 197–98.
[22] *House Miscellaneous Document*, 37 Cong., 2 sess., No. 31 (1862).

While conceding the right of fugitive slaves and free Negroes to claim adequate legal protection, northern public sentiment continued to sanction the political and social inferiority of the African race. By 1860, the five states which granted equal-suffrage rights — Massachusetts, Maine, New Hampshire, Vermont, and Rhode Island — contained only 6 per cent of the total northern Negro population. Proposals to extend the suffrage appeared on the ballot in various states during the 1850's, but none were approved. In addition to maintaining disfranchisement, constitutional conventions and legislatures in four states — Illinois, Indiana, Iowa, and Oregon — agreed between 1850 and 1857 to prohibit the further entry of Negroes, and white voters gave these enactments their overwhelming approval. Not only did Negroes continue to face political, social, and economic proscription, but they also encountered a large number of petty persecutions. The Ohio state senate, for example, voted to expel a Negro editor from his seat in the reporter's section and justified this unprecedented action by observing that the laws of nature and the moral and political well-being of both races required a strict separation.[23]

While southern congressional spokesmen continued to cite the proscription of the Negro in the free states, a growing number of northern proslavery pamphleteers, anxious to offset the influence of abolitionist tracts and broadsides, further lampooned the inferior race. Bearing such titles as *Abolitionism Unveiled!*, *Is the North Right!*, *The Laws of Race*, and *Free Negroism*, these publications varied little in content and emphasis. Divine or natural laws, they claimed, had destined the Anglo-Saxon race to command and the African race to obey. Using pseudo-scientific, biblical, and moral arguments, these pamphleteers further contended that Negroes could not possibly comprehend or properly exercise the ordinary rights

[23] Forest City *Democrat*, January 23, 24, 30, February 17, 1854, in W.P.A. (eds.), *Annals of Cleveland*, XXXVII, 279–80; *The Liberator*, February 10, 1854.

and privileges of free men. Such a person as Frederick Douglass was an exceptional case, for few Negroes could ever attain so much as he had. Did not the general status of free Negroes in the "abolition-loving states" prove beyond any doubt the inherent inferiority of the Africans, the folly of emancipation, and the utter hypocrisy of antislavery arguments? Agreeing with these critics, George Fitzhugh, a leading southern publicist and slavery apologist, looked at the degraded position of northern Negroes and concluded that "humanity, self-interest, consistency, all require that we should enslave the free Negro." [24] Several southern legislatures, in fact, offered free Negroes at least one legally recognized right: that of selling themselves into permanent bondage. But most northerners recoiled at such a proposal and hoped instead that colonization might provide a permanent remedy.

Against this rather dismal background, northern Negroes sought to organize their forces and effect a change in public opinion and legislation. In Illinois, the Repeal Association was formed to secure the abrogation of the Black Laws; Ohio Negroes organized the Colored American League to assist runaway slaves, to improve the condition of the freedmen, and to encourage Negro communities to form military companies; New York Negroes established the State Suffrage Association to press for a constitutional amendment giving them equal voting rights and the Legal Rights Association to combat continued harassment in the public conveyances. [25]

[24] T. V. Paterson, *Abolitionism Unveiled! Hypocrisy Unmasked! and Knavery Scourged!* (New York, 1850) ; *"Is the North Right!" Or, A Word about Slavery and the Colored Race. Addressed to the People of Massachusetts. By a Fellow Citizen* (Boston, 1855) ; Sidney George Fisher, *The Laws of Race* (Philadelphia, 1860) ; David Christy, "Cotton Is King," in E. N. Elliott (ed.), *Cotton Is King, and Pro-Slavery Arguments* (Augusta, Ga., 1860) ; *Free Negroism; or, Results of Emancipation in the North and the West India Islands* (New York, 1862); George Fitzhugh, *What Shall Be Done with the Free Negroes* (Fredericksburg, Va., 1851).

[25] *Proceedings of the State Convention of Colored Citizens of the State of Illinois* (Chicago, 1856), pp. 7, 13; *Ohio Colored Convention of 1850*, p. 13;

Moreover, Negroes moved toward co-ordinating their efforts nationally. On July 6, 1853, delegates from various states met in Rochester, recorded their grievances, and elected the National Council of the Colored People. But this and other national organizations became involved in factional struggles and accomplished little, thus leaving the primary responsibility for effective action in the hands of the state groups.[26]

The rise of antislavery feeling in the North, coincident with the defiance of the Fugitive Slave Act, also encouraged Negroes to take more aggressive action against southern bondage. By 1858, Negro abolitionism not only incorporated the once controversial appeals of David Walker and Henry Highland Garnet but went even further in some cases and welcomed the overthrow of the American government. To this group, the Fugitive Slave Act and the Dred Scott decision deprived Negroes of legal protection and thus absolved them from any allegiance to the federal union. To support the government and the Constitution upon which it was based, Robert Purvis declared, was to indorse "one of the basest, meanest, most atrocious despotisms that ever saw the face of the sun"; any man claiming self-respect would look upon this "piebald and rotten Democracy" with "*contempt, loathing*, and *unutterable abhorrence*!" Why not, then, Purvis urged, welcome the overthrow of "this atrocious government" and construct a better one in its place? Along similar lines, a delegate to the California Negro convention of 1856 bitterly assailed a patriotic resolution favoring support of the United States against foreign invasion. "I would hail the advent of a foreign army upon our shores," he declared, "if that army provided liberty to me and my people in bondage." Emigrationist leader H. Ford

Proceedings of the State Convention of the Colored Men of the State of Ohio (Columbus, 1857), p. 7; *Frederick Douglass' Paper*, September 7, 14, 1855; New York *Daily Times*, August 27, 1855.

[26] *Proceedings of the Colored National Convention* (Rochester, 1853); *Frederick Douglass' Paper*, July 28, 1854, May 18, 1855.

Douglass agreed. "I can hate this Government without being
disloyal," he said, "because it has stricken down my manhood, and treated me as a saleable commodity. I can join a
foreign enemy and fight against it, without being a traitor,
because it treats me as an ALIEN and a STRANGER, and I am
free to avow that should such a contingency arise I should
not hesitate to take any advantage in order to procure such
indemnity for the future." [27]

Most Negroes did not indorse the sentiments of this small
but vocal minority; nevertheless, they did welcome John
Brown's direct thrust at slavery as the obvious work of a
saint. Prior to his dramatic raid on Harper's Ferry, Brown had
urged Frederick Douglass to join him in a declaration of war
on slavery, but the Negro leader had refused on the grounds
that such an attack was doomed to tragic failure. Once the
plan had been executed, however, Douglass applauded it as
an act of courage and devotion and denounced Brown's de-
tractors as the products of "an effeminate and cowardly age"
which was "too gross and sensual to appreciate his deeds,
and so calls him mad." Any act which created restless nights
for slaveholders, Douglass declared, should be a cause for
rejoicing. Knowing the futility of moral appeals to the South,
Brown had struck at bondage "with the weapons precisely
adapted to bring it to the death." Since slavery existed only
through "brute force," Douglass concluded, why not turn its
own weapons against it? [28]

Brown's raid and subsequent death by hanging aroused
Negro sympathies in the North — he had executed a "glorious
act for the cause of humanity"; he had "rocked the bloody
Bastille" in a desperate attempt to redeem Americans from

[27] *Proceedings of a Convention of the Colored Men of Ohio* (Cincinnati, 1858),
pp. 6–7; *The Liberator*, May 22, 1857, May 18, 1860; *Proceedings of the Second
Annual Convention of the Colored Citizens of the State of California* (San Francisco, 1856), pp. 14, 19; Aptheker (ed.), *Documentary History*, p. 368.
[28] *Douglass' Monthly*, November, 1859.

the national sin of slavery; he clearly deserved commendation, not condemnation. If the historical role assigned to Brown seemed dubious in a terrorized South and a frightened though awed North, it had already been assured in the Negro community, for no white had ever made such a dramatic sacrifice for the cause of human freedom. "The memory of John Brown," one Negro proclaimed, "shall be indelibly written upon the tablets of our hearts, and when tyrants cease to oppress the enslaved, we will teach our children to revive his name, and transmit it to the latest posterity, as being the greatest man in the 19th century." [29]

Despite the impact of John Brown, most American Negroes indorsed political action rather than violence, although neither alternative seemed particularly promising. Violence could result only in tragic failure — Nat Turner and John Brown symbolized the hopelessness of this approach. Disfranchisement severely curtailed the Negro's political power, and in any case the major political parties had little to offer. Until the organization of the Republican party, Negroes either had to adopt a lesser-of-two-evils political philosophy or give their support to third-party movements. Many of them did participate actively in the Liberty and Free Soil parties; in fact, the New York Liberty party went so far as to nominate Frederick Douglass for a state office — the first time such an honor had ever been accorded a Negro. [30] The appearance of the Republican party raised Negro hopes and attracted enthusiastic supporters, but, as some Negroes soon discovered, the new party offered few reasons for any great optimism. It promised to resist southern aggression and keep the territories free — but that was all. This, too, was to be a white man's party devoted to the supremacy of the white race. Although most Negroes

[29] Woodson (ed.), *Mind of the Negro*, pp. 508–10; *The Liberator*, December 16, 1859, March 16, May 18, July 13, 1860.
[30] Wesley, "The Participation of Negroes in Anti-Slavery Parties," p. 69.

continued to favor the Republicans, this often reflected desperation rather than real conviction.

If the Negro had any expectations of a fundamental change in his condition under Republican rule, they were quickly banished as Republicans proceeded to clarify their position in response to partisan attacks. To offset growing Republican popularity in the North, the Democrats seized upon those issues which could excite the most heated passions and prejudices — racial equality, amalgamation, and white supremacy. The Republicans had to be portrayed as a party that would be "soft" on the race issue, as a pro-amalgamation, "nigger loving" political conglomeration bent on raising Negroes to full legal and social equality with whites. Indeed, the very supremacy of the white race would be placed in grave jeopardy. Once in power, Democrats warned, the "Black Republicans" would appoint Negroes to government offices, elect them to legislative bodies, and grant them the right to vote, to act as witnesses in court, and to sit in classrooms with white students. "Negro equality," an Indiana congressman charged, "is the necessary, logical, and inevitable sequence of their principles." [31] Exploiting this issue to the fullest, Senator Stephen Douglas castigated his Illinois rival, Abraham Lincoln, as a friend of the Negro and the candidate of Frederick Douglass and warned that a Republican triumph would cover the western prairies with black settlements. "If you desire negro citizenship," he told a political rally, "if you desire to allow them to come into the State and settle with the white man, if you desire them to vote on an equality with yourselves, and to make them eligible to office, to serve on juries, and to adjudge your rights, then support Mr. Lincoln and the Black Republican party." Douglas, on the other hand, promised to stand on the principle that the American government had

[31] *Appendix to the Congressional Globe*, 36 Cong., 1 sess., p. 282. See also *Congressional Globe*, 36 Cong., 1 sess., pp. 238–39; *Appendix to the Congressional Globe*, 36 Cong., 1 sess., pp. 282–88.

been formed "on the white basis, by white men, for the benefit of white men and their posterity forever." [32]

Seeking to press these charges in a more spectacular manner, some thirty thousand anti-Republicans staged a torchlight procession in New York City a few days before the election of 1860. Many of the floats, placards, and banners identified Republicans with miscegenation and racial equality. One float pictured Lincoln holding a black flag labeled "Discord" and Horace Greeley clutching a *Tribune* while between them sat a thick-lipped Negro embracing a white girl; another depicted, under the standard "Republicanism," a Negro leading a white woman into the White House. The banners carried by the marchers bore such slogans as "Republican Platform — Rails and Wool!"; "No Negro Equality"; "Massa Greeley and Master Sambo"; and "Free Love, Free Niggers, and Free Women." Since a Republican-dominated legislature had voted to place the Negro-suffrage question on the November ballot, these charges appeared to have particular relevance. [33]

Actually, both political parties agreed on the need to contain the menace of racial equality, and each sought to outdo the other in professions of allegiance to the principles of white supremacy. "We, the Republican party, are the white man's party," declared Senator Lyman Trumbull, Illinois Republican leader and a close associate of Lincoln. "We are for free white men, and for making white labor respectable and honorable, which it can never be when negro slave labor is brought into competition with it." [34] Republicans repeatedly stressed this point, assuring the electorate that opposition to slavery

[32] Basler (ed.), *Collected Works of Abraham Lincoln*, III, 9. See also III, 55–56, 112–14, 171–72.

[33] New York *Herald* and New York *Express*, as quoted in *The Liberator*, November 2, 1860.

[34] Address of Senator Lyman Trumbull, delivered at Chicago, August 7, 1858, as quoted in Francis P. Blair, Jr., *The Destiny of the Races of this Continent* (Washington, D.C., 1859), p. 30. See also *Congressional Globe*, 36 Cong., 1 sess., p. 102.

expansion made them "the only white man's party in this country." Taking this one step further, Republican leaders, while denouncing the Dred Scott decision and the Kansas-Nebraska Act, made few efforts to sympathize with the plight of the Negro. This was irrelevant. "The 'negro question,' as we understand it," an Ohio Republican wrote, "is a *white man's question*, the question of the right of free white laborers to the soil of the territories. It is not to be crushed or retarded by shouting 'Sambo' at us. We have no Sambo in our platform. . . . We object to Sambo. We don't want him about. We insist that he shall not be forced upon us." [35]

While stressing this incompatibility of free and slave labor, most Republicans also denied any intention to extend political rights to free Negroes and expressed revulsion at the idea of social intercourse with them. Full legal protection should be accorded both races, but according to Republican logic, it did not necessarily follow that Negroes should be granted the right to vote, sit on juries, or testify in cases involving whites. To the Negro, this must have been a strange logic indeed. In many areas, party leaders contended that any concessions to Negroes would constitute political suicide. In 1860, for example, an Ohio leader declared that a poll of the Republican party in the Old Northwest would not find "one in every thousand" favoring social and political rights for Negroes.[36] Even such a firm and outspoken abolitionist as Congressman Joshua Giddings of Ohio hesitated to commit his party too far on this potentially explosive issue. "We do not say the black man is, or shall be, the equal of the white man," Giddings declared in 1859, "or that he shall vote or hold office, however just such a position may be; but we assert that he who murders

[35] *Congressional Globe*, 35 Cong., 2 sess., p. 981; 36 Cong., 1 sess., pp. 239, 1903, 1910; *Appendix to the Congressional Globe*, 34 Cong., 3 sess., p. 91; Earl B. Wiley, " 'Governor' John Greiner and Chase's Bid for the Presidency in 1860," *Ohio State Archaeological and Historical Quarterly*, LVIII (1949), 261–62.

[36] *Congressional Globe*, 36 Cong., 1 sess., p. 1910.

271

a black man shall be hanged; that he who robs the black man of his liberty or his property shall be punished like other criminals." [37] And few Republicans were as radical as Giddings on this question! Meanwhile, Republican-dominated legislatures and constitutional conventions made few efforts to extend political rights. If their conservatism required any further demonstration, a New York City Republican proudly noted that of the 32,000 who voted for Lincoln in 1860, only 1,600 indorsed the state Negro-suffrage amendment. [38]

The expediencies and compromises of politics only partially explain the Republican aversion to equal rights, for this aversion also reflected the popular conviction that an inferior race had no place in the body politic. Some Republican newspapers not only openly proclaimed the superiority of the Caucasian race over the African, but assured the electorate that the Republican party would preserve this supremacy and protect the nation as much as possible "from the pestilential presence of the black man." [39] Even the professed friends of the Negro — those who went so far as to advocate equal political rights — could claim no immunity from prevailing racial theories and prejudices. William H. Seward, for example, described the American Negro to an 1860 political rally as "a foreign and feeble element like the Indians, incapable of assimilation . . . a pitiful exotic unwisely and unnecessarily transplanted into our fields, and which it is unprofitable to cultivate at the cost of the desolation of the native vineyard." But the Negro still had a right "to such care and protection as the weak everywhere may require from the strong." While indorsing the cause of Negro education in Washington, D.C., abolitionist Senator Henry Wilson of Massachusetts made it clear that he did not believe "in the mental or the intellectual

[37] *Ibid.*, 35 Cong., 2 sess., p. 346.
[38] Nevins and Thomas (eds.), *Diary of George Templeton Strong*, III, 76.
[39] Bernard Mandel, *Labor: Free and Slave* (New York, 1955), p. 150.

equality of the African race with this proud and domineering white race of ours." Fearing no competition from an admittedly inferior race, Wilson could see no reason why Congress should not extend to Negroes educational opportunities and even full citizenship.[40]

Despite this rather clear opposition to racial equality, several Republican leaders felt that something more had to be done before the crucial election of 1860. The party needed a still firmer and more positive position on the troublesome Negro question, one that would appeal to northern and border-state sentiment without altogether alienating the abolitionists. By 1858, this group, which included such party dignitaries as Francis P. Blair, Jr., and Edward Bates of Missouri, Montgomery Blair of Maryland, and Senator James Doolittle of Wisconsin, had found an ideal solution: the Republican party should press for the colonization of American Negroes in Central America under the direction of the federal government. "It would do more than ten thousand speeches," Montgomery Blair wrote, "to define accurately our objects and disabuse the minds of the great body of the Southern people . . . that the Republicans wish to set negroes free among them to be their equals and consequently their rulers when they are numerous." [41]

To promote this plan, Representative Francis P. Blair, Jr., proposed to the House in January, 1858, that a committee inquire into the expediency of acquiring territory in Central or South America for the purpose of Negro colonization. Not only would this check the expansion of slavery into those areas, Blair explained, but it might secure for "a class of men who are worse than useless to us" innumerable opportunities which would never be available to them in the United States. Indeed,

[40] Baker (ed.), *Works of William H. Seward*, IV, 317; *Congressional Globe*, 36 Cong., 1 sess., p. 1684.
[41] Reinhard H. Luthin, *The First Lincoln Campaign* (Cambridge, Mass., 1944), p. 66.

colonization appeared to be the only alternative to forcible expulsion. In the Senate, James Doolittle introduced a similar proposal and spoke in glowing terms of the attractions of Central and South America, including a political and physical climate better adapted to the Negro's constitution and creative energies.[42]

Various Republican and abolitionist spokesmen enthusiastically indorsed the Blair-Doolittle proposals. Senator Trumbull welcomed the plan and wished "Godspeed" to any measure for the removal of the Negro population. Placing more emphasis on the voluntary nature of the plan, Representative Giddings gave his blessing to the Central American project for those Negroes who desired to settle in a more congenial climate. Gerrit Smith, antislavery leader and outspoken critic of the American Colonization Society, told Blair that the proposal had "enlightened and gratified" him, but such emigration would have to be voluntary and "be couched in words that would [not] offend the black, or invade their self-respect." Several Negro emigrationists, including James T. Holly, James M. Whitfield, and J. Dennis Harris, hailed the plan as inaugurating "a new era in their hopes" and promised full co-operation.[43]

The federal government and most Negroes remained unenthusiastic. The old spirit of African colonization had been revived under a new name, one Negro leader charged, but the principle had not changed — "the old snake with a new skin — nothing more, nothing less." Nor did the voluntary nature of the plan increase its attractiveness, for repressive legislation could easily force a "voluntary" departure. Noticing the

[42] Congressional Globe, 35 Cong., 1 sess., pp. 293–98, 3034; Senate Miscellaneous Document, 35 Cong., 2 sess., No. 26 (1858).

[43] Blair, Destiny of the Races, pp. 30, 32, 33–38; J. Dennis Harris, A Summer on the Borders of the Caribbean Sea (New York, 1860), pp. iii, 178. For Edward Bates' support, see Howard K. Beale (ed.), The Diary of Edward Bates, 1859–1866 (Washington, D.C., 1933), p. 113.

rather obvious connection between the new emigration proposals and the Republicans, Frederick Douglass expressed
the hope that Negroes might be able to expect better things
from that avowedly antislavery party. Should the Republican
party triumph in 1860, he wrote, "we earnestly hope and pray,
for its own sake, for the sake of the country, and for the sake
of humanity, that it will first assume a higher level than this
in regard to the black man." Otherwise, Douglass warned, the
white American faced tragic consequences. If enfranchised,
the Negro would remain forever a part of the Union; if further
oppressed, he would "send it into a thousand fragments." [44]

In view of the avowed principles and policies of the Republican party, northern Negroes obviously faced a political dilemma. Although they rejoiced at its vigorous stand against
slavery expansion, Negro leaders found it difficult to register
any great enthusiasm over a party which promised them no
relief from oppressive legislation, recognized the constitutional right of slavery to exist and be protected in the South,
showed an aversion to social and political equality, and ignored the Fugitive Slave Act and bondage in the District of
Columbia. In the current political struggle, one Negro lamented, neither party had any regard for the doctrine of equal
rights: "Despotism is the avowed object of one, whilst self-
interest is the all controlling power and ruling motive of the
other. The philanthropic doctrine of equal rights is totally
ignored. The poor negro, although the cause of this agitation,
is denied by both parties as having any rights in common with
humanity. They both worship at the shrine of Avarice and
Cupidity, and sacrifice the rights of men to propitiate their
gods." [45]

Recognizing the even drearier alternatives, many Negroes
decided that political expediency justified support of the Re-

44 *The Liberator*, May 18, 1860; *Douglass' Monthly*, March, 1859.
45 Charles M. Wilson, "What Is Our True Condition?" *Anglo-African Magazine*, II (January, 1860), 19.

publican party. After all, Frederick Douglass pointed out, the Republicans did symbolize northern antislavery sentiment and might, in time, establish a more favorable climate for equal-rights legislation. In New England, Ohio, and New York, Negro conventions expressed sympathy for the Republican movement, though recognizing at the same time its serious limitations.[46] Such support, although qualified, did not go unchallenged. "No, sir, I am not a Republican," Robert Purvis told the American Anti-Slavery Society in 1860. "I can never join a party, the leaders of which conspire to expel us from the country." Asking forgiveness for having once supported that party, another Negro leader — John Jones of Illinois — charged that the Republicans had impeded the antislavery struggle by making abolitionism an ugly word.[47]

The nomination of Abraham Lincoln afforded little promise of a change in Republican policy. H. Ford Douglass, an Illinois Negro leader, recalled that the Republican nominee had once refused to sign a legislative petition asking for the repeal of the state law barring Negro testimony in cases involving whites. If blacks dared to send their children to the schools of Illinois, the Negro leader charged, "Abraham Lincoln would kick them out, in the name of Republicanism and anti-slavery!" Both parties, he concluded, "are barren and unfruitful. . . . I care nothing about that anti-slavery which wants to make the Territories free, while it is unwilling to extend to me, as a man, in the free States, all the rights of a man." Even Frederick Douglass, otherwise a reluctant Republican supporter, recognized the deficiencies of the victorious Republican candidate and mournfully predicted that Lincoln's administration would probably appease the slavery

[46] *Frederick Douglass' Paper*, August 15, 1856; New York *Daily Times*, July 31, 1856; *The Liberator*, September 5, 1856, April 10, July 3, October 23, 1857, October 1, December 3, 1858, August 1, 1859; *Proceedings of the State Convention of Colored Men* (Columbus, 1856), p. 2; *Ohio Colored Convention of 1858*, pp. 9–10.

[47] *The Liberator*, May 18, 1860; *Illinois Colored Convention of 1856*, p. 18.

interests rather than engage in any effective antislavery activity. But the South did not give Douglass a chance to prove his point.[48]

Always a masterful politician, Abraham Lincoln possessed an extraordinary insight into the public mind. On the question of political and social equality of the races, he accurately and consistently reflected the thoughts and prejudices of most Americans. By November, 1860, candidate Lincoln had apparently convinced a majority of northerners that the Republican party stood for checking the advance of slavery, not for extending political and social rights to an inferior race. Had he held any other position on this explosive issue, his nomination and election would have been problematical. No man who has supported Negro suffrage, a Republican editor asserted, could be elected President of the United States. In 1860, the party had found a "safe" candidate.

As a spokesman for the Republican party, Lincoln made quite clear his position on Negro rights. Even if his own feelings could admit the desirability of racial equality — and he vigorously denied this possibility — he could not make it any less repugnant to most whites. "A universal feeling, whether well or ill-founded," he remarked, "can not be safely disregarded. We can not, then, make them equals." Accordingly, the Negro had to be kept in an inferior position. "I will say then," Lincoln told a political rally in 1858, "that I am not, nor ever have been in favor of bringing about in any way the social and political equality of the white and black races, [applause] — that I am not nor ever have been in favor of making voters or jurors of negroes, nor of qualifying them to hold office, nor to intermarry with white people." Physical differences, he continued, made political and social equality between Negroes and whites impossible. As long as both races

[48] *The Liberator*, July 13, 1860; *Douglass' Monthly*, December, 1860.

remained in the United States, "there must be the position of superior and inferior, and I as much as any other man am in favor of having the superior position assigned to the white race." [49]

The recognition of white supremacy, Lincoln insisted, should not deprive the Negro of common legal protection. Although the Negro could hardly be considered the moral or intellectual equal of the white man, he was still entitled to those natural rights enumerated by the Declaration of Independence: life, liberty, and the pursuit of happiness. "All I ask for the Negro," Lincoln stated, "is that if you do not like him, let him alone. If God gave him but little, that little let him enjoy." Of course legal protection did not imply a recognition of Negro citizenship. Despite the Dred Scott decision, Lincoln defended the right of each state to decide this important question for itself. Anticipating a problem of Reconstruction, he made it clear in 1858 that only a state legislature — not Congress — could recognize Negro citizenship or alter the social and political relations of the races. If Illinois should entertain such a proposal, however, Lincoln assured his followers that he would oppose it. [50] One question Lincoln left unanswered: How could a disfranchised Negro, unable to testify in a case involving a white man or to sit on a jury, enjoy common legal protection at the same time?

Since nearly all whites felt "a natural disgust" for any indiscriminate mixing of the races, Lincoln concluded that colonization offered the only hope of solving the racial problem. Prior to 1860, he had urged that the African be returned to his native climate; this was morally correct and would benefit both races. During the war, Lincoln maintained this position; indeed, the inevitability of emancipation redoubled his efforts in that direction. Addressing a Negro delegation in 1862, the

[49] Basler (ed.), *Collected Works of Abraham Lincoln*, II, 256, III, 145–46.
[50] *Ibid.*, II, 520, III, 16, 179, 299–300.

President stressed the physical incompatibility of the two races and the fact that "on this broad continent, not a single man of your race is made the equal of a single man of ours." Inasmuch as Americans did not desire the further presence of the Negro population, Lincoln urged the black man to look elsewhere — to Liberia, which had had a limited success, or, preferably, to Central America, where location, natural resources, and climate offered splendid opportunities.[51]

On some occasions, Lincoln appeared to temper his advocacy of the political and social proscription of Negroes. In 1858, for example, he told a Chicago audience to discard "all this quibbling about this man and the other man — this race and that race and the other race being inferior, and therefore they must be placed in an inferior position." Instead, Americans should reassert their belief that all men are created equal. Of course Lincoln often reserved these sentiments for strongly antislavery audiences in northern Illinois. This "chameleon-like" position of Republicans in various parts of the state enraged the Democrats. In northern Illinois, Stephen Douglas charged, abolitionists were told to vote for Lincoln because of his advocacy of racial equality, while in the southern portion of the state, white supremacy was emphasized. But Lincoln denied any inconsistency: "Anything that argues me into . . . social and political equality with the negro, is but a specious and fantastic arrangement of words, by which a man can prove a horse chestnut to be a chestnut horse."[52]

Despite Democratic charges of hypocrisy, Abraham Lincoln and the Republican party had correctly gauged public opinion. Protect the Negro's life and property, but deny him the vote, jury service, the right to testify in cases involving whites, and social equality, and — if possible — colonize him outside the United States. Until the death of Lincoln and the triumph of

---

[51] *Ibid.*, II, 405, 409, 521, V, 370–75.
[52] *Ibid.*, III, 16, 105, 176–77, 214–15.

the Radicals, Republicanism refused to advance beyond this position. Northern Negroes, in the meantime, welcomed the success of the Republican party and hoped for a liberalization of its racial policies and a consequent improvement of their own political, social, and economic position.

In 1860, such a change did not seem imminent. Despite some notable advances, the northern Negro remained largely disfranchised, segregated, and economically oppressed. Discrimination still barred him from most polls, juries, schools, and workshops, as well as from many libraries, theaters, lyceums, museums, public conveyances, and literary societies. Although he himself was responsible for this exclusion, the white man effectively turned it against the Negro. Having excluded the Negro from profitable employments, the whites scorned his idleness and poverty; having taxed him in some states for the support of public education, they excluded his children from the schools or placed them in separate and inferior institutions and then deplored the ignorance of his race; having excluded him from various lecture halls and libraries, they pointed to his lack of culture and refinement; and, finally, having stripped him of his claims to citizenship and having deprived him of opportunities for political and economic advancement, the whites concluded that the Negro had demonstrated an incapacity for improvement in this country and should be colonized in Africa. Nevertheless, most Negroes remained in the United States and chose to die on American soil, knowing full well that social proscription would follow them to the grave. Symbolic of the Negro's position in the ante bellum North was the public cemetery, or potter's field, of Cincinnati: whites were buried east to west and Negroes north to south.[53] After all, white supremacy had to be preserved, even among the dead.

[53] Abdy, *Journal of a Residence and Tour*, III, 7.

Bibliographical
Essay

This bibliographical essay will be selective rather than exhaustive. No attempt will be made to discuss every work used in this study, nor will its materials necessarily be limited to those appearing in the footnotes. Instead, the essay will seek out those works — primary and secondary — that proved especially valuable, that might serve as research aids for future historians of the northern Negro, and that provide additional depth in certain areas for the interested scholar or general reader.

GENERAL RESEARCH AIDS AND ACCOUNTS

Still waiting to be superseded as the most thorough bibliographical guide to Negro history is Monroe N. Work, *A Bibliography of the Negro in Africa and America* (New York, 1928). It should be supplemented, however, with Dorothy P. Porter's more recent and exhaustive essay, "Early American Negro Writings: A Bibliographical Study," *The Papers of*

the Bibliographical Society of America, XXXIX (1945),
192–268. A convenient guide to the most important depositories of Negro materials is the preparatory volume of the
Encyclopedia of the Negro (New York, 1945) by W. E. B.
DuBois and Guy B. Johnson.

The general history of the American Negro has been accorded both popular and scholarly treatment. Old but still
valuable is the remarkably thorough work of a nineteenth-
century Negro historian, George W. Williams, *History of
the Negro Race in America* (2 vols.; New York, 1882). More
recent, scholarly, and authoritative is John Hope Franklin,
From Slavery to Freedom: A History of American Negroes
(2d ed.; New York, 1956). Two important sociological contributions to the study of the Negro's past are Gunnar Myrdal,
An American Dilemma (2 vols.; New York, 1944) and
E. Franklin Frazier, *The Negro in the United States* (rev. ed.;
New York, 1957), both of which stress the post–Civil War
period but still contain some useful and suggestive material
on the ante bellum northern Negro. The same emphasis may
be found in Richard Bardolph, *The Negro Vanguard* (New
York, 1959), although this work is more valuable for its
study of Negro leadership in the ante bellum North. Carter G.
Woodson, *Free Negro Heads of Families in the United States
in 1830* (Washington, D.C., 1925) and *A Century of Negro
Migration* (Washington, D.C., 1918) discuss some of the
general problems of the free Negro.

The best sourcebook of Negro history is Herbert Aptheker
(ed.), *A Documentary History of the Negro People in the
United States* (New York, 1951), rich in original materials
and invaluable for any student of Negro history. The northern free Negro is accorded more than adequate attention. This
work should be supplemented with the more limited though
not necessarily repetitious Benjamin Brawley (ed.), *Early
Negro American Writers* (Chapel Hill, 1935) and Carter G.

Woodson (ed.), *Negro Orators and Their Orations* (Washington, D.C., 1925).

There are some valuable general guides to the legal position of ante bellum northern Negroes. Helen T. Catterall, *Judicial Cases Concerning American Slavery and the Negro* (5 vols.; Washington, D.C., 1926–37) is most thorough and indispensable. An old but still useful summary of pertinent legislation is John Codman Hurd, *Law of Freedom and Bondage in the United States* (2 vols.; Boston, 1858). Along similar lines, see Henry W. Farnam, *Chapters in the History of Social Legislation in the United States to 1860* (Washington, D.C., 1938), especially the appendix for its excellent outline — chronological and geographical — of constitutional provisions and legislation pertaining to the Negro.

Among the more notable contemporary accounts of the Negro's general condition, most of them written by abolitionists, are William Jay, *On the Condition of the Free People of Colour in the United States* (New York, 1839); James Freeman Clarke, "Condition of the Free Colored People of the United States," *The Christian Examiner*, LXVI, Fifth Series, IV (1859), 246–65; and William Yates, *Rights of Colored Men to Suffrage, Citizenship and Trial by Jury* (Philadelphia, 1838). More recent and specific are Emil Olbrich, *The Development of Sentiment on Negro Suffrage to 1860* (Madison, Wis., 1912); Charles H. Wesley, "Negro Suffrage in the Period of Constitution Making, 1787–1865," *Journal of Negro History*, XXXII (1947), 143–68; and Leon F. Litwack, "The Federal Government and the Free Negro," *ibid.*, XLIII (1958), 261–78.

The Negro's economic position is carefully examined in Charles H. Wesley, *Negro Labor in the United States, 1850–1925* (New York, 1927). More specific are Robert Ernst, *Immigrant Life in New York City, 1825–63* (New York, 1949) and "The Economic Status of New York City Negroes,

1850–63," *Negro History Bulletin*, XII (March, 1949), 131–32, 139–43; and Arnett G. Lindsay, "The Economic Condition of the Negroes of New York Prior to 1861," *Journal of Negro History*, VI (1921), 190–99. Oscar Handlin, *Boston's Immigrants, 1790–1865* (Cambridge, Mass., 1941) contains some useful information on the Negro's economic position and his often violent relations with competing Irish workers. The Pennsylvania Society for Promoting the Abolition of Slavery and the Society of Friends made several important studies of the Negro's position in that state: *The Present State and Condition of the Free People of Color of the City of Philadelphia* (Philadelphia, 1838); *Register of the Trades of the Colored People in the City of Philadelphia and Districts* (Philadelphia, 1838); *Statistical Inquiry into the Condition of the People of Color of the City and Districts of Philadelphia* (Philadelphia, 1849); and *Statistics of the Colored People of Philadelphia* (Philadelphia, 1856). The accounts of foreign travelers, discussed elsewhere, provide perhaps the most valuable source for the Negro's economic status in the ante bellum North.

On Negro education, Carter G. Woodson, *The Education of the Negro Prior to 1861* (2d ed.; Washington, D.C., 1919) is still the standard work. Indispensable for state segregation policies, and containing more than the title implies, is the *Special Report of the Commissioner of Education on the Condition and Improvement of Public Schools in the District of Columbia, Submitted to the Senate June 1868, and to the House, with additions, June 13, 1870* (Washington, D.C., 1871). Efforts to establish Negro schools or secure the integration of white schools produced several tracts and official documents, none of which are perhaps more important or revealing than the majority and minority special committee reports of the Boston Primary School Board and the Boston Grammar School Board (1846 and 1849), and Charles Sumner's classic argument against separate but equal facilities in *Argument of Charles Sumner, Esq., Against the Constitutionality of Separate Colored Schools, in the Case of Sarah C. Roberts vs. the City of Boston* (Boston, 1849). For a recent discussion of that case, see Leonard W. Levy and Harlan B. Phillips, "The Roberts Case: Source of the 'Separate but Equal' Doctrine," *American Historical Review*, LVI (1951), 510–18. A Negro's defense of segregation may be found in Thomas P. Smith, *An Address Before the Colored Citizens of Boston in Opposition to the Abolition of Colored Schools* (Boston, 1850).

Carter G. Woodson, *The History of the Negro Church* (Washington, D.C., 1921) is a limited though adequate study of organized religion in the Negro community. A discussion of ante bellum sermons may be found in Benjamin E. Mays, *The Negro's God as Reflected in His Literature* (Boston, 1938). For the organization of the independent Negro church, see especially Charles H. Wesley, *Richard Allen, Apostle of Freedom* (Washington, D.C., 1935). No attempt will be made to enumerate the various published histories of independent Negro denominations, many of which have little value for the historian. The classic abolitionist indictments of prejudice within the white churches are James G. Birney, *The American Churches, The Bulwarks of American Slavery* (Newburyport, Mass., 1842); John Jay, *Caste and Slavery in the American Church* (New York and London, 1843); and Harvey Newcomb, *"The Negro Pew:" Being an Inquiry Concerning the Propriety of Distinctions in the House of God on Account of Color* (Boston, 1837).

STATE AND LOCAL STUDIES

Historians have accorded the southern free Negro greater monographic treatment than his northern counterpart. Still the most valuable state study of the northern Negro is Edward

R. Turner, *The Negro in Pennsylvania* (Washington, D.C., 1911), based almost exclusively on manuscript collections, newspapers, state legislative documents, court records, and pamphlets. Emma Lou Thornbrough, *The Negro in Indiana* (Indianapolis, 1957) is based on the same kind of thorough research and focuses much of its attention on the ante bellum period. The same is true of Robert A. Warner's historical-sociological study, *New Haven Negroes, A Social History* (New Haven, 1940). Lorenzo J. Greene, *The Negro in Colonial New England* (New York, 1942) emphasizes the institution of slavery but provides a useful background for a study of the free Negro in that region.

Several other state and local studies might be consulted, with varying degrees of profit: Irving H. Bartlett, *From Slave to Citizen: The Story of the Negro in Rhode Island* (Providence, 1954); Julian S. Rammelkamp, "The Providence Negro Community, 1820–42," *Rhode Island History*, VII (1948), 20–33; John Daniels, *In Freedom's Birthplace. A Study of the Boston Negroes* (Boston and New York, 1914); W. E. B. DuBois, *The Philadelphia Negro; a Social Study* (Philadelphia, 1899); Leo H. Hirsch, Jr., "The Negro and New York, 1783 to 1865," *Journal of Negro History*, XVI (1931), 382–473; A. A. Payne, "The Negro in New York, prior to 1860," *Howard Review*, I (1923), 1–64; Charles T. Hickok, *The Negro in Ohio, 1802–70* (Cleveland, 1896); James H. Rodabaugh, "The Negro in Ohio," *Journal of Negro History*, XXXI (1946), 9–29; Richard C. Wade, "The Negro in Cincinnati, 1800–1830," *ibid.*, XXXIX (1954), 43–57; and Carter G. Woodson, "The Negroes of Cincinnati prior to the Civil War," *ibid.*, I (1916), 1–22.

Examining the Negro's changing legal position on a state or regional basis, in addition to the studies already cited, are James T. Adams, "Disfranchisement of Negroes in New England," *American Historical Review*, XXX (1925), 543–47, an important corrective of previous historical errors; Dixon Ryan Fox, "The Negro Vote in Old New York," *Political Science Quarterly*, XXXII (1917), 252–75, an explanation of the Negro's attachment to the Federalist and Whig parties; and Marion T. Wright, "Negro Suffrage in New Jersey, 1776–1875," *Journal of Negro History*, XXXIII (1948), 168–224. The struggle of Massachusetts Negroes and abolitionists for equal rights is vividly related by Louis Ruchames in "Jim Crow Railroads in Massachusetts," *American Quarterly*, VIII (1956), 61–75; "Race and Education in Massachusetts," *Negro History Bulletin*, XIII (December, 1949), 53–59, 71; and "Race, Marriage, and Abolitionism in Massachusetts," *Journal of Negro History*, XL (1955), 250–73. Two notable contemporary commentaries on the Negro's legal status in Pennsylvania, both of which deny his right to citizenship and reflect prevailing white attitudes, are John Fox, *Opinion . . . Against the Exercise of Negro Suffrage in Pennsylvania* (Harrisburg, Pa., 1838) and John F. Denny, *An Enquiry into the Political Grade of the Free Coloured Population, Under the Constitution of the United States, and the Constitution of Pennsylvania* (Chambersburg, Pa., 1834). Frank U. Quillin, *The Color Line in Ohio: A History of Race Prejudice in a Typical Northern State* (Ann Arbor, Mich., 1913) and J. Reuben Sheeler, "The Struggle of the Negro in Ohio for Freedom," *Journal of Negro History*, XXXI (1946), 208–26, shed light on the Negro's often tenuous existence in that state.

MANUSCRIPT COLLECTIONS

Few ante bellum Negroes left any extensive manuscript collections. Perhaps the largest and certainly the most important are the Frederick Douglass Papers (Washington, D.C.). I found few important letters in the microfilm copy of these papers that could not be found in Philip S. Foner's excellent compilation, *The Life and Writings of Frederick Douglass*

(4 vols.; New York, 1950–55). The difficulty of locating ante
bellum Negro manuscripts makes Carter G. Woodson's published collection of Negro correspondence, *The Mind of the
Negro as Reflected in Letters Written during the Crisis, 1800–
1860* (Washington, D.C., 1926) that much more valuable.
Most of the volume consists of letters to the American Colonization Society and to various antislavery leaders, societies,
and newspapers. See also Dorothy B. Porter, "Early Manuscript Letters Written by Negroes," *Journal of Negro History*,
XXIV (1939), 199–210, and Benjamin Quarles, "Letters
from Negro Leaders to Gerrit Smith," *ibid.*, XXVII (1942),
432–53. The Carter G. Woodson Collection of Negro Papers
(Library of Congress), although not fully catalogued and de-
posited at the time I consulted them, appear to have limited
value for the ante bellum North.

Any serious student of northern Negro history must consult, in addition to the Douglass papers, the manuscript
collections of white abolitionists. Here are to be found correspondence with prominent Negro leaders, information on
Negro activities and conditions in the North, and some excellent insights into abolitionist attitudes toward the Negro.
Along these lines, I consulted with particular profit the anti-
slavery collections at the Boston Public Library, including
the papers of William Lloyd Garrison, Maria (Weston)
Chapman, Anne (Warren) Weston, and Samuel May, Jr.;
the Lewis Tappan Papers (Library of Congress), especially
the manuscript diary, 1836–38; and the Theodore Weld,
Angelina Grimke Weld, and Sarah Grimke Letters (Clements Library, University of Michigan), the most important
of which have been published by Gilbert H. Barnes and
Dwight L. Dumond in *Letters of Theodore Dwight Weld,
Angelina Grimke Weld and Sarah Grimke, 1822–44* (2
vols.; New York, 1834). Of more limited value were the
Elizur Wright, Jr. Papers (Library of Congress) and the

James Birney Papers (Library of Congress and the Clements Library, University of Michigan). Much of the Birney correspondence has been published by Dwight L. Dumond in *Letters of James Gillespie Birney, 1831–57* (2 vols.; New York, 1938).

The voluminous papers of the Pennsylvania Society for Promoting the Abolition of Slavery, located in the Historical Society of Pennsylvania (Philadelphia), shed considerable light on conditions prevailing among ante bellum Pennsylvania Negroes. The manuscript minutes of the Junior Anti-Slavery Society of Philadelphia, also located in the Historical Society, are of particular interest for their discussions of the expediency of Negro membership and social intercourse between the races.

GOVERNMENT DOCUMENTS: FEDERAL AND STATE

The anomaly of the free Negro attracted, and sometimes demanded, the attention of the federal government and most of the state governments. The proceedings of Congress — published as *Annals of Congress* (1789–1824), *Congressional Debates* (1825–37), and *Congressional Globe* (1833–73) — are inadequately indexed and thus often tedious to use, but they afford the patient researcher ample rewards for his labor. The northern Negro attracted particular attention during the debates on the admission of Missouri (16 Cong., 2 ness.) and in the 1850's (see especially 36 Cong., 1 sess.), as various southern and "Doughface" congressmen used the Negro's inferior position in the North to demonstrate the relative beneficence of slavery and the hypocrisy of abolitionist arguments. In addition to this, the congressional debates covered such a variety of topics as colonization in Africa and Central America, the employment of Negroes in the armed forces (27 Cong., 2 sess.), the reception of free Negro petitions (6 Cong., 1 sess.), the right of Negroes to the public domain (26 Cong., 2 sess.; 31 Cong., 1 sess.; 33 Cong., 1 sess.), public schools for Negroes in Washington, D.C. (35 Cong., 1 sess.; 36 Cong., 1 sess.), and the restrictions placed on Negroes in the proposed Oregon Constitution (35 Cong., 1 and 2 sess.). Meanwhile, the Senate and House Documents and Reports gave attention to such matters as the reliability of census statistics on insanity among Negroes, the imprisonment of colored seamen in southern ports, and African colonization.

Any study of the federal government's position on Negro citizenship requires a careful look at the *Official Opinions of the Attorneys General of the United States* (40 vols.; Washington, D.C., 1791–1948), and at Chief Justice Roger B. Taney's classic argument in *Dred Scott vs. Sanford*.

Important statistical information, including a geographical breakdown of the free Negro and slave population, is contained in John Cummings, *Negro Population in the United States, 1790–1915* (Washington, D.C., 1918), and in *A Century of Population Growth: From the First Census of the United States to the Twelfth, 1790–1900* (Washington, D.C., 1909).

The most valuable and voluminous sources for a study of northern white attitudes toward the Negro are the state constitutional conventions. In determining the kind and amount of rights and privileges that were to be exercised by Negroes, these conventions invariably engaged in bitter and often lengthy disputes. While speakers tended at times to exaggerate or distort the Negro's condition, depending on the extent of their own prejudices, the debates contain extensive information on the legal and economic status of the Negro and provide a valuable consensus of white public opinion. Among the most pertinent conventions were those of California (1849), Illinois (1847), Indiana (1850–51), Iowa (1857), Kansas (1859), Massachusetts (1853), Michigan (1835–36), New

York (1821 and 1846), Ohio (1850–51), Oregon (1857), and Pennsylvania (1837–38).

In addition to the convention debates, state legislative documents and the messages of the governors occasionally provide some important materials. The various reports of Massachusetts legislative committees, for example, on Negro immigration restriction (1821–22), the intermarriage ban (1839–41), equal railroad accommodations (1842), and the integration of public schools (1855) were especially useful, as was an Ohio legislative committee report on the proposed repeal of the Black Laws (1845).

NEWSPAPERS AND PERIODICALS

Negro and white abolitionist newspapers provide a rich source of information. Indispensable for any study of northern Negroes are three of their newspapers: *Freedom's Journal* (1827–30); *Colored American* (1837–42; published Jan.–Feb., 1837, as *Weekly Advocate*); and *Frederick Douglass' Paper* (1847–63; published 1847–51 as *North Star*, and 1859–63 as *Douglass' Monthly*). The *Anglo-African Magazine* (1859), edited by Thomas Hamilton, had a short-lived existence, but during that time it provided a literary outlet for Negroes and some often biting commentaries on the Negro in American society. Of particular interest was its reaction to the Republican Party. Still a useful account of early Negro journalism is Irving G. Penn, *The Afro-American Press and its Editors* (Springfield, 1891).

The *Liberator* (1831–65), edited by William Lloyd Garrison, had a comparatively large number of Negro subscribers and supporters. It regularly reported Negro activities, gave substantial attention to the problems of northern Negroes, especially segregation, and reprinted many pertinent articles — both friendly and unfriendly to the Negro — from other newspapers. (The hostile articles appeared in the "Refuge of

Oppression" column.) Among the many other useful abolitionist newspapers and periodicals are the *American Anti-Slavery Reporter* (New York, 1833–34); the *Emancipator and Republican* (New York and Boston, 1833–50; title varies); *The Friend of Man* (Utica, N.Y., 1836–42); the *National Anti-Slavery Standard* (New York, 1840–60); and the *Quarterly Anti-Slavery Magazine* (New York, 1836–37).

Throughout this period, *Niles' Weekly Register* (Baltimore, 1811–49) was an excellent source of information on various subjects relating to the Negro in the North.

TRAVEL ACCOUNTS: FOREIGN AND DOMESTIC

Curious about the workings and prospects of American democracy, a host of foreign travelers descended upon the United States in the ante bellum period, most of them between 1830 and 1860, and recorded their impressions. The descriptions and evaluations of American society varied considerably, ranging from strong sympathy to outright condemnation, depending in some cases on the traveler's predilections before arriving in the United States. Exaggeration, distortion, and misinformation characterized some of the published impressions. Nevertheless, although requiring careful use, many of these accounts remain extremely valuable and provide the historian with a mine of information on almost every aspect of American life.

This study employs the travel account on numerous occasions, for most of these foreign observers had something to say about the Negro's difficult position in northern society. Having previously associated the Negro's plight in America with southern bondage, many of these foreign visitors looked with great surprise, and most with dismay, at northern racial oppression and the tenacity with which whites in that section held to the doctrines of white supremacy. They noted the confinement of Negroes to menial jobs, observed segregation in

the theaters, the lecture halls, the churches, and on the railroads and steamboats, and found that most whites took this
as a matter of course and justified it on the basis of fixed
natural laws which would forever separate the two races.

Two of the most perceptive observers of the American
scene were Alexis de Tocqueville and Gustave August de Beaumont, companions on a trip through the United States in 1831.
Tocqueville, in *Democracy in America*, ed. Phillips Bradley
(2 vols.; New York, 1951), and Beaumont, in a romantic
novel, *Marie; or, Slavery in the United States*, tr. Barbara
Chapman (Stanford, 1958), recorded their observation that
northern Negroes, although legally free, were politically, economically, and socially oppressed. The raw materials upon
which the two Frenchmen based their conclusions may be
found in George Wilson Pierson, *Tocqueville and Beaumont
in America* (New York, 1938).

Reaching almost identical conclusions about the Negro's
position and prospects was Francis Lieber, a German political
exile who remained in the United States and became one of
its most prominent political scientists and educators. Although
opposed to slavery on moral grounds, Lieber pessimistically
concluded in *Letters to a Gentleman in Germany, Written After a Trip from Philadelphia to Niagara* (Philadelphia, 1834)
that emancipation would be meaningless in the fact of prevailing prejudices. Only amalgamation could achieve a true state
of freedom for American Negroes, but this, he warned, would
also lead to the degeneration of the white race. The final object, Lieber decided, must be the colonization of the Negro.

The most thorough study of the northern Negro by a foreign traveler is Edward S. Adby, *Journal of a Residence and
Tour in the United States of North America, from April, 1833,
to October, 1834* (3 vols.; London, 1835). An Englishman
with pronounced antislavery views, Abdy traveled extensively
and based his impressions largely on actual experience, in-

cluding conversations with colored convicts as well as Negro leaders, visits to a Negro lyceum and the Ohio "Black Colonies," and firsthand observations of the Negro in New England, New York, Pennsylvania, and Ohio. Abdy's account should be supplemented with five other particularly extensive observations of the Negro's position in the free states: Thomas Hamilton, *Men and Manners in America* (2 vols.; London, 1834); William Chambers, *Things as They Are in America* (London and Edinburgh, 1854) and *American Slavery and Colour* (London, 1857); Andrew Bell, *Men and Things in America* (London, 1838); and Charles Mackay, *Life and Liberty in America: Or, Sketches of a Tour in the United States and Canada in 1857–58* (2 vols.; London, 1859). Although a somewhat unreliable "debunking" account of American society, Thomas Brothers, *The United States of North America as They Are; Not as They are Generally Described* (London, 1840) includes an appendix, based largely on newspaper articles, describing anti-Negro riots in the North.

Several travelers, including Alexis de Tocqueville and Charles Mackay, made the almost inevitable comparison between the condition of the southern slave and the northern free Negro. Most of them found that few if any differences existed or that southerners generally treated their bondsmen with greater compassion and tolerance. Whatever the differences, most of the travelers deplored northern antislavery sentiment as inconsistent with the treatment accorded Negroes in that section. Among those comparing the slave and the free Negro were Francesco Arese, *A Trip to the Prairies and in the Interior of North America*, trans. Andrew Evans (New York, 1934); Henry Ashworth, *A Tour in the United States, Cuba, and Canada* (London, 1861); William E. Baxter, *America and the Americans* (London, 1855); William Ferguson, *America by River and Rail; or, Notes by the Way on the New World and its People* (London, 1856); Francis J.

Grund, *Aristocracy in America* (2 vols.; London, 1839) and *The Americans in Their Moral, Social, and Political Relations* (2 vols.; London, 1837); Matilda C. J. F. Houstoun, *Hesperos* (2 vols.; London, 1850); David W. Mitchell, *Ten Years Residence in the United States* (London, 1862); Henry A. Murray, *Lands of the Slave and the Free: or, Cuba, the United States, and Canada* (2 vols.; London, 1855); John W. Oldmixon, *Transatlantic Wanderings* (London, 1855); Alfred Pairpoint, *Uncle Sam and His Country; or, Sketches of America, in 1854–55–56* (London, 1857); and Edward Sullivan, *Rambles and Scrambles in North and South America* (London, 1852).

Most valuable for their observations of the emancipated northern slave in the late eighteenth century are Jacques P. Brissot de Warville, *New Travels in the United States of America* (Dublin, 1792); Duke de la Rochefoucault Liancourt, *Travels through the United States of North America, the Country of the Iroquois, and Upper Canada, in the Years 1795, 1796, and 1797* (2 vols.; London, 1799); and Kenneth and Anna M. Roberts (eds.), *Moreau de St. Mery's American Journey* (New York, 1947).

Among other early accounts of the Negro in the North are Isaac Candler, *A Summary View of America* (London, 1824); John M. Duncan, *Travels through Part of the United States and Canada* (2 vols.; New York, 1823); Henry B. Fearon, *Sketches of America. A Narrative of a Journey of Five Thousand Miles through the Eastern and Western States* (London, 1818); James Flint, *Letters from America* (Edinburgh, 1822); Isaac Holmes, *An Account of the United States of America, Derived from Actual Observation, During a Residence of Four Years in that Republic* (London, 1823); and Frances (D'Arusmont) Wright, *Views of Society and Manners in America* (New York, 1821).

To enumerate every travel account that made mention of the

northern Negro would consume considerable space. There are several which have not been noted, however, that merit attention: Carl D. Arfwedson, *The United States and Canada, In 1832, 1833, and 1834* (2 vols.; London, 1834); James Boardman, *America, and the Americans* (London, 1833); J. S. Buckingham, *The Eastern and Western States of America* (3 vols.; London, 1842); Michael Chevalier, *Society, Manners and Politics in the United States* (Boston, 1839); Elizabeth H. Cawley (ed.), *The American Diaries of Richard Cobden* (Princeton, N.J., 1952); Ebenezer Davies, *American Scenes and Christian Slavery; A Recent Tour of Four Thousand Miles in the United States* (London, 1849); Mrs. Felton, *A Narrative of Two Years' City and Country Residence in the United States* (London, 1842); Thomas C. Grattan, *Civilized America* (2 vols.; London, 1859); Sir Charles Lyell, *Travels in North America, Canada, and Nova Scotia* (2 vols.; 2d ed.; London, 1855); Alexander Mackay, *The Western World; or, Travels in the United States in 1846–47* (3 vols.; 4th ed.; London, 1850); Alexander Marjoribanks, *Travels in South and North America* (5th ed.; London and New York, 1854); Captain Frederick Marryat, *A Diary in America, With Remarks on its Institutions* (3 vols.; London, 1839); Harriet Martineau, *Society in America* (2 vols.; New York, 1837); Francis and Theresa Pulszky, *White, Red, Black: Sketches of American Society* (2 vols.; New York, 1853); James Stirling, *Letters from the Slave States* (London, 1857); James Stuart, *Three Years in North America* (2 vols.; Edinburgh, 1833); Joseph Sturge, *A Visit to the United States in 1841* (London, 1842); and William Tallack, *Friendly Sketches in America* (London, 1861).

In addition to the foreign observations, there are some valuable impressions of American society by native travelers. James Fenimore Cooper, for example, in *Notions of the Americans: Picked up by a Travelling Bachelor* (2 vols.; London,

1828), discusses the economic and moral condition of New
York Negroes and concludes that as long as the prevailing
white prejudices persisted, freedom would not be favorable
to the perpetuation of the Negro race. Horace Greeley, *An
Overland Journey from New York to San Francisco, in the
Summer of 1859* (New York, 1860) comments, among other
things, on the political necessity that forces midwestern Republicans to uphold white supremacy with even greater tenacity than the opposition party.

Of particular interest and relevance are the recorded impressions of northern society by southern travelers. To be sure,
the Negro's position in the North attracted immediate attention. Through the character of "Major Jones," William T.
Thompson, in *Major Jones's Sketches of Travel: Comprising
the Scenes, Incidents, and Adventures, in His Tour from
Georgia to Canada* (Philadelphia, 1848), describes "nigger
freedom" in Philadelphia, the wretched condition of the Negro
there, the hypocrisy of northerners on the race question, and
the comparative benefits of slavery. One can find this same dim
view of northern Negro freedom and white inconsistency in
A. A. Lipscomb, *North and South, Impressions of Northern
Society Upon a Southerner* (Mobile, Ala., 1853); William M.
Bobo, *Glimpses of New-York City* (Charleston, S.C., 1852);
J. C. Myers, *Sketches on a Tour through the Northern and
Eastern States, the Canadas and Nova Scotia* (Harrisonburg,
Va., 1849). For other southern views of the Negro in the North,
as reported by a northern traveler, see Frederick Law Olmsted,
The Cotton Kingdom, ed. Arthur M. Schlesinger (New York,
1953).

Although little is known about the author's background,
Joseph W. Wilson, writing as "A Southerner," has furnished
us with a most valuable and apparently authoritative study of
the northern Negro: *Sketches of the Higher Classes of Colored
Society in Philadelphia* (Philadelphia, 1841). After discussing

the social distinctions that divided Philadelphia Negroes, Wilson ably describes the composition, intellectual interests, political aspirations, and social life of the "higher classes" of Negro society. The final chapter enumerates the Negro literary and debating societies of Philadelphia.

ABOLITIONISM: WHITE

For the early (pre-Garrisonian) antislavery movement — a largely neglected subject — the standard works are still Mary S. Locke, *Anti-Slavery in America, 1619–1808* (Boston, 1901) and Alice D. Adams, *The Neglected Period of Anti-Slavery in America, 1808–31* (Boston, 1908). Indispensable as original sources are the annual reports of the American Convention for Promoting the Abolition of Slavery and Improving the Condition of the African Race (1794–1837). These contain valuable information on the condition of the emancipated northern slave as well as moralistic appeals to the Negro population. Some of the reports and appeals have been reprinted in *The Journal of Negro History*, VI (1921), 103–12, 200–240, 310–74. For the work of the early societies, see also Benjamin Lundy's newspaper, *Genius of Universal Emancipation* (1821–38); Edward Needles, *An Historical Memoir of the Pennsylvania Society, for Promoting the Abolition of Slavery, the Relief of Free Negroes Unlawfully Held in Bondage, and for Improving the Condition of the African Race* (Philadelphia, 1848); and Thomas Drake, *Quakers and Slavery in America* (New Haven, 1950). The papers of the Pennsylvania Society for Promoting the Abolition of Slavery (Historical Society of Pennsylvania) are an important source of information for early attempts to improve the Negro's position.

The most recent account of post-1830 abolitionism is Louis Filler, *The Crusade Against Slavery, 1830–60* (New York, 1960), which includes a much needed bibliographical essay on antislavery materials. An older study, with a different emphasis, is Gilbert H. Barnes, *The Anti-Slavery Impulse, 1830–44* (New York, 1933). Unfortunately, the author's attempt to downgrade the importance of the Garrisonians in relation to the western abolitionists results in an unbalanced treatment. Moreover, Barnes almost totally ignores the Negro antislavery leaders and incorrectly describes the first national colored convention as a white abolitionist-inspired effort to gain publicity for a Negro school project.

The official reports of the American Anti-Slavery Society, the New England Anti-Slavery Society, the American and Foreign Anti-Slavery Society, and the various state and local abolition societies provide considerable material on the legal and economic condition of the Negro and regularly report the progress made to improve his status. The value of abolitionist newspapers and manuscripts has been cited elsewhere. Francis and Wendell P. Garrison, *William Lloyd Garrison, 1805–79* (4 vols.; Boston and New York, 1894) provides additional material on Garrison's efforts to secure equal rights for northern Negroes. Among the innumerable abolitionist memoirs, Samuel J. May, *Some Recollections of Our Anti-Slavery Conflict* (Boston, 1869) is especially useful, particularly its vivid portrayal of the Prudence Crandall affair in Connecticut. See also May, *The Right of Colored People to Education, Vindicated* (Brooklyn, Conn., 1833).

ABOLITIONISM: NEGRO

Little attention has been accorded the role of the Negro in the abolitionist movement. Some brief but scholarly accounts are Herbert Aptheker, *The Negro in the Abolitionist Movement* (New York, 1941) and "Militant Abolitionism," *Journal of Negro History*, XXVI (1941), 438–84. Richard Bardolph, *The Negro Vanguard* (New York, 1959) and Vernon Loggins, *The Negro Author* (New York, 1931) include discussions of leading Negro abolitionists. See also Charles H. Wesley, "The

Participation of Negroes in Anti-Slavery Political Parties," *Journal of Negro History*, XXIX (1944), 32–74 and "The Negroes of New York in the Emancipation Movement," *ibid.*, XXIV (1939), 65–103; and Benjamin Quarles, "Ministers without Portfolio," *ibid.*, XXXIX (1954), 27–42. Three older but still useful accounts are William C. Nell, *The Colored Patriots of the American Revolution* (Boston, 1855), a more general study than the little implies; William Wells Brown, *The Black Man, His Antecedents, His Genius, and His Achievements* (4th ed.; Boston, 1865); and William J. Simmons, *Men of Mark: Eminent, Progressive and Rising* (Cleveland, 1887).

Among the biographical studies of leading ante bellum northern Negroes, all of them active at some time in the struggle for equal rights, are Philip Foner (ed.), *The Life and Writings of Frederick Douglass* (4 vols.; New York, 1950–55); Robert A. Warner, "Amos Gerry Beman — 1812–74, A Memoir on a Forgotten Leader," *Journal of Negro History*, XIII (1937), 200–221; Henry N. Sherwood, "Paul Cuffe," *ibid.*, VIII (1923), 153–229; Ray Allen Billington, "James Forten: Forgotten Abolitionist," *Negro History Bulletin*, XIII (November, 1949), 31–36, 45; William M. Brewer, "Henry Highland Garnet," *Journal of Negro History*, XIII (1928), 36–52, and "John B. Russwurm," *ibid.*, XIII (1928), 413–22; Monroe N. Work, "The Life of Charles B. Ray," *ibid.*, IV (1919), 361–71; and Dorothy B. Porter, "David Ruggles, An Apostle of Human Rights," *ibid.*, XXVIII (1943), 23–50.

Besides the numerous fugitive slave memoirs, most of which stress the agonies of bondage rather than the problems of freedom, several Negroes published tracts in which they candidly discussed the inferior position of their people and the means by which it must be improved. David Walker's controversial tract, *Walker's Appeal, in Four Articles* (Boston, 1830), directed its message to both slaves and free Negroes. It called for violent resistance to southern bondage and beseeched northern Negroes to improve their position economically and intellectually in order to demonstrate their manhood to the world. For the impact of Walker's tract on the South, see Clement Eaton, "A Dangerous Pamphlet in the Old South," *Journal of Southern History*, II (1936), 323–34.

Of varying value are the tracts of early Negro leaders, most of them orations given at local anniversary celebrations of the abolition of slavery and the African slave trade. One that deserves a special comment, however, is Joseph Sidney, *An Oration, Commemorative of the Abolition of the Slave Trade in the United States; Delivered before the Wilberforce Philanthropic Association, in the City of New-York, on the Second of January, 1809* (New York, 1809). Reflecting the political bias of many, if not most, New York Negroes, Sidney reviews the accomplishments of the Federalists and the decline of American prosperity under Jeffersonian Republicanism and calls upon Negro voters to reject the Republican Party as the party that sanctions slavery.

Among the later Negro tracts, by far the most valuable is Martin R. Delany, *The Condition, Elevation, Emigration, and Destiny of the Colored People of the United States* (Philadelphia, 1852). A strong advocate of emigration to Central America, Delany reviews the historical past of American Negroes, their political and economic condition, their contributions to the Revolution and the War of 1812, and to the arts and sciences. He concludes that the United States is still determined never to grant Negroes equal rights, that the abolitionists — although sincere — have failed to implement their avowed goals, and that Negroes must henceforth look elsewhere for salvation and real freedom — to a "Promised Land" outside the territorial limits of the United States.

Other Negro tracts and memoirs that may be profitably consulted are Frederick Douglass, *My Bondage and My Freedom* (New York, 1855) and *The Life and Times of Frederick*

Douglass (Hartford, Conn., 1884); William G. Allen, *A Refugee from American Despotism. The American Prejudice Against Color* (London, 1853); William Wells Brown, *The American Fugitive in Europe* (Boston, 1855); Hosea Easton, *A Treatise on the Intellectual Character, and Civil and Political Condition of the Colored People of the United States; and the Prejudice Exercised Towards Them* (Boston, 1837); and John Malvin, *Autobiography* (Cleveland, 1879). Two eloquent Negro appeals for equal rights, among the many published, are the *Appeal of Forty Thousand Citizens, Threatened with Disfranchisement, to the People of Pennsylvania* (Philadelphia, 1838) and the *Memorial of Thirty Thousand Disfranchised Citizens of Philadelphia to the Honorable Senate and House of Representatives* (Philadelphia, 1855).

The proceedings of the ante bellum Negro conventions are indispensable for any study of the northern Negro. In addition to providing material on virtually every aspect of Negro life, the convention proceedings provide an excellent progress report on the Negro's organizational activity and the nature of his demands. Among those consulted for this study were the national colored conventions (New York and Philadelphia, 1831–35; Buffalo, 1843; Troy, 1847; Rochester, 1853; Philadelphia, 1855), the national emigration convention (Cleveland, 1854), the Moral Reform Society proceedings (Philadelphia, 1837), the General Convention for the Improvement of the Colored Inhabitants of Canada (Amherstburgh, C. W., 1853), and the state conventions of California (1856), Connecticut (1849), Illinois (1853 and 1856), Michigan (1843), New Jersey (1849), New York (1851), Ohio (1849–53, 1856–58), and Pennsylvania (1848).

For a recent analysis of the Negro conventions, see Howard H. Bell, *A Survey of the Negro Convention Movement, 1830–61* (Unpublished Ph.D. Dissertation; Northwestern University, 1953), and two articles by the same author:

"The Negro Convention Movement, 1830–60: New Perspectives," *Negro History Bulletin*, XIV (February, 1951), 103–5, 114, and "National Negro Conventions of the Middle 1840's: Moral Suasian vs. Political Action," *Journal of Negro History*, XLII (1957), 247–60.

COLONIZATION

There is no adequate history of the American Colonization Society or of other efforts to colonize the Negro outside the United States. Early Lee Fox, *The American Colonization Society, 1817–40* (Baltimore, 1919) and Frederic Bancroft, "The Colonization of American Negroes, 1801–65," in Jacob E. Cooke, *Frederic Bancroft* (Norman, Okla., 1957) are both useful but the subject requires further work. See also Charles I. Foster, "The Colonization of Free Negroes in Liberia, 1816–35," *Journal of Negro History*, XXXVIII (1953), 41–66, and Henry N. Sherwood, "The Formation of the American Colonization Society," *ibid.*, II (1917), 209–28, and "Early Negro Deportation Projects," *Mississippi Valley Historical Review*, II (1916), 484–508.

The best insights into the American Colonization Society and its attitude toward the free Negro are still to be gained by going directly to the sources: the annual reports of the American Colonization Society (1818–60), *The African Repository* (Washington, D.C., 1825–92), and the many pamphlets published by the national society and the state auxiliaries.

The classic abolitionist indictments of colonization are William Lloyd Garrison, *Thoughts on African Colonization: or An Impartial Exhibition of the Doctrines, Principles and Purposes of the American Colonization Society, etc.* (Boston, 1832) and William Jay, *Inquiry into the Character and Tendency of the American Colonization, and American Anti-Slavery Societies* (2d ed.; New York, 1835). The Negro condemnation of colonization came much earlier and is perhaps best summed up by Samuel E. Cornish and Theodore S. Wright in *The Colonization Scheme Considered in its Rejection by the Colored People, in its Tendency to Uphold Caste, in its Unfitness for Christianizing and Civilizing the Aborigines of Africa and for Putting a Stop to the African Slave Trade* (Newark, N.J., 1840).

The merits of non-Liberian colonization are debated by Negro leaders Frederick Douglass, William J. Watkins, and James M. Whitfield in *Arguments, Pro and Con, on the Call for a National Emigration Convention, to be held in Cleveland, Ohio, August, 1854* (Detroit, 1854), and are indorsed vigorously in Martin R. Delany, *The Condition, Elevation, Emigration, and Destiny of the Colored People of the United States* (Philadelphia, 1852) and in the *Proceedings of the National Emigration Convention of Colored People; held at Cleveland, Ohio, . . . the 24th, 25th and 26th of August, 1854* (Pittsburgh, Pa., 1854). For Negro support of the American Colonization Society, limited though it was, see Carter G. Woodson (ed.), *The Mind of the Negro as Reflected in Letters Written during the Crisis, 1800–1860* (Washington, D.C., 1926).

Index

Abdy, Edward S.: English traveler, 292–93; on Negro crime, 96; on segregation in Quaker meeting halls, 206; on racial prejudices of French abolitionists, 219

Abolition of slavery: in the North, 3–14; economic explanation of, 4, 60; influence of War of Independence on, 6–12, 14–15; Quakers and, 12–13; antislavery societies and, 13–14; Virginia judge explains southern objections to, 14–15

Abolitionism Unveiled! 263

Abolitionists, Negro: antislavery activities of, 33–34, 231–37, 244–46; condemn Dred Scott decision, 63; attack racial discrimination, 74, 86, 94, 105–11, 120, 137, 142–51, 181, 208–11, 235, 237, 264; as religious leaders, 187, 188, 189–90, 203; publications of, 232–35, 238, 241, 245; divisions among, 237–43, 244–45, 265; oppose Fugitive Slave Act, 250–51, 252; on support of federal government, 265–66; praise John Brown, 266–67; *see also* Douglass, Frederick; Negro conventions, national; Negro conventions, state

Abolitionists, white: pre-Garrisonian, 13–14, 17–19, 121, 171; fate of, in the South, 19–20; attitudes of, to colonization, 26–28, 254–56, 273; attack racial discrimination, 74, 86, 105–11, 137–39, 143–51, 162, 197, 206–7; support Negro education, 118, 121–22, 123–31, 137–38; encourage Negro economic improvement, 170–74, 176–77; on Negro class distinctions, 185, 186; Negro criticism of, 203, 226–29, 239, 239–40, 242–43, 245; organization and aims of, 214–15; racial prejudices of, 216–30; on Negroes in antislavery societies, 216–17, 218–19, 221–22, 222 n., 236; on social intercourse with Negroes, 216, 217–18, 219–23; effectiveness of, 229–30; on *Walker's Appeal*, 234–35; divisions among, and the Negro, 237–44, 244–45; on merits of separate Negro conventions, 239; oppose Fugitive Slave Act, 250–51, 252; *see also* American and Foreign Anti-Slavery Society; American Anti-Slavery Society; American Convention of Delegates from Abolition Societies; Garrison, William Lloyd; *Liberator, The*; New

cized for admitting Negroes, 109; segregated schools in, 137, 143; attack on segregated schools in, 143–50; occupations of Negroes in, 155; Negro sections of, 168; Negro churches in, 195; fugitive slave rescues in, 250–51, 252
Boston *Courier*, 125
Boston *Daily Bee*, 56
Boston *Evening Telegraph*, 150
Boston Primary School Committee, 144–46, 148
Boston Vigilance Committee, 250–51
Bowdoin College (Me.), 139
Brown, John, 245, 246, 266–67
Brown, William Wells, 182, 237, 249
Buchanan, James, 54
Bucks County, Pa., 85–86, 167
Buffalo, N.Y., 244–45
Buffum, Arnold, 205–6, 226
Business, Negroes in, 101, 155, 179, 180–81

Caldwell, Elias B., 23
Calhoun, John C., 33, 42–43, 45
California: restricts Negro testimony, 93; fear of Negro labor competition in, 161; Negroes and Chinese in, 167–68; Negro convention opposes emigration, 259; Negro petitioners support colonization, 262; Negro denounces patriotic resolution, 265; *see also* Sacramento
Canaan, N.H., 117–20, 120 n.
Canada: welcomes Negro "exiles," 73; Negro emigration to, 73, 249; support of emigration to, 235, 262
Canterbury, Conn., 126–31
Carey, Matthew, 24
Cass, Lewis, 56
Catholics, 204, 204 n.
Cemeteries, 65, 97, 204 n., 279; *see also* Segregation of races
Census of 1840, 40–46
Central America, 29, 258–59, 261, 262, 272–73, 278
Chandler, Peleg W., 147, 148
Channing, William Ellery, 216, 224

Chicago, 243
Child, Lydia, 223
Chinese, 59, 167–68
Christiana, Pa., 251
Church, Negro: importance of, 187–89, 196; sermons in, 188–89, 190; and antislavery protest, 188, 189–90, 203, 211; conservative influence of, 190, 211; independence of, 191–96; criticism of, 192, 195–96, 211–13; *see also* Baptists, Negro; Congregationalists, Negro; Episcopalians, Negro; Methodists, Negro; Presbyterians, Negro
Church, white: and abolition of slavery, 12–13; segregation of Negroes in, 191, 196–99, 206–7; attack on segregation of Negroes in, 191, 196–98, 204, 206–7, 208–11, 213; and Negro churches, 192–93, 194, 199–201, 204; discrimination in theological seminaries of, 201–3, 203–4; and antislavery protest, 203, 204; *see also* Catholics; Episcopalians, white; Methodists, white; Presbyterians, white; Quakers; Segregation of races
Cincinnati: race riots in, 73, 100; migration of Negroes from, 73; Negro schools in, 122, 151, 222; racial discrimination in, 160, 279; Negro sections of, 168, 170
Cincinnati *Gazette*, 73
Citizenship, Negro: House of Representatives recognizes, 32; debated in Congress, 34–39; Attorneys General of U.S. on, 50–54; Secretaries of State on, 54–57; Dred Scott decision and, 59–62; Republicans on, 62–63, 277
Class stratification, Negro: basis of, 179–81; nativity and, 181–82; white ancestry and, 182–83; education and, 183–84; effects of, 184–86; criticized, 185, 186
Clay, Cassius, 173
Clay, Henry, 24, 252
Clayton, John M., 54, 55
Cleveland, Ohio, 259–61

314

INDEX

lic conveyances of, 111–12, 264; segregated schools in, 121, 132–33, 134, 136, 144, 151; occupations of Negroes in, 155, 157, 166; economic discrimination against Negroes in, 159; Negro and white barbers organize in, 160; longshoremen strike in, 160–61; Irish and Negroes in, 163–64, 165, 166; Negro section of, 168; tuberculosis among Negroes in, 169; Negroes organize American League of Colored Labourers, 177–78; Negro discrimination against Negroes in, 180–81; Negro churches in, 195, 203; Negroes establish the *Colored American*, 238; anti-Republican parade in, 269

New York *Evening Post*, 54–55, 88–89
New York *Herald*, 149–50, 163
New York *Journal of Commerce*, 125
New York Manumission Society, 14, 81, 121
New York *Tribune*, 44, 90, 269
New York *World*, 90–91
Newark, N.J., 198
Newspapers, Negro; *see* Negro press
North American Review, 44
North Carolina, 234
North Star, 212–13, 241, 242; *see also* Douglass, Frederick; *Frederick Douglass' Paper*

Oberlin, College (Ohio), 139–41
Occupations of Negroes: during slavery, 4; after emancipation, 154; in Boston, 155; in New York, 155, 157, 166; in Philadelphia, 155, 159, 166; and class stratification, 179–80; *see also* Economic Condition of Negroes; Labor, Negro
Ohio, 66; prohibits slavery, 3 n.; opposition in, to Negro immigration, 69–70, 167; restricts entry of Negroes, 70 n., 72–74; repeals restrictions on entry of Negroes, 74; restricts Negro right to petition legislature of, 74; restricts Negro testimony, 93, 94; repeals restriction on Negro testimony, 94; segregated schools in, 114, 151;

opposition to Negro education in, 115, 116, 122; Negroes establish schools in, 121; Negro conventions in, 181, 211, 243, 245, 259, 275; Negro Methodists in, 195, 211; legislature supports separate territory for Negroes, 253; Negroes oppose emigration, 259; senate expels Negro reporter, 263; Negroes organize Colored American League, 264; Republican leader, on the "negro question," 270; Negroes support Republican party, 275; *see also* Cincinnati; Cleveland; Troy; Zanesville
Ohio Anti-Slavery Society, 224–25
Onderdonk, Benjamin T., 202
Oneida Institute (N.Y.), 142
Oregon, 70, 70 n., 71, 93, 263
Oregon Territory, 49, 70 n.
Otis, Harrison Gray, 34, 104
Otis, James, 8–9
Owen, Robert Dale, 67, 67 n.

Parker, Theodore, 109
Passports, 54–57
Paul, Nathaniel, 231
Paul, Thomas, 118, 195
Payne, Daniel A., 187
Pease, Elizabeth, 206–7
Pennington, J. W. C., 187
Pennsylvania, 17, 66; abolition of slavery in, 3 n., 7, 12–13; merchants oppose duty on importation of Negroes, 5; early antislavery societies in, 13, 17–18, 19, 121, 171; economic discrimination against Negroes in, 17, 158, 162; considers restriction of Negro immigration, 36, 69; Constitution of, cited, 54; support of colonization in, 69, 101; Constitutional Convention of 1837–38, 69, 77, 79, 84–85, 86; Negroes vote in, 75, 80, 84, 85; disfranchisement of Negro in, 75, 77, 84–87; disfranchisement of Negro in, opposed, 79, 80, 86–87; Negro crime in, 95; segregated schools in, 114, 121; occupations of Negroes in, 154, 155; Irish and Negroes in,

315